Toward Finance With Meaning

The Methodology of Finance: What It Is and What It Can Be

**CONTEMPORARY STUDIES IN
ECONOMIC AND FINANCIAL ANALYSIS, VOLUME 80**

Editors: Robert J. Thornton and J. Richard Aronson
Lehigh University

Contemporary Studies in Economic and Financial Analysis
An International Series of Monographs

Edited by **Robert J. Thornton** and
J. Richard Aronson, *Lehigh University*

Volume 1 - **Hunt L.** - Dynamics of Forecasting Financial Cycles

Volume 2 - **Dreyer, J.S.** - Composite Reserve Assets in the International Money System

Volume 3 - **Altman, El.,** et al. - Application of Classification Techniques in Business, Banking and Finance

Volume 4 - **Sinkey, J.F.** - Problems and Failed Institutions in the Commercial Banking Industry

Volume 5 - **Ahlers, D.M.** - A New Look at Portfolio Management

Volume 6 - **Sciberras, E.** - Multinational Electronic Companies and National Economic Policies

Volume 7 - **Allen, L.** - Venezuelan Economic Developement: A Politico-Economic Analysis

Volume 8 - **Gladwin, T.M.** - Environment Planning and the Multinational Corporation

Volume 9 - **Kobrin, S.J.** - Foreign Direct Investment, Industrialization and Social Change

Volume 10 - **Oldfield, G.S.** - Implications of Regulation on Bank Expansion: A Simulation Analysis

Volume 11 - **Ahmad, J.** - Import Substitution, Trade and Development

Volume 12 - **Fewings, D.R.** - Corporate Growth and Common Stock Risk

Volume 13 - **Stapleton, R.C.** and **M.G. Subrahmanyam**- Capital Market Equillibrium and Corporate Financial Decisions

Volume 14 - **Bloch, E.** and **R.A. Schwartz**- Impending Changes for Securities Markets: What Role for the Exchange

Volume 15 - **Walker, W.F.** - Industrial Innovation and International Trading Performance

Volume 16 - **Thompson, J.K** - Financial Policy, Inflation and Economic Development: The Mexican Experience

Volume 17 - Omitted from Numbering

Volume 18 - **Hallwood, P.** - Stabilization of International Commodity Markets

Volume 19 - Omitted from Numbering

Volume 20 - **Parry, T.G.** - The Multinational Enterprise: International Investment and Host-Country Impacts

Volume 21 - **Roxburgh, M.** - Policy Responses to Resource Depletion: The Case of Mercury

Volume 22 - **Levich, R.M.** - The International Money Market: An Assessment of Forecasting Techniques and Market Efficiency

Volume 23 - **Newfarmer, R.** - Transnational Conglomerates and the Economics of Dependent Development

Volume 24 - **Siebert, H.** and **A.B. Anatal** - The Political Economy of Environmental Protection

Volume 25 - **Ramsey, J.B.** - Bidding and Oil Leases

Volume 26 - **Ramsey J.B.** - The Economics of Exploration for Energy Resources

Volume 27 - **Ghatak, S.** - Technology Transfer to Developing Countries:
The Case of the Fertilizer Industry

Volume 28 - **Pastre, O.** - Multinationals: Bank and Corporation Relationships

Volume 29 - **Bierwag, G.O.** - The Primary Market for Municipal Debt:
Bidding Rules and Cost of Long Term Borrowing

Volume 30 - **Kaufman, G.G.** - Efficiency in the Municipal Bond Market:
The Use of Tax Exempt Financing for "Private" Purposes

Volume 31 - **West, P.** - Foreign Investment and Technology Transfer:
The Tire Industry in Latin America

Volume 32 - **Uri, N.D.** - Dimensions of Energy Economics

Volume 33 - **Balabkins, N.** - Indigenization and Economic Development:
The Nigerian Experience

Volume 34 - **Oh, J.S**. - International Financial Management:
Problem, Issues and Experience

Volume 35 - **Offlcer, L.H.** - Purchasing Power Parity and Exchange Rates:
Theory Evidence and Relevance

Volume 36 - **Horwitz, B.** and **R. Kolodny** - Financial Reporting Rules
and Corporate Decisions: A Study of Public Policy

Volume 37 - **Thorelil, H.B.** and **G.D. Sentell** - Consumer Emancipation
and Economic Development

Volume 38 - **Wood, W.C.** - Insuring Nuclear Power: Liability, Safety and
Economic Efficiency

Volume 39 - **Uri, N.D.** - New Dimensions in Public Utility Pricing

Volume 40 - **Cross, S.M**. - Economic Decisions Under Inflation: The Impact of
Accounting Measurement Error

Volume 41 - **Kautman, G.G**. - Innovations in Bond Portfolio Management:
Immunization and Duration Analysis

Volume 42 - **Horvitz, P.M.** and **R.R. Pettit** - Small Business Finance

Volume 43 - **Plaut S.E.** - Import Dependence and Economic Vulnerability

Volume 44 - **Finn, F.J.** - Evaluation of the Internal Processes of Managed Funds

Volume 45 - **Moffitt, L.C.** - Strategic Management: Public Planning at the Local Level

Volume 46 - **Thornton, R. J., et al**. - Reindustrialization: Implications for U.S.
Industrial Policy

Volume 47 - Omitted from Numbering

Volume 48 - **Von Pfeil, E.** - German Direct Investment in the United States

Volume 49 - **Dresch, S.** - Occupational Earnings,1967-1981: Return to Occupational
Choice, Schooling and Physician Specialization

Volume 50 - **Siebert, H.** - Economics of the Resource-Exporting Country Intertemporal
Theory of Supply and Trade

Volume 51 - **Walton, G.M.** - The National Economic Policies of Chile

Volume 52 - **Stanley, Q** - Managing External Issues: Theory and Practice

Volume 53 - **Natziger, E.W.** - Essays in Entrepreneurship, Equity and
Economic Development

Volume 54 - Omitted from Numbering

Volume 55 - **Slottje, D.** and **J. Haslag.** - Macroeconomic Activity and Income Inequality in the United States

Volume 56 - **Thornton, R.F.** and **J.R. Aronson.** - Forging New Relationships Among Business, Labor and Government

Volume 57 - **Putterman, L.** - Peasants, Collectives and Choice: Economic Theory and Tanzanian Villages

Volume 58 - **Baer, W.** and **J.F. Due** - Brazil and the Ivory Coast: The Impact of International Lending, Investment and Aid

Volume 59 - **Emanuel, H., et al.** - Disability Benefits: Factors Determining Applications and Awards

Volume 60 - **Rose, A.** - Forecasting Natural Gas Demand in a Changing World

Volume 61 - Omitted from Numbering

Volume 62 - **Canto V.A.** and **J.K Dietrich** - Industrial Policy and Industrial Trade

Volume 63 - **Kimura, Y.** - The Japanese Semiconductor Industry

Volume 64 - **Thornton, R., Hyclak, T.** and **J.R. Aronson** - Canada at the Crossroads: Essays on Canadian Political Economy

Volume 65 - **Hausker, A. J.** - Fundamentals of Public Credit Analysis

Volume 66 - **Looney, R.** - Economic Development in Saudi Arabia: Consequences of the Oil Price Decline

Volume 67 - **Askari, H.** - Saudi Arabias Economy: Oil and the Search for Economic Development

Volume 68 - **Godfrey, R.** - Risk Based Capital Charges for Municipal Bonds

Volume 69 - **Guerard, J.B** and **M.N. Gultekin** - Handbook of Security Analyst Forecasting and Asset Allocation

Volume 70 - **Looney, R.E** - Industrial Development and Diversification of the Arabian Gulf Economies

Volume 71 - **Basmann, R.L., et al.** - Some New Methods for Measuring and Describing Economic Inequality

Volume 72 - **Looney, R.E.** - The Economics of Third World Defense Expenditures

Volume 73 - **Thornton, R.J.** and **A.P. O'Brien** - The Economic Consequences of American Education

Volume 74 - **Gaughan, P.A.** and **R.J. Thornton** - Litigation Economics

Volume 75 - **Nafzinger, E. Wayne** - Poverty and Wealth: Comparing Afro-Asian Development

Volume 76 - **Frankurter, George** and **Herbert E. Phillips** - Forty Years of Normative Portfolio Theory: Issues, Controversies, and Misconceptions

Volume 77 - **Kuark, John Y.T**. - Comparative Asian Economics

Volume 78 - **Stephenson, Kevin** - Social Security: Time for a Change

Volume 79 - **Duleep, Harriet Orcutt** and **Wunnava, Panindra V.** - Immigrants and Immigration Policy: Individual Skills, Family Ties, and Group Identities

Volume 80 - **Frankfuter, G.M.** and **McGoun, E.G.** - Toward Finance with Meaning The Methodology of Finance: What It Is and What It Can Be

Toward Finance With Meaning

The Methodology of Finance:
What It Is and What It Can Be

by   GEORGE M. FRANKFURTER
Louisiana State University
and
ELTON G. MCGOUN
Bucknell University

 JAI PRESS INC.

Greenwich, Connecticut   *London, England*

332
F82t

Library of Congress Cataloging-in-Publication Data

Frankfurter, George M.
  Toward finance with meaning : the methodology of finance, what it
is and it can be / by George M. Frankfurter and Elton G.
McGoun.
    p.   cm. — (Contemporary studies in economic and financial
analysis ; v. 80)
  Includes bibliographical references (p.   ) and index.
  ISBN 0-7623-0163-5
  1. Finance.   2. Finance—History.   3. Risk. 4. Business
mathematics.   I. McGoun, Elton George, 1950-   .   II. Title.
III. Series.
HG173.F69   1996
332—dc21   96-04849
                                                    CIP

Copyright © 1996 JAI Press Inc.
55 Old Post Road, No. 2
Greenwich, Connecticut 06836

JAI PRESS LTD.
38 Tavistock Street
Covent Garden
London, WC2E 7PB
England

ISBN: 0-7623-0163-5

Library of Congress Catalog Number: 96-40849

Manufactured in the United States of America

CONTENTS

		Page
Preface		xiii

SECTION 1.   INTRODUCTION AND PHILOSOPHICAL BACKGROUND

I.	Introduction	3
	Finance and Philosophy	4
	Finance as Social Science	5
	Finance Without Meaning	6
	Toward Finance With Meaning	7

II.	Scientism	9
	Science as Philosophy	10
	The Enlightenment	11
	Medieval Scholasticism	11
	The Philosophy of the Enlightenment	13
	Post-Empiricism	16
	Conclusion	18

SECTION 2.   THE METHODOLOGICAL FOUNDATIONS OF FINANCIAL ECONOMICS

III.	The Philosophical Justification: Friedman's Positivism	25
	Logical Positivism	25
	Friedmanian "Positivism"	26
	Data	27
	Assumptions	29
	Concluding Remarks	32

		Page
IV.	**A Critique of Friedman's Positivism**	**35**
	Friedman and the Philosophy of Science	35
	Popper$_n$ and Popper$_s$	35
	Popper and Friedman	36
	The Pitfalls of Friedmanian Instrumentalism	38
	Data	38
	"Cordelia's Dilemma"	39
	Data Mining	39
	Data "Snooping"	40
	Data Dredging	40
	Data Conjuring	40
	Data Storking	41
	Assumptions	41
	Summary	43
V.	**The Paradigms of Finance and their Evolution**	**45**
	Corporation Finance	47
	The Irrelevance Contentions	47
	The MM Theory of Cost-of-Capital—Irrelevance #1	47
	Miller-Modigliani Dividend Policy Theory—Irrelevance #2	49
	Post—MM Theories of Cost of Capital	50
	The Trade-Off Theory	51
	MM in General Equilibrium	52
	Informational Asymmetry and Agency Theory	53
	Ad Hoc Scenerios	54
	An "Organizational" Theory of Capital Structure	55
	Dividend Policy	56
	Dividend Signaling	58
	Agency Theory Explanations	58
	Capital Asset Pricing	59
	The EMH	61
	The APT	62
	Other Pricing Models	65
	Pricing of Contingent Claims	66
	Market Micro-Structure	

SECTION 3.   LOGICAL INCONSISTENCIES: THE CASE OF FINANCE AND RISK

VI.	**Positive, Normative, and Useful Finance (or is it a Plane, a Bird, a Man): The History of the CAPM**	**73**
	The Alternative CAPMs	74

The Positive, and Normative CAPMs   76
CAPM-U   77
The Predecessors of the CAPM   79
The Expected Return-Variance Maxim   79
Testing the Normative Hypotheses   80
The Original CAPM   83
Tobin's Liquidity Preference Model   83
Sharpe's Original CAPM   84
The Maturing CAPM   86
Testing the CAPM   87
The CAPM Today   88
The Failure of the CAPM—P   88
More About the Useful CAPM   90
The Notoriety of the CAPM   92
The Sociological Explanation: Academics and Practitioners   92
The Psychological Explanation and
the Academic Community   94

VII. **Risk, Uncertainty, and Probability: Language and Concepts   99**
Finance, Language, and Translation   99
Probability Theories   102
The Theories Defined   102
The Theories Explained   103
The Theories and the Languages   106
The Probability Calculus and Economic Risk   109
The Concepts   109
The Concepts, the Theories, and the Languages   111

VIII. **The History of Risk Measurement   115**
Probability and Risk in Economics until 1930   116
Interest Before 1900   116
Excitement from 1900 to 1920   118
Caution from 1920 to 1930   121
The Rejection of Probabilistic Measurement of Risk   123
The Restoration of the Probabilistic Measurement of Risk   124
Hick's Initial Reaction   124
The First Austrian Assault   126
The Brief Skeptical Backlash   128
The Triumph of Statistical Measurement of Risk   130
The Final Solution   132

SECTION 4.   PRACTICE AND LANGUAGE

		Page
IX.	**The Language of Mathematics**	139
	Science and Mathematics	139
	From Numerology to Science	139
	From Science to Numerology	141
	Mathematics in Theory Creation	142
	Finance and Statistics	143
	Hypothesis Testing in Event Studies	143
	Problems with Statistical Significance	148
	Other Problems with Statistical Significance	151
X.	**The Language of Finance: A Duality of Culture**	157
	Figures of Speech	157
	The Jargon of the Street	157
	Metaphors in Finance	159
	Catch-All Metaphors in Finance	162
	"Abnormal Returns—A Possible Mumpsimus?"	162
	The Dangerous Metaphor—The Implicit	165
	Equilibrum Assumption	168
	The Duality of the Language—Academic Finance and	169
	Practitioner Finance	169
	World View and Content	172
	Method	174
	Style	175
	Conclusion	175

SECTION 5.   THE SOCIOLOGY OF
FINANCIAL ECONOMICS

XI.	**How and Why this Happened**	181
	What is Useful and to Whom	182
	If Practitioners Use It	182
	If Academics Use It	184
	The Rationale for the Positivist Methodology in Finance	185
XII.	**The Profession and Practice**	189
	A Model of Scientific Activity	190
	The Elements	190
	The Process	192
	Modigliani and Miller: An Example	193
	Influence on the Intellectual Environment	195

The Process   195
Modigliani and Miller   195
Informal Extractions from the Environment   196
The Process   196
The Case of Financial Economics   198
Modigliani and Miller   199
The Influence on the External Environment   200
The Process in Financial Economics   200
Modigliani and Miller   202
Implications for Finance   203
Beyond Positivism   203
The Methology of Finance   204
Counterintuitive Macrobehavior   205

SECTION 6.   FINANCE WITH MEANING

XIII.   Meaning   **211**
    Meaning   212
    Structuralism   212
    Hermeneutics   214
    Critical Theory   216
    Modernity and Post-Modernity   218

XIV.   Alternative Methods   **223**
    The Quantitative Research Tradition   223
    New Directions in Finance   229
    Alternative Methods   231
    Grounded Field Theory   231
    Ethnographic Analysis   233
    Historical Techniques   234
    Case Study Research   234
    Action Research   235

XV.   Concluding Remarks   **239**

   References   **243**

   Index   **255**

Preface

The idea of writing a book about the methodology of finance was a matter of both coincidence and necessity. Had it not been for a special session of the Eastern Finance Association on Alternative Perspectives on Finance, during the 1993 meetings in Richmond, Virginia, we most likely would have never met nor talked to each other. It happened that William Lane, who was the program chair at that meeting, showed a paper of Elton McGoun's to George Frankfurter and asked him his opinion. Lane was aware that Frankfurter had been seriously questioning the [non-existent] philosophical tenets of the field, and thought the McGoun article conveyed a similar message.

Indeed, the article was so appealing to Frankfurter that he decided to publish it in one of the early issues of *The International Review of Financial Analysis*. One thing led to another, and the two of us decided to cooperate on an article critiquing the methodology of finance. In a short time, we realized that it was impossible to cope with a subject so complex within the framework of a paper, even if we were assured (and we were not) that such a work would be published.

Soon it became clear that the only way to deal with this multifarious subject was to write a treatise. A brief search of the literature revealed that such work had not been done since the publication of Fred Weston's careful manuscript, *The Scope and Methodology of Finance*, published by Prentice Hall in 1966. A cursory reading of the Weston book revealed, however, that either by choice or timing, Weston covered almost nothing of the paradigm now widely accepted in the field. Consequently, we decided to fill the void by writing a book on the subject. After developing an outline and prospectus that served as a blueprint for the work here, we began our search for a publisher.

It soon became clear that finding a publisher who would pursue the project not strictly for wealth maximization would be more than difficult. Indeed, the main-stream textbook publishers (with one exception) shied away from the idea in an instant. Luckily, JAI Press, which specializes in treatises, was quick to respond with its support of the project.

During our search for a publisher, the editor of economics and finance at a major publisher of textbooks showed a keen interest in philosophy and personally tried his very best to underwrite the endeavor. His effort culminated in seven reviews, which he shared with us. We believe that excerpts from these reviews (some positive, some negative) would serve as a better testimony of the need for this book, and a justification for what follows, than a million of our own words.

The referees of our outline and prospectus are not known to us. They were numbered 1 to 7 by the textbook editor. We reproduce, herein, for ease of reference the prospectus that was sent to these referees.

TOWARD FINANCE WITH MEANING
THE METHODOLOGY OF FINANCE:

What it is and What it Can be

Prospectus and Outline

*By **George M. Frankfurter** and **Elton G. MCGoun*** In 1966, J. Fred Weston published his monograph, "The Scope and Methodology of Finance." Conspicuous by their absence from the list of references are articles by Markowitz (1952), Sharpe (1963, 1964), Miller and Modigliani (1961) and many others in print at that time. These papers are regarded as having shaped what has come to be known today as modern finance, or in the parlance of a leading school of thought: financial economics. Of course, the monograph makes no mention of Agency, Pecking Order and Signaling Theories and/or the burgeoning literature of Micro Structure and the Market for Corporate Control, all of which appeared subsequent to its publication.

Thus, nearly all of the dominant theories and models that are built on the paradigm upon which research in finance is conducted are missing from Weston's work. In spite of this, the book remains the most recent and possibly the only attempt to define the scope and methodology of finance. The purpose of the proposed work is to provide an up-to-date critique of the methodology of finance, and concurrently, to consider why it is that finance pays so little attention to what it is doing and why this subject has been largely ignored for 27 years.

It will be argued that modern finance is but a lax compilation of ad hoc theories and models, connected by little other than the presupposition that the only relevant human behavior is wealth maximization. Other factors that might explain the activities of corporations, investors, financial analysts and institutions but cannot coexist with this rationality of wealth maximization are ignored. Any activity that contradicts this maxim is either overlooked or considered an anomaly.

The methodological thinking by which such theories and models are created and tested is based upon two doubtful canons: (1) that complex problems can be decomposed to simple parts which in turn can be mathematically expressed and manipulated to arrive at a solution after which they can be put back together again and (2) that the underlying human behavior can be inferred from the statistical analysis of aggregate market data.

While building the intricate structure of financial economics upon such dubious foundations is a serious problem, there are others. The present monograph will also explain that (1) the structure contains a number of internal contradictions, rendering it logically unsound, and (2) its methods of analysis are biased and distorted in ways which presuppose the outcomes, mocking scientific rigor.

Additionally, it will be shown that this state of affairs did not emerge by default or lack of recognition that the paradigm is fundamentally flawed. The current state is a result of an academic reward system in which the "production" of scientific papers and their subsequent publication in the "nobility" press is the gauge of intellectual capability—modern day jousting of sorts. Accordingly, the search for knowledge and understanding is subjugated to methods by which one can better enhance one's vita. Articles published in the leading organs of the field become a measure of one's marketability.

The concluding section of the proposed monograph offers some alternative ways and means of thinking to provide a new avenue for scientific research in finance.

OUTLINE[1]

SECTION I. INTRODUCTION AND BACKGROUND
Chapter 1 Introduction: the purpose and structure of the monograph
Chapter 2 Modernism and scientism
SECTION II. THE METHODOLOGICAL FOUNDATIONS OF FINANCIAL ECONOMICS
Chapter 3 The philosophical justification: Friedman's positivism.
Chapter 4 The critiques of Friedmanian positivism.
Chapter 5 The fundamental postulates of finance and their refutations.

SECTION III. LOGICAL INCONSISTENCIES AND FALLACIES
Chapter 6 The purpose of finance versus its methodology
Chapter 7 Probability and the concept and measurement of risk
Chapter 8 Economic rationality, epistemological rationality and statistical independence
SECTION IV. THE PRACTICE OF SELF DECEPTION
Chapter 9 The deceptive language of metaphors
Chapter 10 Deceptive statistical methods
SECTION V. THE SOCIOLOGY OF FINANCIAL ECONOMICS
Chapter 11 How and why this happened
SECTION VI. FINANCE WITH MEANING
Chapter 12 Observations and analyses of social phenomena
Chapter 13 Alternative methodologies and methods
Chapter 14 Suggestions for new avenues of research
Chapter 15 Concluding remarks

REFERENCES

Markowitz, Harry M. 1952. "Portfolio Selection." *Journal of Finance* 7:77-91.
Miller, Merton H. and Franco Modigliani. 1961. "Dividend Policy, Growth and the Valuation of Shares." *Journal of Business* 34:411-433.
Sharpe, William F. 1963. "A Simplified Model of Portfolio Analysis" *Management Science* 9:277-293.
———— . 1964. "Capital Market Prices: A Theory of Market Equilibrium Under Conditions of Risk." *Journal of Finance* 14:425-442.
Weston, J. Fred. 1966. *The Scope and Methodology of Finance*. Englewood Cliffs: New Jersey.

Now, the reviews:

> Wealth maximization, or any other form of optimization, is just but a convenient way to simplify and analytically track problems. Nobody ever claimed it IS [referee's capitals] reality but the litmus test is how closely reality fits the models derived from such blatantly flawed assumptions. That is why a significant portion of articles published actually deal with empirical tests of the models: this is the only way researchers get a degree of comfort with the models themselves.

> ... I do agree with the statement that the review process may be unduly biased toward "accepted" methodologies but I would certainly stay shy of blaming the reward system for this state of affairs (Referee #1)

If these passages had been written on Milton Friedman's lap, they could not have been truer to the spirit of the man who transplanted defunct positivism/instrumentalism into economics. Nevertheless, this referee thinks that "... the concern of the authors with the underlying assumptions in financial research is indeed warranted and it would be a very interesting contribution to the research process itself."

It is time for a synthesis, or is this the S&M of Finance?! Weston's work, *not cited in the prospectus* [it was—our italics] was significant at a time when managerial was displacing descriptive. Perhaps it is time for us to take another look at the scope and methodology of finance.

The topical outline of this proposal includes not only the "scope and methodology," something that will sell if packaged right, but possibly a "grilling" of the Finance journal "insiders" who have led the field astray. The latter half of the outline, always looking for a publication outlet, would be interesting and controversial. I cannot decide if this proposal is "leading edge" or "crackpot!" (Referee #2).

Is there a difference?

There are books, readings and journals that cover new theories as well as criticism and tests of those theories. Consider the impact of the Fama-French article dealing with the CAPM. It has stimulated numerous articles, books and dissertations. Therefore restating theories and controversies about them does not seem to warrant a book. While it is true that some of our methodology is flawed, stating that it is "mocking scientific rigor" is pushing it too far. Although I will concede that some journals are more rigorous than others. So what is the contribution of this monograph? Neither the prospectus nor the outline provided me with an answer to that question. (Referee #3)

The reference to the now-famous Fama and French (1992) article begs a comment. As Jahnke tells his story in *The Journal of Investing*:

The CRSP Seminars, as they were called, provided an ideological home for those desirous of promoting an efficient market agenda.... The few brave souls venturing to the CRSP seminars with evidence contradicting CAPM were met by a band of academics known as "Murderers Row," who usually made quick work of dispatching the heretic (Jahnke 1994, pp. 7-8).

Fama was not just a card-carrying member of that "band of academics," but one *primus inter pares*, and subsequently helped to extend the ranks of "Murderers Row" to include leading academic and professional journals in financial economics. The "Murderers" were instrumental, therefore, as early as the CRSP seminars, in suppressing work that not only anticipated their 1992 conclusions, but, on occasion, also rigorously demonstrated these conclusions. It is a sad commentary on the moral and intellectual state of the field that other academics consider the Fama and French (1992) work iconoclastic, rather than raise the moral and ethical question whether, of all people, these two were qualified to tear down their own church with the same method of analysis with which they erected it and ensured its sanctity for a quarter of a century.

In fairness to the authors, I am not sure what it is they want to do. For example, their proposal begins by belaboring the fact that Weston's "Scope and Methodology of

Finance" is out of date. Few students and faculty members are probably aware of this book nowadays; so, I wonder why it is considered a central deficiency.

...I distinguish "scope and methodology" from theoretical paradigms. For example, I would consider the study of capital markets to be part of the scope of finance; and, the use of statistical methods as part of the methodology. Likewise, I would consider the "efficient market" to be a central paradigm of modern finance. Now, if the authors are suggesting that psychological aspects of behavior should be included within the scope of financial theory, I don't think that's such an earth-shaking or even controversial notion; certainly, the main premise of agency theory is that the behavior of agents may be at odds with the preference of shareholders. Likewise a good deal of "modern" financial research is based on clinical (?) case studies which focus more on contractual arrangements than an statistical methods [sic]. So, I see nothing radically different there. (Referee #4)

The brief proposal for "Towards Finance with Meaning" has been a difficult one to me to evaluate. The statement in the 2nd paragraph that the dominant theories and models of finance are built upon a paradigm missing from Weston's work the authors take as a criticism of the models of finance. It seems to me more simply evidence that Weston's work was less than complete, or to be more charitable, evidence that Weston's work in 1966 was relatively soon after the 63 and 64 ground breaking work of Sharpe and so did not consider it as it might have done had Weston wrote a few years later. In any case, the fact that Weston did not include these things in a 1966 trade book, is not, to me, prima facie evidence that the whole paradigm of finance is fatally flawed. The authors seem to consider it as just such evidence. (Referee #5)

We reproduced the prospectus and the outline to show to the unbiased reader that we made no claim that there is anything wrong with the Weston monograph, except that the field evolved after his writing. Apparently, if there is freedom of speech, there must be freedom of reading, too. Accordingly, one can impute anything one wishes to the best of one's understanding.

Despite the authors' concern over the parochialism of finance scholarship, the outline does not suggest very convincingly that there is a way out. Is there a new unifying principle that can be applied to direct future research? How can one go about constructing theory that relies on alternative assumptions about wealth seeking behavior? Is there an alternative paradigm? What are the consequences of continuing the current course of research?

...What they seem to want to say is important, but I am unconvinced that they can say it in an alluring way. I suggest they organize a conference around the themes that are noted in the prospectus. (Referee #6)

We certainly hope that the reader of this work will conclude that we have answered some of the questions of this referee without having to organize a conference on the themes.

Fred Weston was a recognized pioneer in finance in 1966, and it thus was appropriate
for him to author a monograph, THE SCOPE AND METHODOLOGY OF FINANCE
in that year. Fred remains active, he continues to be a pioneer for finance, and it would
be no less appropriate for him to prepare an update on the status of the finance field.
In fact, I wish Fred would do that!

And, can the authors really ignore the fact that Professors Markowitz, Miller, and Sharpe
shared the 1990 Nobel Prize in that year for that very work they propose to add in this
monograph? That singular award suggests to me that finance as a discipline is much
more coherent and focused.(Referee #7)

No, we cannot and will not ignore the fact, precisely because the 1966 pioneer
did not talk about that work at all. By the way, if you see Fred, say hello
to him from us. We also have great respect for him, although we vehemently
disagree with many of his conceptualizations in the *Scope and Methodology
of Finance*.

Perhaps the most shocking aspect of these critiques is not what they
say, but what they do not say. It seems that none of these distinguished
referees realize that we are challenging the philosophical tenets of the
finance field—the very same foundations that they seem to accept for
granted.

Extra Ecclesiam Nulla Salus (there is no salvation outside the church)
has long been a canon of the Catholic church. In this book, we challenge
the canon (as it pertains to finance), for the church of positive economics.

Several chapters of this book contain concepts and ideas we discussed in
papers, both published and unpublished, that we wrote either jointly or
separately. We feel that it is important to put these papers together in a
volume that will reflect our perception of the field and the direction it is
following at present.

The following is a partial list of material taken from our previous,
published workd, and the chapters in this book they appear:

McGoun:
"Machomatics in Egonomics." *The International Review of Financial Analysis*, forthcoming,
Chapter II.
"The CAPM: A Nobel Failure." *Critical Perspectives on Accounting 1992, Chapter VI.*
"The History of Risk Measurement." *Critical Perspectives on Accounting 1995, Chapter VIII.*
"The New Pythagoreans: Metaphysical Mathematics in Finance." *Slovene Economic Review*
1994, Chapter IX, X.
"On the Knowledge of Finance." *The International Review of Financial Analysis* 1992, Chapter
XII.
Bettner, Robinson, and McGoun:
"The Case for Qualitative Research in Finance." *The International Review of Financial
Analysis* 1994, Chapter XIV.
Frankfurter:
"The End of Modern Finance?" 1993. *The Journal of Investing* Chapter VI.

"The Rise and Fall of the CAPM Empire." *Financial Markets, Institutions and Instruments* 1995, Chapter VI.
Frankfurter and Lane:
"The Rationality of Dividends." *International Review of Financial Analysis*, 1992, Chapter V.
Frankfurter and McGoun:
"The Event Study: An Industrial Strength Method." *The International Review of Financial Analysis*, 1993, Chapters IX, X.
"But It Looked So Good on My Vita." *The Journal of Financial Education* 1996, Chapters XI, XV.
Frankfurter and Philippatos:
"Financial Theory and the Growth of Scientific Knowledge: From Modigliani and Miller to An Organizational Theory of Capital Structure." *International Review of Financial Analysis*, 1992, Chapter V.
Frankfurter and Phillips:
"Normative Implications of Equilibrium Restricted Models: Homogeneous Expectations and Other Artificialities." *Journal of Economic Behavior and Organization*, Forthcoming, Chapter VI.

ACKNOWLEDGMENTS

We are grateful to many of our students, who were not only an inspiration, but also source of knowledge for us. Sincere thanks are due to Ms. Ivonne Lewis Day for her expert editing of this book. Also, we recognize the great help we received from our graduate assistants, Mr. Armand Kosedag and Ms. Kim Edwards. We are indebted to our friends-coauthors, Professors Bettner, Lane, Philippatos, Phillips and Robinson.

Without the fascinating debates we conducted with our colleagues at Bucknell University, Louisiana State University, and the University of Ljubljana on many of the topics covered in the book, and without their encouragement this work would have never seen the light of day. Last, but not least, our heartfelt gratitude is extended to our spouses who, for reasons unfathomable, put up with our chosen profession.

Athough it might seem that we are too critical, the reader should know that this manuscript is a labor of love.

NOTE

1. We reproduce here the original outline, as it was sent for review, in the interest of authenticity. Naturally, as the manuscript evolved, changes had to be made which are reflected in the Table of Contents of the finished work.

Section 1

INTRODUCTION
AND PHILOSOPHICAL BACKGROUND

Chapter I

Introduction

The word *"methodology,"* which appears in the title of this book is used frequently in finance. Unfortunately, it is used most often as a synonym for *method*, to refer to the technique of data acquisition and analysis in research, when it should instead refer to the underlying philosophy and logical structure of the process. If methods are the building blocks of a science, methodology is the cornerstone. Since the term *methodology* is inaccurately used in finance, it is not surprising that its importance has not been recognized. Whereas there have been countless publications regarding the "methods" of financial research, there have been disappointingly few regarding methodology. The most ambitious appeared more than a quarter-century ago (Weston, 1966), predating most of the papers that are today thought to form the core knowledge of the subject.

Another word appearing in the title of this book (*meaning*) is never used in finance. Along with methodology, meaning has become subordinate to method as the research process has become divorced from its subject matter. While data acquisition and analysis are the central concerns of finance, what the results of that analysis might mean for the finance community, how this meaning is determined by the original data and the processes by which it is analyzed, and how research itself unknowingly alters meaning are rarely, if ever, considered.

The objective of this book is to advance methodology and meaning as important concerns of finance. To accomplish this objective, it is necessary: first, to convince financial economists that philosophical content such as methodology and meaning matter; second, to articulate the implicit philosophical substructure upon which the work of finance has evolved; third, to show what the failure to consider philosophy has led to; fourth to explain why philosophy has been so broadly ignored by those who have contributed the most to shaping the discipline; and fifth, to suggest alternative philosophies that might contribute to a better understanding of financial behavior. Without understanding methodology and meaning, finance cannot hope to resolve fundamental issues, avoid inconsequential research, and achieve real knowledge.

FINANCE AND PHILOSOPHY

The Capital Asset Pricing Model (CAPM, subsequently) (Sharpe, 1964) is an excellent example of finance without methodology and meaning. For a very simple valuation model first published in 1964 to be seriously controversial more than three decades later does not speak well for the capabilities of finance research as it now stands. It is not that the controversy itself matters, for a spirited interplay among conjectures and refutations is said to mark the advancement of all sciences (Popper, 1963); rather, it is that the controversy continues to drag on fruitlessly after so many years of intense effort. There is still no agreement on whether the CAPM is a descriptive model; if so, whether it is testable; and if so, whether it has been tested—questions that one would expect to have been answered long ago for a model considered to be a fundamental achievement of modern finance theory. The CAPM's successors, the multiperiod CAPM (Merton, 1973) and the arbitrage pricing theory (APT) (Ross, 1976), have fared no better.

Although it is true that conventional finance research has eschewed anything explicitly philosophical, an implicit philosophy of the science is unavoidable. What there is to know (ontology) and how it is known (epistemology) are questions fundamental to all sciences, including finance, yet research in finance rarely confronts questions of ontology and epistemology. By working according to a research tradition, program, or paradigm within which answers to these questions are implicit, one can sidestep the questions. Historically, however, immature sciences and sciences in crisis have turned to philosophy for understanding and renewal. This is what finance must do to cure the methodological rigidity that has caused it to stagnate. Unfortunately, it is a difficult task to convince someone who has absorbed the research conventions of any science that philosophy matters.

Why, then, does it matter? Consider the natural sciences, most of the research in which is predicated upon the belief that there are immutable laws governing the universe (the ontology) and that these laws can be discovered by the "scientific" method of forming hypotheses and testing their implications against observations or experiences of reality (the epistemology). Few natural scientists—at least in their work as scientists— would believe it to be any other way, attributing the very existence of modern society to this approach.

In the centuries prior to Descartes, beliefs and the "sciences" built upon them were quite different. Nowadays, most would regard these beliefs as primitive or naive. Yet, in recent times, quantum physicists and philosophers (of pragmatism, structuralism, post-empiricism, hermeneutics, critical theory, and post-modernism among others) have again come to challenge the prevailing ontological and epistemological beliefs and to propose different "scientific" methods. The scientific basis of modern society is no longer thought to be quite so simple or so straightforward as it once appeared. Likewise, the scientific basis of finance is more complex than current research would indicate, and the dearth of consequential research reflects the failure to confront this complexity.

Although the preceding paragraphs have suggested the importance of a philosophical perspective on finance, the case is not complete without a comprehensive discussion of what the philosophy of finance is, what the philosophy of finance might be, and why philosophy has not mattered in finance thus far. Such discussion is comprised in the remainder of the book and is organized as follows.

FINANCE AS A SOCIAL SCIENCE

Chapter 2 looks at traditional science and its underlying belief structure. If there are immutable laws, as is the dominant belief in the natural sciences, then one understands why an event occurred in terms of a covering law and the conditions that brought that law to bear upon the event. In the social sciences, however, one can also understand what an event "means" in terms of the intentions of the actors. Meaning is not a matter of laws, but of the unique personal, social, and historical conditions surrounding the event. Although knowledge in finance has excluded meaning, a full understanding of finance is not possible without it; hence, the title of the book reflects its purpose.

In a well-thought-out essay, Merton (1995) provides what is perhaps the most concise and accurate normative definition of the theory of finance:

> The core of finance theory is the study of the behavior of agents in allocating and deploying their resources, both spatially and across time, in an uncertain environment. Time and uncertainty are the central elements that influence financial behavior (p. 7).

The focal element of Merton's definition is behavior: "the behavior of agents" and "financial behavior." Yet this aspect of the theory of finance is one that has been studied very little. Instead, for almost the entire existence of the discipline, researchers have focused on method—staring at, categorizing, analyzing, rehashing, and interpreting data in ever-increasing mass and frequency[1] with the aid of electronic storage media and high-speed computers. The purpose of all this analysis is to make inferences from the data regarding the behavior of the agents, rather than observing that behavior directly in the first place. Ostensibly concerned with behavior, but unconcerned with meaning, finance has become a social science masquerading as a natural science.

The social sciences got their start (and their name) by emulating the natural sciences (hence, the application of the term *science* to the study of society). It was the discovery of statistical regularities in social phenomena that suggested to Quetelet and others that there are laws governing societies just as there are laws governing the physical universe (Porter, 1986). In a similar vein, some social scientists began to imitate the mathematical models of physics with simple mathematical models of society. To them, the natural sciences and social sciences were united by a common philosophy of inquiry or methodology. Other social scientists, however, were concerned with what they perceived to be significant differences between the social sciences and the natural sciences.

Within some social science disciplines, a rigorous philosophical and methodological debate between the two positions ensued. Although there was some dissent among economists, that discipline (from which finance is descended) clearly cast its lot with the unity of science; that is, that social science and natural science rested upon the same beliefs and were to be conducted in the same way. Milton Friedman's (1953) essay, "The Methodology of Positive Economics," discussed in Chapter III, became the definitive statement of such beliefs—beliefs to which finance now adheres with a greater tenacity than its economics parent.

Even if one were to believe in the methodological unity of the natural and social sciences, which belief is itself controversial, the philosophy of natural science that Friedman appropriated for economics and that was transferred to finance was largely moribund by the time he seized it. It had already been discredited by philosophers, and, after its publication, was severely criticized by a number of economists.

What appears surprising in light of the severe deficiencies summarized in Chapter IV is that Friedman's beliefs continue to dominate economics and to monopolize finance. As described in Chapter V, the science of finance is built upon an underlying foundation of postulates that may be all too easily refuted, and the only justification for employing such a dubious methodology in the social science of finance is a misguided philosophy of natural science.

FINANCE WITHOUT MEANING

Finance has been able to dismiss the insecurity of its foundations by disregarding its underlying philosophy. It has been equally indifferent to its internal inconsistencies. Internal contradictions are disturbingly common. Although the flaws are subtle and easy to ignore in the interest of preserving cherished beliefs, their impact is devastating. If the purpose of finance is a positive description of the laws governing the behavior of financial agents (under conditions of uncertainty), and if hypotheses are tested against that behavior, then finance is robbed of its social meaning as it can have no influence on those agents. If, on the other hand, the purpose is a normative prescription of the principles for improved performance by financial agents, then its hypotheses must be tested against a value-laden (extra-scientific) objective. This thesis is developed in Chapter VI through a discussion of the intellectual history of the CAPM, a model that is quite problematic with regard to the issue of positive versus normative.

One of the underlying assumptions of the CAPM—in fact such a deeply buried assumption that is usually taken for granted and never made explicit—is that risk can be measured statistically. But if risk is to be measured statistically, then one must assume a relative frequency theory of probability. Within a relative frequency theory of probability, however, that type of risk does not exist, as is shown in Chapter VII. The curious story of how this severe problem came to be ignored is addressed in Chapter VIII, which introduces the notion that the profession may sweep its problems beneath the rug in order to sustain its chosen ways of "doing things."

Abuse of probability—statistics in particular, and mathematics in general—is both theoretical and empirical. To ensure that it generates "results," finance routinely violates the necessary conditions of valid statistical testing, misinterpreting and overstating the outcomes of its tests, as presented in Chapter IX. Another way of protecting itself from its shortcomings is for finance to cloak itself in a language of deceptive terms and metaphors and to use a different vernacular for academics and professionals. That subterfuge is the subject of Chapter X. Chapter XI concludes that the reward system and social structure of the academic profession of finance research explain how and why this has happened, and Chapter XII concludes that the profession has an impact on practice that it fails to take into account.

TOWARD FINANCE WITH MEANING

To restore some rigor to its methodology, finance must revoke the license granted by Friedman and resist the more mercenary lures of the profession. False postulates, faulty logic, misleading terminology and sloppy tests have no place in a discipline that desires to emulate the natural sciences. But if the science of finance truly seeks to understand financial behavior, then it must challenge the notion of the "unity of science" and incorporate meaning.

Although the philosophy and methodology of the natural sciences undoubtedly have a role to play in finance, this role must not be the only one. The dominance of instrumentalism/empiricism has to be broken. Chapter XIII argues that social phenomena are much different than natural phenomena and suggests different philosophies.

Taking into account these alternative philosophical perspectives, Chapter XIV describes alternative methods by which finance as a social science can be studied. Chapter XV envisions the research opportunities that would arise if finance were to broaden its scope to accept new methodologies and methods, and to broaden its reward structure to recognize the accomplishments of researchers who apply them.

Once-promising avenues of exploration in financial theory have led nowhere, yet they continue to be overcrowded. Once-promising methods of discovery have yielded little understanding, but they continue to be overused. With a dearth of fresh ideas, finance muddles on, assiduously mining the data with the latest mathematical or statistical method, trying to extract something of value from theories long since depleted by others. However one defines success in the sciences, finance has had too few successes in view of the resources that have been and continue to be expended. If this work serves as a modest beginning toward a change in this state of affairs, then the authors' return on investment more than justifies the risk they have taken breaking with tradition.

NOTE

1. In fact, the first conference of high frequency data in finance, titled HFDF-I was held in Zürich, Switzerland in March, 29-31, 1995.

Chapter II

Scientism

You do not get to philosophy by reading many and multifarious philosophical books, nor by torturing yourself with solving the riddles of the universe, but solely and surely by not evading what is essential in what you encounter in your ... academic studies (Heidegger 1984, p. 18).

In the Introduction, we stated that immature sciences and sciences in crisis have turned to philosophy for understanding and renewal.[1] Many may disagree that finance falls into either of these categories; therefore, any discussion of philosophy may seem to them inappropriate, if not unnecessary. Elsewhere in the Introduction, however, we stated that, either implicitly or explicitly, all sciences must answer questions of ontology (what there is to know) and epistemology (what it means to know it), and finance is no exception.[2] Indeed, it is the answers to these questions that make science "science"; therefore, to fully understand what finance *is* (and *does*), one must understand its philosophy.

It would not be an exaggeration to say that science does not just *have* a philosophy; it *is* a philosophy. To those who regard science and philosophy as very different, even irreconcilable, methods of inquiry, this is a controversial statement that challenges the privileged position of science in modern society. Science is supposed to be experimentation, not speculation; fact, not belief; proof, not rhetoric.[3]

The purpose of this chapter is to show that science is indeed a philosophy. As we like to think of them, "experimentation," "fact," and "proof" are unattainable ideals—science is as much speculation, belief, and rhetoric as philosophy is held to be. The first section of this chapter discusses why science must be a philosophy; the second section, the historical origins of the philosophy of modern science; and the third section, the contrast between the image of science as "science" and the reality of science as philosophy. Given the privileged position of science in modern society, it is no wonder that finance has tried to be more "scientific." In doing so, however, it has adopted a philosophy at odds with its subject matter and cultivated an image that is not only deceptive but also dangerous.

9

SCIENCE AS PHILOSOPHY

What is the purpose of a science? The answers to this fundamental question are the same for all sciences: to predict something, to control something, to solve the problems of something, to understand something, to explain something, or to find the truth of something. These answers separate nicely into two groups of three each: "practical" purposes and "knowledge" purposes.

One observation we might make is that the practical purposes are not peculiar to science. As long as there have been humans, or even as long as there has been life on this planet, humans and all other living things have had to predict, to control, and to solve problems in order to survive. In fact, a definition of "life" might well include the ability to perform these functions (De Duve 1991). Another observation we might make is that the practical and knowledge purposes are closely related. To solve the problems of something or to control something, a living thing must be able to "predict" (in some way or another) the effects of its actions. To predict the effects of its actions, it must "understand" (in some way or another) why the effects occur, be able to "explain" (in some way or another) why the effects occur, or "know" (in some way or another) the true relationships between its actions and their effects. Science is simply one source of the skill and knowledge all living things must have; therefore, it is not what science is supposed to do that distinguishes it from non-science.

Perhaps it is the *methods* of science; that is, how it does what it is supposed to do, that distinguish it from non-science. In the introduction to this chapter, we contrasted science and philosophy as "methods" of inquiry, and in the discussion of the Enlightenment in the following section, we make it clear that its "method" is a characteristic attribute of science.[4] Indeed, the "scientific method"—formulate a theory, build a model, generate a hypothesis, and test it—is featured in the introduction of most elementary science textbooks.

Unfortunately, the "scientific method" is more an *ex post* "rational reconstruction" of what scientists did than a description of what they do.[5] The "scientific method" is not the real method of science. Furthermore, it would not be difficult to show that all living things can, in fact, be said to behave "as if" they formulate theories, build models, generate hypotheses, and test them in the sense that we can find psychological, physiological, or evolutionary activities analogous to our usual definitions of these terms. This is reflected in the earlier uses of the phrase "in some way or another." The "scientific method" can be as much a method of non-science as it is of science. Although science is often characterized by its "scientific method" of operation,[6] it is not the method in and of itself that distinguishes science from non-science.

Rather, science is distinguished by its answers to the philosophical questions of where inquiry begins and where it ends. Where inquiry begins is the ontological question of what there is to know; where inquiry ends is the epistemological question of what it means to know it. Science believes in a certain way that the universe is structured (what there is to know) and believes in a certain type of statement with which to describe that structure (what it means to know it). Science cannot *know* how the universe is structured; it can only *believe* that it is structured in a certain way and, on the basis of that *belief*, proceed with its method. Science cannot *know* how to describe the universe; it can only *believe* that it can be described by certain types of statements and, on the basis of that *belief*, use its method to produce those statements. All scientific knowledge *is* (and indeed *must be*) based upon philosophical belief.[7] This is a familiar observation;[8] however, it is one that is too easy to overlook.[9]

We recognize that this defense of the statement that science must be a philosophy has been abstract. A more complete understanding should follow from the next section on the historical origins of the philosophy of modern science, in which we discuss what the traditional ontological and epistemological beliefs of science are and how they came about.

THE ENLIGHTENMENT

Medieval Scholasticism

Associated with the work of Galileo, Kepler, Descartes, and Bacon in the seventeenth century, the Enlightenment was a methodological revolution of sorts against medieval scholasticism, an amalgam of Christian theology and Aristotelian philosophy. Medieval scholars, or "schoolmen," sought the answers to profound theological, philosophical, and scientific questions[10] by building grand schemes for the structure and function of the universe out of material gathered from classical texts and idiosyncratic observations. By the early seventeenth century, scholasticism was marked by labyrinthine systems teased out of gross oversimplifications, and mastery of arcane terms and subtle debating points was required to achieve academic distinction (Cottingham 1986). The scholastic controversy over how many angels could dance on the head of a pin has become the archetype of scholarly decadence.

Before considering the nature of the Enlightenment and the age of Modernity of which it marks the beginning, there are lessons in humility we might learn from the experience of the schoolmen. Since most of us have been educated in the modernist tradition, it is far more difficult for us to understand the schoolmen than to understand the early modernists who treated them with contempt.[11] We must be cautious, however, about criticizing an intellectual perspective with which we may be not only unfamiliar but also unable to comprehend. For example, Rucker (1982) suggests that the controversy over how many angels could dance on the head of a pin was in fact a struggle over the meaning of infinity; thus, it was a debate we would agree to be consequential, although it was conducted in terms we find peculiar.

In the preface to *The Essential Tension*, Kuhn (1977) makes the following recommendation that arose out of his own experience with Aristotle:

> When reading the works of an important thinker, look first for the apparent absurdities in the text and ask yourself how a sensible person could have written them. When you find an answer, ... when those passages make sense, then you may find that more central passages, ones you previously thought you understood, have changed their meaning (Kuhn 1977, p. xii).

In *Greek Science*, Benjamin Farrington also makes the point that there are different sciences for different societies.

> Fully to understand the science of any society, we must be acquainted with the degree of its material advancement and with its political structure. There is no such thing as science *in vacuo*. There is only the science of a particular society at a particular place and time. The history of science can only be understood as a function of the total life of society (quoted in Harris 1980, p. 32).[12]

Like scholasticism, all intellectual traditions have their practical and epistemological limits, and again like scholasticism, all intellectual traditions have an eventual tendency to lose their rigor and drift into pedantry. Finance theory would be hard-pressed to defend itself against the charge that it is a labyrinthine system built on gross oversimplifications, and the finance profession would be similarly hard-pressed to defend itself against the charge that mastery of arcane terms, of subtle debating points, and of the requisite rhetorical flourishes was required to achieve academic distinction.[13] To dismiss out-of-hand scholasticism or any other intellectual tradition[14] admits ignorance of one's inherent prejudices and blindness to the likely fate of one's own philosophy.

The Enlightenment ushered in Modernity with a methodological revolution that created "science" and, at the same time, produced the schism between science and philosophy that has persisted through today. In place of classical texts and idiosyncratic observations, scholars gathered their information in the form of reproducible measurements (objectivity); in place of arcane terms and rhetorical flourishes, they used plain, common language (clarity); in place of grand schemes and labyrinthine systems, they built simple structures of logic and mathematics (rationality). The very term *Enlightenment* implies the inherent superiority of these values (objectivity, clarity, and rationality).[15]

Although we share a belief in these values with Galileo, Bacon, Descartes, and Newton, we must bear in mind that it is only a belief. We are not "right" and the schoolmen "wrong"; rather, we hold a different philosophy.[16] This does not mean that our philosophy is not in some ways "more successful" than that of the schoolmen, but our definition of "success" is itself a part of that philosophy, and, for the schoolmen, "success" was likely to have been something quite different.

The Philosophy of the Enlightenment

We begin our brief discussion of the philosophy of the Enlightenment with Descartes' statement of his "rules" (or method) for the conduct of inquiry and the acquisition of knowledge; then we proceed to consider their implications.

> The first rule was never to accept anything as true unless I recognized it to be certainly and evidently such: that is, carefully to avoid all precipitation and prejudgement, and to include nothing in my conclusions unless it presented itself so clearly and distinctly to my mind that there was no reason or occasion to doubt it. The second was to divide each of the difficulties which I encountered into as many parts as possible, and as might be required for an easier solution. The third was to think in an orderly fashion when concerned with the search for truth, beginning with the things which were simplest and easiest to understand, and gradually and by degrees reaching toward more complex knowledge, even treating, as though ordered, materials which were not necessarily so (Descartes 1960, p. 15).

Perhaps the most striking characteristic of Descartes' method is its reliance on what might be termed a "mechanical" metaphor. Just as the performance of a machine is a simple sum of the functions of its individual subassemblies, nothing is either gained or lost from dividing something (a problem, the universe) into its pieces or assembling something from its pieces.[17] This is explicit in his second rule that problems might be divided into parts, and the solution to the whole problem can be assembled from the solution of each of its component sub problems. The mechanical metaphor is implicit in his third rule that the solution to a complex problem can be achieved by beginning with a simpler (hypothetical) problem and proceeding through a series of increasingly more complex problems until reaching a solution, and also implicit in his first rule in which he feels free to divide the universe into a subject (himself) and an object (everything else)[18]

We find this same mechanical metaphor and this same method in finance, most strikingly in the capital structure problem. First, we believe that we can separate the capital structure decision from other corporate finance decisions, especially the investment decision. Second, we believe that we can solve the capital structure problem by stripping it to its bare essentials

(Modigliani and Miller 1958) and then adding complications in small increments (countless references too numerous to cite). Third, we believe that our research has no effect on the capital structure decisions we observe firms make.[19]

Underlying Descartes' method are other beliefs less explicit than those associated with the mechanical metaphor. One is the ontological belief that there is something "out there" to know. The universe works according to laws that exist independently of time and space. Such laws govern not only the physical world (the *cosmos*) but the social world (the *polis*) as well. This belief is aptly described by Toulmin (1990) as a contrast to Renaissance humanism.

> After the 1630s, the tradition of Modern Philosophy in Western Europe concentrated on formal analysis of chains of written statements, rather than on the circumstantial merits and defects of persuasive utterances. Within that tradition, *formal logic was in, rhetoric was out....* Modern moral philosophy was concerned not with minute 'case studies' or particular moral discriminations, but rather with the comprehensive general principles of ethical theory. In a phrase, *general principles were in, particular cases were out....* When modern philosophers dismissed ethnography and history as irrelevant to truly 'philosophical' inquiry, they excluded from their enterprise a whole realm of questions that had previously been recognized as legitimate topics of inquiry. From then on, *abstract axioms were in, concrete diversity was out....* From Descartes' time on, attention was focused on timeless principles that hold good at all times equally: *the permanent was in, the transitory was out* (Toulmin 1990, p. 30).[20]

More than three centuries later, we see these same ontological principles unchanged in finance. Although finance theories are often accompanied with stories describing their "economic rationale," their acceptance or rejection is formally dependent upon the logic of their mathematical derivations and statistical tests. Although individual cases may suggest avenues of inquiry, only aggregate data can justify a theory. Although individual cases are full of confusing detail, this confusion is a consequence of our inability to distinguish the individual contributions of a number of general principles and not that the cases themselves are fundamentally unique. Finally, our theories are timeless, and the longer a series of data we can acquire to test them, the better the test.

Another belief underlying Descartes' method is the epistemological belief that, with the application of this method, we can know the laws of the universe. Although he did not cast his method in a form that we recognize as our own "scientific method," he clearly believed in the efficacy of an appropriate combination of observation and reason. The methods of the schoolmen, concerned as they were for their historic texts and divorced as they were from experience, were hopelessly inadequate.

I will say nothing of philosophy except that it has been studied for many centuries by the most outstanding minds without having produced anything which is not in dispute and consequently doubtful and uncertain (Descartes 1960, p. 8).

For it seemed to me that I might find much more of truth in the cogitations which each man made on things which were important to him, and where he would be the loser if he judged badly, than in the cogitations of a man of letters in his study, concerned with speculations which produce no effect, and which have no consequences to him except perhaps that the farther they are removed from common sense, the more they titillate his vanity, since then he needs so much more wit and skill to make them seem plausible (Descartes 1960, p. 9).[21]

Through the application of Descartes' method, and only through the application of his method, was it possible to gain explanation, understanding, and truth and the ability to predict, control, and solve problems. This is "scientism," variously defined as "[the belief that] science is the only measure of what counts as knowledge and reality" (Bernstein 1983, p. 48); "[the claim] that it is the natural sciences alone that provide the model and the standards for what is to count as genuine knowledge" (Bernstein 1983, p. 112); "the conviction that we can no longer understand science as one form of knowledge, but rather must identify knowledge with science" (Habermas 1971, p. 4); or "[the belief that] the meaning of knowledge is defined by what the sciences do and can thus be adequately explicated through the methodological analysis of scientific procedure" (Habermas 1971, p. 67).

Although he also uses the term *scientism*, Bernstein subsumes Descartes' ontological and epistemological beliefs under the term *objectivism*.

By "objectivism" I mean the basic conviction that there is or must be some permanent historical matrix or framework to which we can ultimately appeal in determining the nature of rationality, knowledge, truth, reality, goodness, or rightness.... Objectivism is closely related to foundationalism and the search for an Archimedean point (Bernstein 1983, p. 8).

He goes on to point out that there is a very strong emotional component to a belief in objectivism—the "Cartesian Anxiety."

It is the quest for some fixed point, some stable rock upon which we can secure our lives against the vicissitudes that constantly threaten us. The specter that hovers in the background of this journey is not just radical epistemological skepticism but the dread of madness and chaos where nothing is fixed, where we can neither touch bottom nor support ourselves on the surface.... But at the heart of the objectivist's vision and what makes sense of his or her passion, is the belief that there are or must be some fixed, permanent constraints to which we can appeal and which are secure and stable (Bernstein 1983, p. 18).

Although we as yet have offered only brief examples from finance, no one who is familiar with finance can fail to see its "scientism" and its descent from the Enlightenment. Of course, we cannot claim that the philosophy has not changed at all in 350 years,[22] and, in the next chapter, we will discuss its refinement as "positivism," the form to which it has evolved.

Before doing so, however, we would like to return to our assertion at the beginning of this chapter that science does not just *have* a philosophy; it *is* a philosophy. We have regularly referred to ontological and epistemological *beliefs*, rather than ontological and epistemological *realities*, although we recognize that many still may disagree. As we have discussed, there is not only a centuries-old tradition of seeing the universe in a certain way, there is also a very real (Cartesian) anxiety associated with not seeing it in that way. Of course, the best defense of our assertion would be to present a selection of alternative philosophies, but we prefer to wait until Chapter XIII to do that. In the concluding section of this chapter, we would like to discuss the point of the post-empiricists that the "scientific method" is not the real method of science. If the accomplishments of science have been achieved with methods that flout the supposed ontological and epistemological realities, then perhaps those "realities" really are just "beliefs."

POST-EMPIRICISM

The startling (or perhaps not-so-startling) insight of the post-empiricist historians and philosophers of science is that science has not worked the way it claims to work. The scientific method is an ideal, honored in principle but not practiced in fact, despite the fact that if the universe has a Cartesian structure, then the scientific method is *the* way to know that structure.[23] Historical accounts of applications of the scientific method are likely to be *ex post* reconstructions of an event that do not reflect what actually occurred.

Thomas Kuhn's *The Structure of Scientific Revolutions* (1970) is usually cited as the seminal post-empiricist work, although there were earlier works in which similar ideas were introduced (Miller 1993). It is impossible to do justice to such a provocative and controversial work in a few sentences here. The fundamental idea, which has perhaps become too familiar, is that science is characterized by periods of "normal science" conducted within a circumscribed paradigm[24] and periods of "revolutionary science" with contending paradigms. Although Kuhn has been criticized for ambiguity in the use of the term *paradigm*[25] and the situation has undoubtedly gotten worse as *paradigm* has passed into common usage and has even become a "buzzword," a working definition is that it is a commonly accepted way of thinking about a science and doing the science. We might say that a paradigm in its most general terms is a philosophy and its attendant methods.

One of the things that makes Kuhn controversial is that his revolutions do not conform to the ideal of the "scientific method."

> No process yet disclosed by the historical study of scientific development at all resembles the methodological stereotype of falsification by direct comparison with nature (Kuhn 1970, p. 77).

Another historian and philosopher of science, Paul Feyerabend, has gone much further in *Against Method* (1975).

> We find then, that there is not a single rule, however plausible and however firmly grounded in epistemology, that is not violated at some time or other. It becomes evident that such violations are not accidental events, they are not results of insufficient knowledge or of inattention which might have been avoided. On the contrary, we see that they are necessary for progress.... More specifically, one can show the following: given any rule, however "fundamental" or "necessary" for science, there are always circumstances when it is advisable not only to ignore the rule, but to adopt its opposite (1975, p. 23).[26]

Unfortunately, both Kuhn and Feyerabend have been accused of relativism: that anyone's opinion of what is rational is as good as anyone else's.[27] This is an unfair characterization. Although there may be no fixed standards, it is still possible for a scientific community to reach a working consensus. In Chapter XIII, we will have more to say about how this is to occur.

Ironically, finance has managed to ignore Kuhn's message regarding the relevance of the history of the conflict between what scientists say and what they do,[28] but has seized Kuhn as a justification for the preservation of the methodological status quo—that it takes a new paradigm to topple the old one.

> Once a first paradigm through which to view nature has been found, there is no such thing as research in the absence of any paradigm. To reject one paradigm without simultaneously substituting another is to reject science itself (Kuhn 1970, p. 79).

Therefore, finance can never adopt another philosophy or methodology. It is sustained by a Catch-22. Criticism is forbidden without an alternative, but alternatives are impossible without criticism. Anything that looks different is considered bad finance or considered not finance at all, and developing an alternative is hazardous to one's career.

What must be questioned, however, is whether finance has ever had what Kuhn would call a paradigm.

Paradigms gain their status because they are more successful than their competitors in solving a few problems that the group of practitioners has come to recognize as acute (Kuhn 1970, p. 23).

As we will show in subsequent chapters, the finance of the last four decades has had no real successes, especially with acute problems such as asset valuation, capital structure, and dividend policy; therefore, finance's so-called paradigm has nothing to do with any scientific achievement, but with a supposedly "scientific" method. Finance's paradigmatic method is justified by its rhetorical elegance and not by its results. It cleverly accomplishes nothing. Even if we agree that one paradigm must be replaced by another, then for finance, this only means new methods.

CONCLUSION

The purpose of this chapter was to show that philosophy matters to finance. Indeed, what makes finance a "science" is its commitment to the philosophy of the Enlightenment. In addition, we hope to have made two important points. The first is that "scientism," the belief in the efficacy of the scientific method for the acquisition of knowledge, is just that—a belief. The scientific method cannot justify itself. The second is that the ideal of the scientific method is more honored than practiced. The undoubted accomplishments of science must be attributed to some other form of inquiry.[29]

Before we consider what those other forms of inquiry might be, we will discuss the philosophy of finance in greater detail and some of the serious problems these beliefs have caused.[30]

NOTES

1. "It is, I think, particularly in periods of acknowledged crisis that scientists have turned to philosophical analysis as a device for unlocking the riddles of their field" (Kuhn 1970, p. 88).

2. "Effective research scarcely begins before a scientific community thinks it has acquired firm answers to questions like the following: What are the fundamental entities of which the universe is composed? How do these interact with each other and with the senses? What questions may legitimately be asked about such entities and what techniques employed in seeking solutions" (Kuhn 1970, p. 4).

3. This paragraph highlights the familiar contrast between science and philosophy as "methods of inquiry." In the following section in our discussion of the Enlightenment, we contrast science with authority, tradition, religion, ideology, myth, and superstition as "sources of knowledge" (Gadamer 1993; Winch 1958; Habermas 1987; Foucault 1994; Borgmann 1992). In chapter 12 in our discussion of alternative methodologies, we contrast science with narrative as "forms of knowledge" (Lyotard 1984). "Method of inquiry," "source of knowledge," and "form of knowledge" are all phrases that capture different (but overlapping) aspects of "science."

4. "Science asserts the priority of method over substance, because we can reliably inform ourselves about substance only with the aid of scientific modes of procedure" (Habermas 1971, p. 75).

5. The third section of this chapter discusses this point in detail.

6. "[Modern science operates] like a machine, reliable in accomplishing obviously very useful things, a machine everyone can learn to operate correctly (Husserl, quoted in Held 1980, p. 167). Husserl did not mean this as a compliment, although it could be taken as one.

7. The "scientific method" itself is contingent upon these beliefs, which is why it is the *beliefs*, and not simply the *method*, that distinguish science from non-science.

8. Fortunately, there can be agreement about the fact that there is only one logic of scientific investigation [the scientific method]—but also that it is not sufficient, since at any given time the viewpoints that select the relevant topics of inquiry and foreground them as subjects of research cannot themselves be derived from the logic of investigation (Gadamer 1993, p. 554).

9. One reason is that philosophical controversies are never explicitly dealt with in the education of most scientists.

> At least in the mature sciences, answers (or substitutes for answers) to [ontological and epistemological] questions … are firmly embedded in the educational initiation that prepares and licenses the student for professional practice. Because that education is both rigorous and rigid, these answers come to exert a deep hold on the scientific mind (Kuhn 1970, p. 4).

10. We, of course, differentiate theological, philosophical, and scientific questions in ways the schoolmen did not.

11. De Wulf (1956) quotes a number of vitriolic descriptions of scholasticism. Vives (p. 4): "[They] rave and invent absurdities that only they themselves can understand." Taine (p. 5): "Three centuries at the bottom of that gloomy abyss did not add a single idea to man's intellectual inheritance." Bacon (p. 4): "Their science degenerated into subtile, vain and unwholesome questions like a decomposing organism."

12. Gadamer (1993) extends this reasoning to logic itself in terms that are especially relevant to the experience of the schoolmen.

> A large part of the trouble here arises from the fact that he [Pareto] has not seen the point around which the main argument of this monograph revolves: that criteria of logic are not a direct gift of God, but arise out of, and are only intelligible in the context of ways of living or modes of social life. It follows that one cannot apply criteria of logic to modes of social life as such. For instance, science is one such mode and religion is another; and each has criteria of intelligibility peculiar to itself. So within science or religion actions can be logical or illogical: in science, for example, it would be illogical to refuse to be bound by the results of a properly carried out experiment; in religion it would be illogical to suppose that one could pit one's own strength against God's; and so on. But we cannot sensibly say that either the practice of science itself or that of religion is either illogical or logical: both are non-logical (Gadamer 1993, p. 100).

13. Consider whether the following descriptions of scholasticism might also apply to finance:

... drawing consequences *ad infinitum* without verifying principles, these remaining above examination." (M. Fouille, quoted in De Wulf 1956, p. 34) and "[having a] striking tendency to hasty generalizations, and [a] mania for making the facts of experience square with the needs of some preconceived theory in order to fit them by force into the current philosophical synthesis (De Wulf 1956, p. 88).

14. Including, of course, those philosophies that we offer in Chapter 14 as alternatives to the current philosophy of finance.

15. This [Jeffersonian] way of looking at modernism asserts itself in the term we commonly use for the modern project—Enlightenment. We think of the Enlightenment as the liberating dawn of reason that dispelled the darkness of medieval superstition and dogmatism, oppression and authoritarianism (Borgmann 1992, p. 25).

16. We must also bear in mind the vast differences between our stated philosophy and the reality of our actions. This is the subject of the section *Post-Empiricism* in this chapter.

17. Bloor (1976) has his own list of four characteristics of "the methodological style of Enlightenment "thought," one of which is relevant here. "First, it is individualistic and atomistic. This means that it conceives of wholes and collectivities as being unproblematically equivalent to sets of individual units" (Bloor 1976, p. 54).

18. Although Descartes does not employ the expressions subject and object in the ways in which they have come to be used by post-Cartesian philosophers (he still draws on the scholastic tradition), nevertheless his metaphysical and epistemological dichotomies provide the basis for this systematic distinction (Bernstein 1983, p. 115).

19. We will not comment on the first or second beliefs except to say that the failure to solve the capital structure problem ought to call them into question. The third belief clearly conflicts with another belief—that finance courses matter to students. Chapter 12 expands on the epistemological implications of the interaction between the profession and practice.

20. Bloor also captures these principles in his list of the characteristics of the "methodological style of Enlightenment thought."

> Second, this individualism is closely associated with a static approach to thinking. Historical variation is subordinated to a concern for the timeless and the universal.... These points are intimately related to the third feature of Enlightenment thought, which might be called abstract deductivism. Typically, particular social phenomena or cases of individual behavior are illuminated by being related to abstract general principles whether of morality or reasoning or scientific law (Bloor 1976, p. 54).

21. Thus, it seems as if Descartes would approve of finance academics' becoming involved in real finance. He does, however, share their reluctance to listen to practitioners.

> Furthermore, it seemed to me that to learn people's true opinions, I should pay attention to their conduct rather than to their words, not only because in our corrupt times there are few who are ready to weigh all that they believe, but also because many are not aware of their own beliefs, since the mental process of knowing a thing is good or bad is distinct from, and can occur without, the mental process of knowing that we know it (Descartes 1960, p. 18).

22. Toulmin (1990) is an excellent account of the evolution of Enlightenment thought, including those elements that have been abandoned. Especially, refer to the list and discussion beginning on p. 109.

23. Nevertheless the search for an algorithm of theory choice, or for clear and explicit criteria for demarcating science from nonscience, or for reconstructing the permanent standards that it is believed ought to govern the validation of scientific hypotheses and theories are legacies of Cartesianism in contemporary analytic philosophy of science. They reflect the demand that the philosopher of science be able to state explicit, determinate, fixed criteria and standards (Bernstein 1983, p. 23).

24. Mopping up-operations are what engage most scientists throughout their careers. They constitute what I am here calling normal science. Closely examined, whether historically or in the contemporary laboratory, that enterprise seems an attempt to force nature into the preformed and relatively inflexible box that the paradigm supplies. No part of the aim of normal science is to call forth new sorts of phenomena; indeed those that will not fit the box are often not seen at all (Kuhn 1970, p. 24).

25. One critic counted 64 meanings for *paradigm* in Kuhn's monograph.

26. To express it differently: in the history of science, standards of justification often forbid moves that are caused by psychological, socio-economic-political and other 'external' conditions, and science survives only because these moves are allowed to prevail (Feyerabend 1975, p. 166).

To sum up; whatever examples we consider, we see that the principles of critical rationalism (take falsification seriously; increase content; avoid *ad hoc* hypotheses; be 'honest'—whatever *that* means; and so on) and, *a fortiori*, the principles of logical empiricism (be precise; base your theories on measurement; avoid vague and unstable ideas; and so on) give an inadequate account of the past development of science and are liable to hinder science in the future. They give an inadequate account of science because science is much more 'sloppy' and 'irrational' than its methodological image. And, they are liable to hinder it, because the attempt to make science more 'rational' and more precise is bound to wipe it out (Feyerabend 1975, p. 179).

27. The relativist not only denies the positive claims of the objectivist but goes further. In its strongest form, relativism is the basic conviction that when we turn to the examination of those concepts that philosophers have taken to be the most fundamental—whether it is the concept of rationality, truth, reality, right, the food, or norms—we are forced to recognize that in the final analysis all such concepts must be understood as relative to a specific conceptual scheme, theoretical framework, paradigm, form of life, society, or culture. Since the relativist believes that there is (or can be) a nonreducible plurality of such conceptual schemes, he or she challenges the claim that these concepts can have a determinate and univocal significance. For the relativist, there is no substantive overarching framework or single metalanguage by which we can rationally adjudicate or univocally evaluate competing claims of alternative paradigms (Bernstein, 1983, p. 8).

28. "History, if viewed as a repository for more than anecdote or chronology, could produce a decisive transformation in the image of science by which we are now possessed" (Kuhn 1970, p. 1).

29. Awareness has been growing that attempts to state what are or ought to be the criteria for evaluating and validating scientific hypotheses and theories that are abstracted from existing social practices are threatened with a false rigidity or with pious vacuity and that existing criteria are always open to conflicting interpretations and applications and can be weighted in different ways. The effective standards and norms that are operative in scientific inquiry are subject to change and modification in the course of scientific enquiry. We are now aware that it is not only important to understand

the role of tradition in science as mediated through research programs or research traditions but that we must understand how such traditions arise, develop, and become progressive and fertile, as well as the ways in which they can degenerate (Bernstein 1983, p. 24).

30.   A belief is a behavioral rule, but not the habitually determined behavior itself. Behavioral certainty is the criterion of its validity. A belief remains unproblematic as long as the modes of behavior that it guides do not fail in reality. As soon as a behavioral habit is rendered uncertain by the resistance of reality, doubt arises with regard to the orientation that guides behavior. The undermining of habits awakens doubt in the validity of the corresponding beliefs (Habermas 1971, p. 120).

Section 2

THE METHODOLOGICAL FOUNDATIONS
OF FINANCIAL ECONOMICS

Chapter III

The Philsophical Justification: Friedman's Positivism

LOGICAL POSITIVISM

The origin of twentieth-century positivism is perhaps with the French social theorist Claude Henri de Rouvroy, comte de Saint-Simon (1760-1825), who is best known for his theory of "evolutionary organicism." Evolutionary organicism postulated history as an orderly progression culminating in an industrial, harmonious society ruled by a scientific elite on the basis of a division of labor. de Rouvroy's ideas influenced August Comte, Karl Marx, and Herbert Spencer, among others. Logical positivism (LP, subsequently), in contrast is a twentieth-century philosophical movement in the tradition of analytic and linguistic philosophy. LP had close ties to the British empiricism of Bacon and Mill, which meant the acceptance and advancement of the natural sciences and the rejection of metaphysics.

The bastion of LP was an ensemble of German and Austrian philosophers, referenced after its evolution as the Vienna Group. Organized by Moritz Schlick (1882-1936), a professor of philosophy at the University of Vienna, the Vienna Group published its own journal. The group included such names as Herbert Feigl, Kurt Gödel, Hans Hahn, Friedrich Waismann, and Rudolf Carnap.

The Vienna Group was much influenced by Ludwig Wittgenstein (1889-1951), an Austrian philosopher and mathematician (not a positivist himself), who argued that propositions are "logical pictures" of possible facts. This argument implied that a proposition is not meaningful unless it determines a precise range of circumstances in which it is true. A partial exception was made for tautologies—propositions that say nothing, since they are, respectively, true or false no matter what.

In contrast, metaphysics, according to Wittgenstein tries to say something about reality as a whole, making claims supposedly so general and fundamental as to be indifferent to the particular facts of the world. In Wittgenstein's theory of language, such claims are literally nonsensical: words without meaning.

The logical positivists used Wittgenstein's argument to refute and sneer at metaphysical propositions, interpreting Wittgenstein in a way that Wittgenstein almost certainly did not mean to be interpreted. Wittgenstein had distinguished in an abstract way between elementary and complex propositions. The positivists took his elementary propositions to be reports of observations. This was the source of their central idea, the verification principle, which said that any meaningful proposition, other than the tautological, or, as they came to be called, "analytic" propositions of logic and pure mathematics, had to be verifiable by means of observation.

Metaphysical statements were not the only ones that did not bode well with the logical positivists. Ordinary moral judgments seemed to fail them, too. One way this was dealt with was by saying that such judgments were expressions of emotion, rather than genuine propositions.

With metaphysics out of the picture, everything was seen as the logical clarification of scientific statements and theories—for example, putting informally stated theories in strict axiomatic form, so as to distinguish clearly their analytical from their empirical elements.

Nevertheless, controversy surrounded the interpretation of the principles of LP. One of these controversies (directly tied to "Friedmanian positivism," which, in fact, is not positivism, but instrumentalism) was about the verification of scientific laws. Because these laws apply to a potentially infinite number of instances, they cannot be verified with absolute conclusiveness. To escape the quagmire, the notion of *verification* gave way to the weaker idea of *confirmation*. Attempts to make this notion precise, however, were not successful. The more the verification principle was qualified, the harder it became to distinguish LP from other forms of logical empiricism.

FRIEDMANIAN "POSITIVISM"

Jerry Giedymin (1978), enumerating the underlying tenets of the logical positivist doctrine, remarked that there are 64 (2^6) possible definitions of positivism. Friedman ported over to economics a relatively simplistic, weak, mutated strain of the logical positivist philosophy and infused it with his strong ideological beliefs in neo-classical economics. In essence, Friedman is an instrumentalist (an offshoot of positivism) in the sense that for him a theory is an instrument for action, the validity of which is measured by success. This is in stark contrast to Dewey's[2] perception of logical thought and action, for example, in which thoughtful action is measured by its success at discovering the truth. For Friedman, the discovery of truth, if there is such a thing in economics as truth, is marginal, if it is even an issue at all.

Friedman's work is strictly philosophical: in part, his interpretation of positivism; in part, watered-down Popperian precepts as set forth in *Conjectures and Refutations* (Popper 1968), and in part, "getting even" with his colleagues on the Cowles Commission. Friedmanian positivism/ instrumentalism can be briefly described as the following set of propositions:

1. The primary requisite of a theory is to produce acceptable forecasts.
2. The secondary requisite of a theory is to be simple and fruitful.
3. The assumptions of the theory *must be* unrealistic to satisfy requisites 1 and 2.

There is no mention in "positive economics" of the discovery of truth, either as the ultimate goal or as a scientific principle. Somehow this discovery is assumed to take form through the acceptability of forecasts (By whom? With what yardstick?). Accordingly, when a theory's forecasts are no longer acceptable (Again by whom? With what yardstick?), a paradigm, hypothesis or model is replaced.

Data

It might be useful to examine in greater detail the logical foundations of Friedmanian instrumentalism. Friedman (1953) begins with accepting John Neville Keynes' definition of what is positive science, what is normative science, and what is art, and states that his concern is "... with certain methodological problems that arise in constructing the 'distinct positive science' Keynes called for ..." (p. 3).

As language, theory has no substantive content. It is just a set of tautologies, to serve as a filing system for empirical material (observable phenomena?). Only the laws of formal logic can show whether theory as a language is complete and consistent, that is, whether its propositions are "right" or "wrong."

But,

> Viewed as a body of substantive hypotheses, theory is to be judged by its predictive power for the class of phenomena which it is intended to "explain." Only factual evidence can show whether it is "right" or "wrong" or, better, tentatively "accepted" as valid or "rejected." As I shall argue at greater length below, the only relevant test of the *validity* of a hypothesis is comparisons of its predictions with experience. The hypothesis is

rejected if its predictions are contradicted ("frequently" or more often than the predictions from an alternative hypothesis); great confidence is attached to it if it has survived many opportunities for contradiction. Factual evidence can never "prove" a hypothesis; it can only fail to disprove it, which is what we generally mean when we say, somewhat inexactly, that the hypothesis has been "confirmed" by experience (1953, p. 9).

From here on, Friedman uses the words *theory* and *hypothesis* interchangeably.[3] This practice, unfortunately, becomes no small cause for confusion, notwithstanding, that the subjective ground rules of Friedmanian's instrumentalism are laid down in what follows. Who is to say what is "frequent" enough and what is not? Better yet, given the system of "scientific" communication, how is one to know how often a cherished theory did not fail to be disproved, because some or all tests that would have shown such non-failure never filtered through the net cast by the promoters of a revered theory?[4]

But Friedman does not stop here with subjectivity. A bit later we learn that the validity of a hypothesis is not a sufficient condition to choose among alternative hypotheses, because observed facts are finite in number, but hypotheses are not. For each hypothesis that is consistent with observable facts there is an infinite number of hypotheses which are also consistent with the observable facts. In essence, what Friedman tells us here is that we have to choose somehow, and that the choosing is left to us.

Thus, the choice among competing hypotheses must be somehow "arbitrary." Friedman uses the criteria of "simplicity" and "fruitfulness" that, according to his own admission are "... notions that defy completely objective specification." With all fairness, Friedman follows up with his definition what "simplicity"[5] and "fruitfulness"[6] mean, but, unpropitiously, his definitions do not help much to mitigate subjectivity. Moreover, given one's cherished ideology, both "simplicity" and "fruitfulness" can be used to support one's chosen dogma. Perhaps there is no branch of economics, other than financial economics, in which the combination of ideology and methodology are so protective of the orthodoxy of the neo-classical church.

The importance of data, positive economics' *totum factum*, is further advanced in Friedman's edict that, although strictly controlled experiments cannot be conducted in economics,[7] this fact does not constitute " ... a basic difference between the social and the physical sciences both because it is not peculiar to the social sciences... and because the distinction between controlled experiment and uncontrolled *experience* [our italics] is at best one of degree" (p. 10).

Friedman goes on asserting that there is no such thing as a completely controlled experiment, and that "every *experience* [our italics] is partially

controlled, in the sense that some disturbing influences are relatively
constant...." In our opinion, the presence of "disturbing influences" is
precisely the element that makes economic *experience*, meaning the gazing
into and sorting through massive ex post data, incomparable to controlled
experiments. We discuss this adversity in more detail when we take a closer
look at the contribution and influence of event studies to the field of finance.

But data are a must for another purpose as well:

> Empirical evidence is vital at two different, though closely related, stages: in constructing
> hypotheses and testing their validity. Full and comprehensive evidence on the
> phenomena to be generalized or "explained" by a hypothesis, besides its obvious value
> in suggesting new hypotheses, is needed to assure that a hypothesis explains what it
> sets out to explain—that its implications for such phenomena are not contradicted in
> advance by experience that has already been observed. Given that the hypothesis is
> consistent with the evidence at hand, its further testing involves deducing from it new
> facts against additional empirical evidence (pp. 12-13).

In footnote 11, attached to the quote above, Friedman does "battle" with
his colleagues on the Cowles Commission, who are "guilty" of classifying
and selecting models that are "identified"; that is, " ... [make] systematic
use of available statistical evidence and theory." They are also culpable of
applying the principles of "Occam's razor," clearly not the "simplicity"
criterion of Friedman as we have already noted.

At this juncture, a little rumination about Koopmans' (1947) words would
not be remiss:

> ...rigorous testing of hypotheses according to modern methods of statistical inference
> requires a specification of the form of a joint probability distribution of the variables.
> In principle, such specification does not need to take a "parametric" form, as when
> linear, parabolic or exponential functions, or normal distributions, are specified—
> although parametric assumptions usually admit more accurate estimation and powerful
> tests whenever they are justified. In any case, however, it is necessary to hypothesize
> in what manner randomness enters into the formation of economic variables. It is for
> this reason that the form of each structural equation should be specified and/or
> determined to the point where at least a conceptual insolation of the random influences
> at work is attained (Koopmans 1947, p. 198).

There is a chasm as wide as an ocean between Friedman and Koopmans.
Unfortunately, many a financial economist has tried to jump this chasm
in two leaps.

Assumptions

The bulk of Friedman's paper, surprisingly, deals with the assumptions
of a theory. In the 43 pages of the essay, Friedman keeps returning to the

assumptions over and over, rather like explaining to a hard-to-learn person how assumptions must be unrealistic and how one must not judge a theory by its assumptions. Perhaps this is an acknowledgment that his view of assumptions was the most controversial part of the essay and the hardest part of his philosophy to swallow. But let's try to follow his line of reasoning (which is not necessarily in the order of the pages in the essay).

Perhaps the most determining statement is the oft-quoted passage:

> …the important question to ask about the "assumptions" of a theory is not whether they are descriptively "realistic," for they never are, but whether they are sufficiently good approximations for the purpose at hand. And the question can be answered only by seeing whether the theory works, which means whether it yields sufficiently accurate predictions (p. 15).

An "under-the-microscope" examination of this statement reveals the following components:

1. a declaration dependent entirely on Friedman's perception of reality and the force with which this perception is stated, that assumptions are never descriptively realistic; and
2. two subjective qualifications: "sufficiently accurate," and "for the purpose at hand."

These two components complete a logical circle that, basically, gives economists the opportunity to develop theories consistent with their *beliefs*. As long as it is possible to find empirical evidence, meaning some kind of test from compiled data, in which the theory does not fail, and as long as one is loud enough declaring that this is so, the theory holds. Remember: "Factual evidence can never 'prove' a hypothesis; it can only fail to disprove it" (p. 9). In fact, the theory not only holds, but carries with it theories of the same religion.

This very same prescription and logic gave Sharpe (1964) the idea to carry Friedman forward (or perhaps, away) one, extra and critical step in advancing his breed of capital asset pricing:

> … since the proper test of theory is not the realism of its assumptions but the acceptability of its implications, and since these assumptions imply equilibrium conditions which form a major part of classical financial doctrine, it is far from clear that this formulation should be rejected (p. 434).

Although Sharpe builds on Friedman (the test of a theory is not the realism of the assumptions), the distinction between the two is critical. Sharpe moves from Friedman's acceptance of a theory if it provides a "sufficiently good approximation" of reality "for the purpose at hand" to adopting a doctrine based on the "acceptability of its implications." In essence, Sharpe eschews dependence on predictive ability (as Friedman's litmus test of the quality of a theory) and instead, condones logical consistency with accepted doctrine. It is sufficient for such logical consistency to exist when a model's mathematical structure is internally consistent and/or when the theory's extra-mathematical implications are not in conflict with rudimentary economic precepts that dominate, indeed rule, the literature. In other words, any theory that tells us not to put all of our eggs in one basket is a good theory.

Friedman also makes it clear that it is a necessary, but not sufficient, condition that assumptions must be unrealistic:

> Truly important and significant hypotheses will be found to have "assumptions" that are wildly inaccurate descriptive representation of reality, and, in general, the more significant the theory, the more unrealistic the assumptions (in this sense) (p. 14).

The other important building block in the structure of positive economics is immunization of the theory from one's scrutiny of the assumptions.[8] But let Friedman speak for himself:

> The difficulty in the social sciences of getting new evidence for this class of phenomena and of judging its conformity with the implications of the hypothesis makes it tempting to suppose that other, more readily available, evidence is equally relevant to the validity of the hypothesis—to suppose that hypotheses have not only "implications" but also "assumptions" and that the conformity of these "assumptions" to "reality" is a test of the validity of the hypothesis *different from* or *additional to* the test by implications. This widely held view is fundamentally wrong and productive of much mischief (p. 14).

Mischief?

Friedman then goes on arguing that efforts to separate valid from invalid assumptions do no more nor less than confuse the issue, promote misunderstanding of the empirical evidence (just how?), misdirect intellectual efforts that should have been devoted otherwise to the development of theories consistent with the tenets of positive economics (God forbid), impede consensus, and, might, quite possibly, be the source of all malaise in this neck of the universe (this last caveat is our rude and sarcastic addition).

The rest of Friedman's (1953) essay is devoted to belaboring the same notion, that a theory cannot be judged by the realism of its assumptions. Friedman goes to great lengths to demonstrate this contention, first with examples from the natural sciences (to which positivism and, because of it, positive economics show great affinity, sometimes ironically referred to as "physics envy"), but later with examples from "economic theory." The impressions these attempts make is tantamount to "preaching to the choir."

It is not our intention to belabor the problems one might have with this perception through a large number of direct quotations from the essay. Nevertheless, as a closing argument, perhaps it would be wise to let Friedman have the final word:

> Complete "realism" is clearly unattainable, and the question whether a theory is realistic "enough" can be settled only by seeing whether it yields predictions that are good enough for the purpose in hand or that are better than predictions from alternative theories. Yet the belief that a theory can be tested by the realism of its assumptions independently of the accuracy of its predictions is widespread and the source of much of the perennial criticism of economic theory as unrealistic. Such criticism is largely irrelevant, and, in consequence, most attempts to reform economic theory that it has stimulated have been unsuccessful (p. 41).

Although the final words here are much weaker than the contentions Friedman makes earlier, the implication of the argument stay, nevertheless, intact.

CONCLUDING REMARKS

It is impossible to review and make an exposition of Friedman's positivism/ instrumentalism without pointing to the weaknesses, flaws, and inconsistencies inherent in this philosophy. At the same time, and with all fairness to Friedman, we are guilty of being subjective where we should have observed utmost objectivity. And, without a doubt, our critics will point to this fault of our own. Yet, this is the nature and course of all philosophical debates, which is exactly what we have in this section of the book. As we pointed out in the previous chapter, all science is a matter of belief. And beliefs are influenced to no small degree by technology.

The next chapter, which is more an explicit critique of the "results" of the adoption of Friedman's philosophy than a critique of the philosophy itself, is a window on the futility of positive financial economics in the process of discovery. Ergo, it is a verification that, consistent with Keynes' (1891) definition of art, financial economics is "a system of rules for the attainment of a given end." What this "end" really is will be discussed in Chapter XI of this book.

NOTES

1. Substantial parts of this section come from Grolier's *1996 Encyclopedia for Windows*. Credit, thus, is due to Michael Williams. For more details about the subject, see the bibliography listing of the encyclopedia under the headings "Logical Positivism" and "Positivism."
2. John Dewey (1859-1952), American philosopher, educator, and psychologist.

3. The *American Heritage Dictionary for Windows* defines "theory" and "hypothesis," respectively, as:

Theory: Systematically organized knowledge applicable in a relatively wide variety of circumstances, especially a *system* [our italics] of assumptions, accepted principles, and rules of procedure devised to analyze, predict, or otherwise explain the nature or behavior of a specified set of phenomena.

Hypothesis: 1. A tentative explanation that accounts for a set of facts and can be tested by further investigation; a theory.
             2. Something taken to be true for the purpose of argument or investigation; an assumption.

Although, in casual conversation, a hypothesis can be considered a theory, as in "I have a theory that behind every successful man there is a strong-willed woman," in more exact parlance, an assumption, as defined in item 2, a hypothesis cannot also be "a system of assumptions, accepted principles, and rules of procedure." On the contrary, hypotheses are built on systems of assumptions. Unfortunately, Friedman interchanges the words *hypothesis* and *assumption* whenever it is convenient for him to make his case.

4. See "data mining" in the next chapter.

5. A theory is simple the less a priori knowledge one must possess to make *predictions*. This is in unequivocal contrast to the principle of Occam's razor, one of the cherished postulates of any branch of science, according to which a theory is preferred to another if it requires fewer *assumptions* to explain the same phenomenon. Assumptions are quite another "story" in Friedman's positivism.

6. A theory is "fruitful," if its predictions are more precise (how precise is precise?), the more ground the predictions can cover, and the more ideas it suggests for the development of other theories.

7. This is again a completely subjective statement, mainly because Friedman is neither trained in nor aware of the possibilities experimental psychology offers. This is so, because Friedman is essentially a macro-economist, which branch of economics does not venture into laboratory experiments. Experimental economics, especially the work of Vernon Smith of the University of Arizona, comes to mind to illustrate the predispositions of Friedman.

See also in Chapter V work in financial economics that is inspired by experimental psychology.

8. As we will argue in the next chapter this immunization is a major concern of Popper, because through such immunization the theory can be made almost totally irrefutable.

Chapter IV

A Critique of Friedman's Positivism

FRIEDMAN AND THE PHILOSOPHY OF SCIENCE

At this juncture, it would be useful to compare and contrast Friedman's (1953) instrumentalism with Popper's philosophy of science. To do so, we must reexamine the difference between Popper of natural sciences and Popper of social sciences.

Popper$_n$ and Popper$_s$

The principles of what constitutes truth, rationality and scientific progress, according to the Popperian philosophy of science,[1] appear in a succinct form in Popper (1979). For the benefit of the reader who is not familiar with these principles, we repeat them here (for more detail, see Popper 1979):

1. a new theory should proceed from some simple, new, powerful and underlying idea about observable relations;
2. a new theory should be independently testable; that is, besides the ability to explain all the explicada that it sets out to resolve, it must have testable consequences leading to phenomena that so far have not been observed; and
3. a new theory should be capable of withstanding some novel and severe tests (examinations to which the older theory could not have been subjected).

In addition, Popper states that a theory must be refutable (falsifiable) and truthful, thus reflecting Tarski's (1943-1944) formulation of truthfulness as "correspondence to facts."

In later writings, Popper acknowledged differences between the natural and the social sciences and supported situational logic as the basis of a scientific methodology applicable to the latter. In brief, situational logic is a rational reconstruction of the actions a person takes in response to a problem situation, explaining why the person did what he or she did (Popper 1972).

The potential logical conflict that exists between Popper's more famous falsificationalism in the natural sciences and situational logic in the social sciences puzzled Hands (1985). If one accepts Popper the falsificationalist, one cannot accept Popper the situational logicist. To solve the dilemma, Hands suggested that we accept the existence of two Poppers: Popper for the natural sciences, **Popper**$_n$, and Popper for the social sciences, **Popper**$_s$ ("s" for either social, or situational logic). But this interpretation is a paradox in itself, because Popper was a zealous supporter of the idea of methodological monism (unity of science).

There exists an extensive literature in economics, dedicated to the resolution of this impasse, too voluminous and too tangential to review and to discuss in this chapter. Our advice to the interested reader is to see Caldwell (1991) as a starting point. Our summary of the different interpretations of Popper scholars in economics is that the Popperian philosophy boils down to critical rationalism. In its most simple and straightforward form, it means that theories must be criticized, even by their own creators, and, of course, by their opponents, in order to make sure (as much as possible) that they are not false.

To use an analogy from jurisprudence, theories are innocent until proven guilty—in this case, of the crime of not being truthful—but one must always be an aggressive prosecutor. And, of course, a theory can and should be tried as often as possible for the crime. Friedmanian instrumentalism agrees that theories are innocent until proven guilty, but takes the side of the defense in that every effort must be made to accumulate evidence of innocence in the form of accurate predictions. And through the shrewd use of "wildly unrealistic" assumptions, it is even possible that theories can be immunized against guilty verdicts.[2]

An acceptance of critical rationalism necessarily casts financial economics' positivist (or instrumentalist) methodology out of the domain of science, for finance is anything but critical. Indeed, as we will argue later, financial economics as it is practiced in its many journals today is art, if it is anything else.[3]

Popper and Friedman

There is one common aspect to Popper's principle of critical rationalism and Friedman's instrumentalism: they both argue the necessity of using data. The former uses data to scrutinize the theory and reject it if it does not correspond to the facts (in the data); the latter, to corroborate the theory if it is reasonably good (in the sense that it is a better predictor of the future than other theories).[4] The first approach is to criticize a theory, whoever the critics might be, in order not to advocate/espouse a false theory. The second approach is not concerned much with truth, but only with surface reality for the sake of a specific use (either forecasting, or not being able to prove that the model/paradigm is false).

According to the latter approach, and especially when it is infused with strong ideological beliefs (as is the case in financial economics[5]) theories can be immunized by a set of cleverly selected assumptions such that the theory is internally consistent. Other, competing doctrines, based on different methodologies, are dismissed on the grounds that they are not "scientific enough," meaning that they do not "pack" mathematical power. These theories are filtered out through the publication process, with the argument that whatever the data show (or do not show) is not good enough. But as Caldwell (1991) observes:

> ... because the empirical basis is theory impregnated (the "facts" one sees depend upon the theory one holds), its content will vary as theories change (Popper 1983, pp. xxii-xxiv) (p. 3).

To put this in sportscasters' lingo: Friedmanian instrumentalism sees it as it calls it. Thus, to overthrow a revered and deeply rooted theory, the data must provide such overwhelmingly contradictory evidence that only the blind, the fanatic, or both could still embrace the theory.[6]

The contrast between Popper and Friedman, therefore, is critical. Popper advocates criticism (whether it is outright falsificationalism or its milder recasting for the social sciences, critical rationalism). Friedman seeks corroboration: what is a good forecast and how one is to use it in decision making. Because it is also infused with an ideology—the preconceived notion that markets know best and that the shareholder must be the ultimate and only beneficiary of everything corporations do—this methodology is especially dangerous, and ultimately futile.

Few papers question the epistemological bases of key finance paradigms. One of the fewer-than-the-fingers-on-one-hand papers is by Ryan (1982). Ryan argues that the epistemological agreement held by the founders of capital market theory has broken down and that the capital asset pricing theory that was developed within this epistemological framework overemphasized the role of empirical testing in the validation of scientific theories. In addition, the positivist perspective on science leads the academic finance community to place an unwarranted reliance on empirical testing to settle *theoretical* [our emphasis] disputes.

What we have is empirical testing and, consequently, data rule. As more and different data come to the public domain (thanks to the incredible growth opportunities of electronic storage), the model is refuted (because it has no predictive ability!), just to be validated again (because it has predictive ability!), and *moto perpetuo*. Yet, if assumptions mattered, and if such fictions as equilibrium and homogeneous expectations are recognized for what they are (fantasy), then why would one wish to presume that a realistic theory will follow?[7] And if it is fiction, then why would one expect it to have normative use?

As we quoted Keynes (1891) in the previous chapter, art is "a system of rules for the attainment of a given end," and we concluded that so is positive model building, as much as composing music is. They both have their strict rules and provide beauty for the cognoscenti/connoisseur/aesthete. Beyond that, to expect usefulness is both unwise and unfair. As Frankfurter and Phillips (forthcoming) observe, there is nothing particularly wrong with the CAPM as a positive model, built in the Friedmanian tradition. Imputing normative implications to this kind of a model, on the other hand, has been, possibly, the cornerstone of the imbroglio surrounding the CAPM.

THE PITFALLS OF FRIEDMANIAN INSTRUMENTALISM

One major fallacy of Friedman's methodology is the view that the same data can be used both to develop a theory and to verify it. This belief, long known in the natural sciences, has been recognized for economics by Koopmans (1947), under the heading, "Measurement Without Theory."

Koopmans' point is quite simple: one cannot verify a scientific theory by the data one uses to formulate the theory. Besides, it does not make sense to presuppose that the very same data can serve the purpose of refuting an alternative theory not suggested by the data, unless it was stated before the data were known. (If Koopmans were a Cajun, born and reared in Louisiana, he would have said one fishes for sacalait not scientific theory.) Koopmans' contention is well known by all who heed the basic doctrines of the philosophy of science. Unfortunately, very few financial economists are aware of or care much about philosophy.[8]

The problems this license to "peek-and-theorize" granted to financial economists have been the source of much frustration, name-calling and futile and inconclusive research in finance. There are several sources of this misuse and abuse, which we turn to discuss now.

Data

The instrumentalist "deal" offered to financial economists involved the surcease from realism of assumptions at the price of accuracy (however subjective) of predictions. Although Sharpe (1964) stretched the bargain a bit further, by reducing predictive ability into "acceptability of implications," for most financial economists, in most of the key issues of the paradigm, what data show remained the ultimate proof (see Ryan above). That necessarily leads to perhaps the ugliest effect of Friedmanian instrumentalism on financial research. Data do not speak (or even scream, as one of our reviewers once put it) for themselves. We put words into their mouth.

Fischer Black (1993), in a heroic and passionate attempt to salvage the CAPM which Fama and French (1992) rechristened "the SLB model" (Sharpe, Lintner, Black), raises the issue of "data mining," "data snooping," and "data dredging," which he eventually lumps together under "hindsight." In our opinion, these aspects of "after-the-fact" manipulations of data to satisfy ex post prediction accuracy go much deeper and are more delicate than the oversimplifying catch-all phrase of "hindsight." The following is one possible classification of the many forms we use to show whatever is "dear"[9] to us.

"Cordelia's Dilemma"[10]

Cordelia's Dilemma is basically the practice of not reporting bad news (hence the name, coined by Stephen Jay Gould, borrowing the concept from Shakespeare's *King Lear*). The dilemma can take on two forms: (1) the publication filter, when a reviewer rejects a paper on the grounds that the results are contrary to "overwhelming" evidence, or because the results differ from the beliefs of the particular reviewer, and (2) self-discipline, where the author(s) voluntarily bury results that they "believe" are not going to be published, saving (often substantial) submission fees.

Data Mining

Data mining is the application of "sophisticated methods" to find in the data whatever we want to prove is there. The crudest form of data mining is a variety of "transformations," most popular of which is logarithmic transformation (which receives an additional "seal of approval" from econometrics by being one procedure for getting rid of a scale effect, if present). The aim, of course, is getting a significant coefficient, which has the "right" sign, according to the hypothesis. As the adage goes: "Keeping one eye on the hypothesis, and one eye on the data."

The surprising aspect of this reasoning is that what we do is supposed to be market "unanimity." But, although we personify the market,[11] in the final analysis we use a statistical model. Whatever the model is, or is not, the results are some kind of average of market activity (buying and selling) of people who acted upon their individual beliefs, preferences, and understanding. Where do we get the gall to pretend that individuals develop a multi-variate regression structure (what most of our empirical work boils down to when everything else is peeled away) interspersed with logarithmic variables? And, although the coefficients line up, eventually, according to theory, the adjusted multiple correlation coefficient of the model is around 0.014. This means that the model explains 11.83 percent, but the unexplained portion of the model is around 99.30 percent ($\sqrt{1.0\text{-}0.014}$).

Another twist of data mining is the search for the right statistical model. Here, the more fireworks the model has, the more "scientific" it is considered. Thus, we do two- and three-stage least squares, random coefficient, ridge, error in and instrumental variables, and other obscure types of regressions, "Scholes-Williams betas" or whatever else the "market will buy" at the moment. Worse, we infer the motivation of people when in fact we have nothing more than estimated coefficients of models that fit the data the best.

Data "Snooping"

Data snooping is the violation of the scientific principle Koopmans, (1947) quoted earlier, warns us about. That is, we formulate our hypothesis by eye-balling the data, and then we use the same data to accept the hypothesis we eye-balled from the very same data.

Data Dredging

Data dredging is scraping the bottom of the barrel to find the data that will be consistent with a cherished theory. A more dangerous and, strictly speaking, dishonest variant of data dredging is data conjuring.

As we said, Black (1993) lumps data mining, data dredging, and data snooping under the common heading of "hindsight." We, on the other hand, believe that this is a too casual and too superfluous a grouping of shortcomings and faults of differing degrees of honesty, and the respective damage they can cause.

Data Conjuring

Data conjuring is selecting the sample based on a preconceived criterion and then finding a story that fits the "sample." For instance, using a large electronically addressable database, one selects stocks that, on a given date had a positive/negative prediction error (see our discussion about event studies in Section III of this book) of, say, greater than 5 percent. Then, one sifts through the *Wall Street Journal* to find an "event" that would fit a story common to these stocks. Presto, one not only has an event study on hand, but also very significant results, before even trying to run the first regression.

A downright felonious form of data conjuring is the case where data is not found to fit one's perceived conclusions, but is artificially created, conjured up. We have no evidence of these kinds of practices in finance, but the fact that there are journals (e.g., the *Journal of Money, Credit and Banking*) that require the submission of all output in case the paper is accepted for publication indicates that there might have been problems with certain authors in the past. This dissolute and deplorable practice is known to exist in other branches of the social sciences, psychology, for example.

Data Storking

We derive the term *data storking* from the classical example of statistics in which the fairy-tale of the stork bringing the babies to the world is statistically proven through the correlation between the frequency of stork nest sightings and the number of babies per household. In general, rural families have a significantly larger number of children per family than urban families. Storks, as well, prefer to nest in rural house chimneys. Otherwise, of course, there is no connection. Yet, the theory serves well those who, for religious or other reasons, prefer postponing sex-education until it is no more of use.

Black (1995), as quoted in *Euromoney* puts it more succinctly: "I feel that econometric studies of time-series data tell us little about the economy.... Econometric studies can tell us about variances and covariances, including autocovariances." The time-series studies of stock market data gave us the real *esoterica extraordinaire*, inventing new concepts of economic time, as opposed to real or calendar time (see, e.g., Lamoureux and Lastrapes 1993) and event-induced variances (Boehmer, Musumeci and Poulsen 1991), to mention just a few of the more recondite examples of the lot.

But the "quants," as the street (Wall Street, that is) calls these model builders, do not stop here. They port over chaos theory, fractals, and, ultimately, neural networks.

These are all "works" in the best tradition of positive economics, yet they give us very little understanding of the true processes that necessarily involve, like everything else in the social sciences, the human element. The much sought-after statistical significance replaces substance, and tells us almost nothing about cause and effect. May the stork nest on your chimney!

Assumptions

Perhaps this is where positive economics "freed" financial researchers from the burden of creating something of value to the practitioners of finance, for the small price of being consistent with economic dogma. The Friedmanian requirement of predictive ability was soon abandoned, or was relaxed to the point where superficial "correspondence" to the facts, achieved by more or less naive, and/or more or less nefarious manipulation of data for the sake of logical consistency, was sufficient. Logical consistency became tantamount to what Sharpe (1964) called "acceptability of implications," more often than not a result that was not at variance with the tenets of neo-classical economics (or folk proverbs).

The element of unrealistic assumptions as the cornerstone of financial model building was broadly criticized at the time the first sophisticated models of financial economics surfaced in the literature. It is important to remember that the many critics of Modigliani and Miller's (1958) seminal work pointed out how unrealistic the assumptions were and how, because of this fault, the arbitrage mechanism, central to the Modigliani and Miller theory, could not possibly work.

Also, remember that even six years after Modigliani and Miller (1958), the first referee of the Sharpe (1964) paper and ultimately, the editor of the *Journal of Finance* found the assumption of homogeneous expectations of all investors "preposterous" (see, Note 7). Indeed, not only are investors' expectations not homogeneous, but also we have very little idea, or factual knowledge of how investors formulate expectations and under what circumstances those expectations are grossly inconsistent with the tenets of value maximization.

But as financial economics' model building embarked on the Friedmanian path, less and less criticism was directed toward the realism of the assumptions. In fact, models that were built on top of the early models took the implications of the earlier models for granted, in many instances completely forgetting the original assumptions upon which the earlier models were built.

As we got enveloped in the positive methodology, criticism died out, or was totally disregarded. For instance, Myers' (1972) thoughtful paper in which it was shown that there is no such thing as an equilibrium-constrained regression was forgotten even by Myers himself (1978), when the CAPM (to be discussed in great detail in Chapter VI) application to problems of cost of capital and capital budgeting became rampant.

The logical inconsistency of Friedmanian instrumentalism reaches its *ne plus ultra* in the entanglement, following the Fama and French (1992) devastating empirical findings about the SLB model (*de facto*, the CAPM in sheep's clothes) mentioned earlier. Fama and French (1992) declare that the SLB model has no predictive power (the ultimate failing in the instrumentalist methodology). Roll and Ross (1994) set out to put Fama and French (1992) in "their place" on the bases of the Roll (1977) proof that the market portfolio must be ex ante efficient and with the magic of matrix algebra. They make no secret about their true *beliefs* right at the outset:

> But the true cross-sectional expected-return beta relation is exact when the index is efficient, so *no* variable other than beta can explain any part of the true cross-section of expected returns. Conversely, if the index is not efficient, the ex-ante cross-sectional

relation does not hold exactly and other variables can have explanatory power. Indeed, any variable that happens to be cross-sectionally related to expected returns could have discernible explanatory power when the index proxy is ex ante inefficient (p. 101).

What Roll and Ross conveniently fail to mention is that, for this "law of nature" to hold, *all other* assumptions (piled on top of a simple linear regression, like a house of cards) of the SLB model must hold. Because if we do not have equilibrium, and homogeneous expectations of all one period, expected utility maximizer investors, then we do not have a market portfolio. And if we do not have a market portfolio, we cannot care less whether an index that proxies for this portfolio is efficient or not.

So what we have are data that show one thing and assumptions that are "wildly" unrealistic. In fact, they are so unrealistic that they preclude any possibility of having a grip on the predictive ability of the paradigm. Ergo, we cannot have an idea how "accurate" the predictions are for whatever purpose we have at hand. What we have is the logical melt-down of Friedman's instrumentalism as modified by Sharpe (1964).

From the simpler, earlier models, we moved on to the more "sophisticated" ones: models that have an insatiable appetite for more and more unrealistic (even obscure and bizarre) assumptions, which serve no purpose other than to hold complex mathematics together on their way to explain some observable phenomenon with the rationale of the *homo economicus*. Archetypical of these models are models of dividend signaling and separating equilibrium, to be discussed in greater detail in Chapter V.

Perhaps the worst use of the methodology of positive economics is when the model builder sets out to prove a preconceived notion with the careful selection of unrealistic assumptions. In such cases, not only does the model builder overlook the minimum requirement of "predictive ability" for him/herself, but also makes it impossible for others to do the "job," because some, or many, of the variables of the model are unobservable. A classic example of this kind of model is Grossman and Hart's (1982) free rider model.

SUMMARY

In this chapter, we have scrutinized positive economics from the vantage point of the direction into which it funneled research and the process of discovery in financial economics. Our conclusion is that, far from labeling positive economics as wrong or mistaken, we must realize that it has turned financial economics into an art, instead of its being science or quasi-science. Practitioners of academic finance are not willing, of course, to admit this because then their efforts to masquerade as scientists would be foiled. The other side of the issue is why intelligent and well-educated people stick to this methodology, which by its construction cannot turn financial economics into science, if indeed this is the real quest of its practitioners. This is not an economic, or methodological, issue but a sociological one. We return to examine this imbroglio in Section V.

In the next chapter, we consider a selection of examples of the positivist/instrumentalist paradigms of finance, discussing how they came about and how their so-called "logic" defies what most would regard as logic. Rather than confronting important questions head-on, finance has a tendency to cling to the same old dubious nostrums as long as they yield "familiar" implications.

NOTES

1. Note that the unmodified word *science* in this work refers exclusively to the natural sciences.

2. A good example to illustrate this point is the many dividend signaling models. For instance, the John and Williams (1985) model of dividend signaling requires 17 explicit and implicit assumptions, most of which are completely unrealistic. In addition, some of the key variables of the model are not directly observable, making any empirical validation efforts impossible. In other words, every guilty verdict must be declared a mistrial.

3. Note that art, as Friedman (1953) quotes Keynes (1891), "... is a system of rules for the attainment of a given end" (P. 3).

4. Here the "artist" has a nearly inexhaustible arsenal of statistical models/mathematical transformations that, with a little perseverance, will prove that a cherished model is a reasonably good predictor. We expand upon this in Chapter IX.

5. A casual survey of the leading textbooks in finance reveals an intersection of sets representing a bevy of no more than eight fundamental paradigms. Although this set is constantly changing, the common factor that remains is that all are based on the tenets of neo-classical economics in which the market is the avatar of God.

6. This is precisely the fate of the CAPM today.

7. An interesting footnote in this regard is the story Gans and Shepherd (1994) tell. Quoting Bernstein (1992), Gans and Shepherd note that Sharpe's (1964) paper was rejected by the editor of the *Journal of Finance* in 1962 when it was submitted for publication consideration. The editor informed Sharpe that the reviewer judged the assumption of homogeneous expectations of all investors "preposterous" and that he, the editor, concurred with the referee. In 1964, the *Journal* changed editors. The paper was resubmitted and quickly published in the September issue.

8. In a private conversation, a distinguished member of this school remarked to one of the authors of this book that he knew very little about philosophy and that other financial economists knew much less than he did.

9. The adjective *dear* in this context, reflects some kind of preference, and it is, in the words of Henry Kissinger "benignly vague." In later chapters of this book, we deal explicitly with the issue of what are the motivating forces of doing research and the reward system that has become the determinant of what research is being done.

10. See Stephen Jay Gould (1993).

11. We speak of the market as if it were a single person, for example, the market punishes, disciplines, rewards, and so on.

Chapter V

The Paradigms of Finance and Their Evolution

Finance is a relatively new discipline, the exact birthdate and parentage of which are difficult to pinpoint. There is general agreement, however, that finance as a field is analytical and that its first analytical model is the DuPont method.[1] If this consensus is accurate, then two conclusions can be drawn:

1. finance as a discipline was born in the mid-1940s; and
2. its parent was the field of accounting.

The DuPont method, as the name suggests, was developed by the DuPont Corportation in the early-1940s (to create a powerful analytical tool of planning and control), is a simple combination of two popular accounting ratios:

$$ROI \doteq TURNOVER \; x \; PROFIT \; MARGIN \qquad (1)$$

where   ROI = Return on Investment;
            TURNOVER = Sales/Total Assets; and
            PROFIT MARGIN = Net Income/Sales.
This equation is a simple identity, because
            ROI = Net Income/Investment;
            TURNOVER = Sales/Total Assets;
            PROFIT MARGIN = Net Income/Sales; and
            Investment = Total Assets.
Hence,

$$\frac{Net \; Income}{Total \; Asssets} \doteq \frac{Sales}{Total \; Assets} \; x \; \frac{Net \; Income.}{Sales} \qquad (2)$$

Because "Sales" cancels out on the right-hand side, both sides, in effect, are the same. By decomposing ROI into two elements, the DuPont corporation created a powerful analytical tool, wherein one factor is a measure of managerial effectiveness (Turnover) and the other is a measure of profitability (Profit Margin), dictated by the market structure within which its divisions operated. The two factors together and ultimately measure overall profitability (the left-hand side of Equation 2), but as separate components they provide a means for both planning and control.

Since the 1940s, when this model was developed, finance has embraced the foundations of positive economics to accomplish two, intertwined objectives:

1. to formulate a distinctive rationale that will distinguish it from accounting; and
2. to espouse a theoretical foundation.

Consequently, three basic canons, either jointly or separately, have become integral to all financial modeling:

1. People (later also referred to as "agents") behave consistent with the logic of the *homo economicus,* whose only concern in life is his/her economic well-being.
2. Human choices are consistent with utility maximization, as set forth originally by Jeremy Benthham and as later expanded, clarified and fitted to cover investment decisions under conditions of uncertainty, by Von Neuman and Morgenstern. Under this umbrella, utility-maximization and wealth-maximization are the same.
3. The principle of marginal analysis.

Drawing on these precepts, two works completed in the 1950s set the mold for academic discourse for the next four decades:

1. Markowitz's (1952) work of portfolio selection; and
2. Modigliani and Miller's (1958) (MM, subsequently) theory of cost-of-capital/capital-structure/value.

The former, a strictly normative work laid the foundations for positive models of asset pricing in equilibrium (to follow later). The latter served as the principal fomenting agent for critical thinking regarding the financial theory of the firm.

A third and somewhat disjointed group of scholarly undertakings comprised the first several attempts of dividend policy modeling. Gordon and Shapiro (1956), Gordon (1963), Solomon (1963), and Walter (1963) introduced a set of models, usually referred to as bird-in-the-hand models, which were based on the same logic and consequently produced similar implications or conclusions.

During the 1950s and early 1960s, a great deal of work was done in normative models, especially on the topics of capital rationing and portfolio theory, applying operations research methods [of mathematical programming] to financial problems. With the introduction of capital asset pricing models (CAPMs) by Black (1972), Treynor (1964), Lintner (1965), Mossin (1964), and most notably, Sharpe (1964), normative models disappear almost entirely, to make room for strictly positive, equilibrium-restricted models. The common underlying methodology of these models is Friedmanian instrumentalism, infused with the ideology of neoclassical microeconomics. The following is a brief survey of the significant models of finance as they evolved in the respective subfields of [what is now generally termed] financial economics.[2]

CORPORATION FINANCE

The Irrelevance Contentions

As we alluded earlier, one of the critical models of corporation finance has been the MM theory of cost of capital/ capital structure/ value (the irrelevance of capital structure thesis), to be followed shortly by Miller and Modigliani's (1961) theory of dividend policy (the irrelevance of dividends). The two theories are closely related, although they cover separate subjects of corporation finance. In subsequent works, model builders of the former theory assume that the latter is a given and vice versa.

The MM Theory of Cost-of-Capital—Irrelevance #1

The issue of cost of capital, along with its *determinand*, value, as a function of capital structure (the mixing of debt with equity)—was a major concern of early theoretical work. Prior to MM's "revolutionary" thesis of irrelevance, there existed two approaches to valuation: the net income approach, or NI; and the net operating income approach, or NOI.[3] From the minor relaxation of some of the assumptions of the NI approach, the so-called classical theory of value emerged. This "classical" theory was, in fact, an implantation of principles of short-term production functions, with particular emphasis on distributable fixed costs for the leverage effect, of neoclassical microeconomic theory under conditions of perfect certainty.

In its bare components, the MM theory of cost of capital, capital structure, value is no more and no less than the NOI approach of valuation. What makes it a scientific theory is the rigorous proof that, given its assumptions, it must hold. The proof is accomplished by the clever invoking of a device (which soon turned into the *deus ex machina* of finance): the arbitrage mechanism.

Because the classical theory of valuation was *ad hoc*, by all reasonable scrutiny of philosophy of science, the MM theory did not just supplant an old theory; it created a theoretical framework where there was none.[4]

The MM theory is constructed as three propositions: two positive statements[5] and the single normative ramification of Proposition 1. The entire analytical structure hinged on a set of carefully selected and strict assumptions (most quite unrealistic, in the best tradition of Friedmanian instrumentalism) and the arbitrage proof. With this proof, MM converted the NOI approach of valuation from a set of mere assertions to solid theory.

The analytical robustness of the original formulation was weakened considerably when MM relaxed some of their most unrealistic assumptions.[6,7] Another problem with the MM theory arose when attempts were made to verify its empirical ramifications. All empirical work—MM's, their supporters', and the critics'—focused on the estimation of the cost of capital. This is both perplexing and understandable. On one hand, one wonders why not a single critic asked for empirical validation of this new theory. On the other hand, one understands why the intellectual quality of the MM theory made it spread like wildfire through the academic community. In the absence of standards, therefore, no one demanded serious empirical validation.[8]

Empirical estimations of the cost of capital showed a marked and significant divergence between the MM estimates and those of their traditionalist opponents (which were much higher than the MM estimates). Although such discrepancies might have been important in hearings of public utility rate structure cases,[9] they did not contribute much to the empirical validation of the theory itself. This point, albeit in a different context, had been clarified by Boness (1964). The only possible way of validation could have been obtained through the empirical verification of Proposition 3. Yet, this would have required testing methods with which neither MM nor other researchers in financial economics felt comfortable.[10]

The basic difference between the MM theory and the classical financial economists' "theory," after all the corrections (for taxes) and the concessions (for a static versus a dynamic model) were made, was in the hierarchy of financial decision making. The latter theorists believed that the financing decision antecedes and is, thus, superior to the investment decision.

This is so, since only through the proper mixing of debt with equity can an optimal capital structure be reached. This structure is optimal since it produces the lowest average cost of capital. This lowest capital cost, in turn, results in the highest net present value of the firm. Thus, the motivational and hierarchical circle of capital structure, cost of capital and value maximization is closed.

In contrast, MM contended that the investment decision is paramount and that the financing decision is either irrelevant (*sans* taxes) or trivial (*cum* taxes). Because of the tax subsidy on debt, the MM theory would predict an all debt capital structure. Because this is rarely, if ever, observable, MM explain the lack of correspondence to the facts as the shortcoming of a static model that is forced on an otherwise dynamic problem. To salvage the theory, Modigliani and Miller (1963) invent the concept of target debt/equity ratio, a mere "cover story" without any theoretical footing.

The major conclusion of the MM theory in its purest, most complete, and most defensible form (the set of original assumptions, *sans* taxes) was that, if there are valuation discrepancies between any two firms in a partial equilibrium framework—that is, in a homogeneous risk class, they emanated from market imperfections (which had been assumed away in the MM analytical structure).

Miller-Modiglinani Dividend Policy Theory—Irrelevance #2

The Miller-Modigliani (1961) dividend irrelevance contention is a direct and logical extension of the MM theory of valuation. This is so, because in a MM "world," created by their assumptions, financing decisions cannot change the real, economic value of the firm. And because of Proposition 3, the wealth-maximizing act is to invest in every project that expects to yield the return (or higher) on a pure equity stream. Given the risk class, the dividend decision is just a financing decision in disguise.

Miller and Modigliani (1961) also raise, for the first time, the possibility that dividends might have a signaling value (a suggestion that, in the late 1970s and during much of the 1980s, created a burgeoning literature on dividend signaling which will be discussed later in this chapter). This "signaling value" might be the reason countless empirical works showed a positive relationship between share-value (measured one way or another) and a "dividend policy" (measured one way or another).

Miller and Modigliani (1961) construct a model, assuming perfect capital markets, and argue that dividend policy is irrelevant. By their reasoning, dividends are a financial illusion, a mere "repackaging" of wealth that cannot alter the value of the firm. Consequently, in the absence of taxes and market imperfections, the act of paying dividends embodies only a change in the form of accumulation, not a change in magnitude, of shareholders' wealth. Miller and Modigliani label the observed reality that dividends affect the value of the firm as "... a result of systematic irrationality on the part of the investing public" (p. 432).

Of course, in the face of double taxation of dividends and a differential tax rate for capital gains and regular, or unearned, income, the irrelevance proposition does not hold. Clearly, dividends are dissipative, in face of the alternatives available to satisfy cash needs of those shareholders who prefer current income over capital appreciation. Three decades of model building have been spent, subsequently, on finding an acceptable model for dividend policy, consistent with the basic canons of finance we postulated at the beginning of this chapter—so far, without much success, as we will see a bit later.

Post-MM Theories of Cost of Capital

Modifications and improvements of the MM theory advanced in two interesting, but conceptually, unrelated directions:

1. reformulation and construction of a new bankruptcy theory from MM, based solely on bankruptcy costs, by Scott (1977), Kim (1978) and others,[11] and
2. the resetting of the MM theory to the fiction of general equilibrium by Hamada (1969, 1972).

Although the strategic precepts in both developments were similar—that is, both rested on modifications of the original assumptions of MM and the introduction of new assumptions—their final edifications were categorically different. The Hamada development was the more intriguing of the two constructs, because it had elements of growth in knowledge, as a more inclusive and comprehensive theory (moving from partial to general equilibrium). This was all the more important since Hamada did not offer alternative explanations of facts or a departure from and replacement of MM.

In contrast, the trade-off theory,[12] though much less complex than Hamada's generalization, offered an explanation of the facts (where MM theory had not succeeded). Because of its lack of ambiguity, the trade-off theory is discussed first.

The Trade-Off Theory

The most appealing aspect of the trade-off theory has been its simplicity. Bankruptcy is a potential consequence of any business dealing, although it is regularly assumed away by financial theorists for the sake of continuity. If one counts both the cost and the probability of operational bankruptcy and factors in the calculus of financial risk (increase in leverage) as well, one is bound to find a point of indifference between the fiscal benefits of leverage and the potential costs of financial distress. On one side of this point of indifference, the benefits of the tax subsidy will outweigh the "cost" of bankruptcy, while, in the other direction, the possibility of financial distress will eliminate the tax advantage. Hence, value-maximizing firms will select their capital structure such that they will be at or very near a point of indifference.

Another advantage of the trade-off theory is the relative ease with which financial model builders can cast this simple idea in mathematical terms. This feature, in turn, endowed trade-off analysis with an aura of exactitude.

By a priori logic, bankruptcy-cost theory seems superior to the original MM work. It surpasses MM by making more precise assertions and explaining more facts. Unfortunately, it is as weak as the MM theory in its correspondence to the facts, such as the explanation of observable traditional leverage.[13]

There is another and equally important problem with the trade-off theory. It lacks a statistical mechanism that can bind observable costs of bankruptcy with probabilities in a consistent and scientifically acceptable fashion. The conclusion, therefore, is that the trade-off or bankruptcy-cost theory is not a useful, nor workable, theory. It is no wonder then that it appeared late and has not been embraced wholeheartedly in financial economics. Although there is some uncertainty about the reasons for this lack of popularity, the predicament of this theory is accepted with contentment.

MM in General Equilibrium

Hamada's (1969) transplantation of MM from its original partial equilibrium milieu to a general equilibrium formulation cannot be considered more than a mere refinement. Yet, it is a major step forward in terms of progress in generalized knowledge.

Hamada embraced the MM theory without questioning or criticism. His motives for confirming MM in a general equilibrium setting can be attributed to two reasons:

1. the unquenchable thirst of economists for theories set in a general equilibrium; and
2. the criticism (empirical in nature) of financial theorists who argued that homogeneous risk-classes, so central to the MM theory, cannot be defined.

Hamada's reformulation of the MM theory in general equilibrium was achieved by connecting the MM theory to, and making the analytical proof contingent upon, the validity of yet another untested theory: The CAPM of Tobin-Lintner-Mossin-Sharpe-Treynor, which will be discussed in great detail in Chapter VI of this book).

Two questions are apropos at this juncture:

1. Can the linking of one theory, untested yet, with another theory be considered progress in knowledge?

2. What was the pragmatic[14] benefit of extending the partial equilibrium framework to the general equilibrium framework?

If one subscribes to the Popperian (1979) principles of growth in scientific knowledge, the answer to the first question must be negative. As for the second question, Hamada's (1969) improvement did not have any pragmatic value. Indeed, it is still not clear whether the theory of corporation finance should be cast in a general equilibrium formulation or not. The reason for this ambiguity is that corporate behavior usually follows specific standards, established for a subset of the environment. Whether these standards are called riskclasses or industry norms is a matter of choice and ultimately boils down to empiricism.

In his polite but critical response to Hamada (1972), Sharpe (1972) indicated that Hamada's empirical validations were weak and unconvincing. These shortcomings, of course, constitute a major void for the usefulness of a paradigm. In summary, the state of corporate financial theory has not been directly advanced by these post-MM developments. This is not to say that their value is nil. It can be argued, in fact, that these post-MM contributions are more important as means of keeping the issues current than as measurable advancements of knowledge in a comprehensive theory.

Informational Asymmetry and Agency Theory

Agency theory, as imported to financial economics by Jensen and Meckling (1976), is founded on the premise that a conflict of interest exists between principals and agents. This conflict originates in the unequal sharing of both risk and return,[15] which in turn affects the relationship between shareholders (principals) and managers (agents). Given the explicit recognition that information is neither costless nor uniformly distributed, the agency scenario becomes truly complicated.

The *raison d'etre* for agency theory, according to Levinthal (1988) is to fill the void left by the traditional theory of the firm under the umbrella of neoclassical economics:

> Thus, agency theory is not a general solution to the problem of organizational design. However, agency theory is the neoclassical response to the void left by the traditional theory of the firm and, in well-defined domains of organizational activity may offer useful insights (p. 155).

This connection is not well known in financial economics, which embraced agency theory as the socio-psychological solution to all the unanswered questions of corporation finance.

Indeed, as Gordon (1994) reminds Jensen and Meckling, they never worked out the "solution" of agency theory for the very large (how large is large?) firm:

> In an article devoted to the agency relations among stockholders, managers and creditors in the public corporation, Jensen and Smith (1985, p. 105) make passing reference to management interest in high earnings retention rates and low leverage rates. There is no consideration, however, of how such behaviour influences the investment, financing and valuation of the corporation. Instead, there is speculation on compensation and institutional arrangements that could be used to compel management to maximize current market value. The implicit and false assumption is that such behavior is optimal because the public corporation is then made to behave like a proprietorship. In fact, proprietorships also do not maximize market value (p. 27).

One of the earliest conceptual formulations of this theory occurs in the classic work of Berle and Means (1932). Berle and Means distinguish between managers who are profit/wealth maximizers and act in the interest of principals and those managers who act, mostly, in their own self-interest. Members of the latter group of managers engage in decisions that might be conceived by the principals as wealth maximizing, when in reality this might not be the case. Such distinction is possible if and only if markets are not perfect (especially with respect to the speed, cost and direction of information dissemination).

Since lenders are aware of this inclination, they constrict the actions of agents, either by contractual arrangements that can be monitored or by increasing the effective rate of borrowing commensurably with the elevation of risk. Eventually, it is up to the market whose original imperfection created this conflict of interest to resolve the discrepancies in expectations through the process of price discovery. Nevertheless, capital structures are different than what they would have been *sans* these agency problems.

Agency theory, thus, provides a broad cover under which corporate-observable phenomena find a logical explanation. These phenomena, though not limited to them, also include decisions made with respect to capital structure. Unfortunately, diametrically opposing behavior can be explained by certain elements of agency theory. More ill-fatedly, empirical research derived from the canons of agency theory is, more often than not, inconclusive, contradictory, or outright discredited, because the variables in question are not directly observable.[16]

Ad Hoc Scenarios

Several ad hoc scenarios have been advanced in conjunction with agency theory. Two of the best known scenarios are the free-cash-flow hypothesis of Jensen (1986) and the pecking-order hypothesis of Myers (1984) and Myers and Majluf (1984).

The underlying logic of the free-cash-flow hypothesis is that, if one leaves uncommitted cash in the hands of managers, they will find a way to squander it. This managerial tendency to waste is manifested either by excessive spending on perquisites[17] or by investing in negative net present value projects. Shareholders are best advised, therefore, to purge free cash by demanding either high dividends or financing that imposes high fixed payments (interest) on management. In essence, the free-cash-flow hypothesis (conjecture, really) is nothing but the tale of the damsel in distress (the shareholder), who is saved by the hero (the omnipotent market, indeed the avatar of God, in neolassical economics), from the villain (the manager) (see, Reiter 1994).

As suggested by Myers (1990), this hypothesis is more an ad hoc stylization of the takeover craze of the 1980s than a defensible theory of corporation finance. Moreover, the hypothesis is based on the implicit assumption that managerial labor markets lack the necessary restraint and are, in effect, inefficient.[18]

The Myers (1984) and Myers and Majluf (1984) pecking-order hypothesis suggests that there is a hierarchy according to which firms issue securities and that dividend policy is "sticky" (in essence, that it is given). Although this theory explains some observable firm behavior, its assumptions are far-fetched and obligating. It creates a scenario in which managers and the market engage in a guessing game whose winner is decided by chance, as long as there is correspondence to facts (empirical results are consistent with the pecking-order hypothesis).

Dozens of published and unpublished empirical papers attempt to reconfirm one or the other of these hypotheses. These works carry the aura of robo-finance; that is, mechanical, robotical constructs that make up for their conceptual deficiencies with unnecessary statistical complexities.

An "Organizational" Theory of Capital Structure

A more recent but unrefined theory of corporation finance has been put forth by Myers (1990). This theory is an economically sophisticated formulation of what is known in the behavioral management literature as organizational slack, along with the related issue of income smoothing.[19] According to this view, management synchronizes spending on perks with increases in income. That is, cost conscientiousness goes hand-in-glove with declines in income. Also, management uses the accounting process to smooth the firm's reported income, as much and whenever it is in its purview.

Myers' (1990) formulation is more sophisticated and structured than its behavioral management's counterpart. He envisions an economic "balance sheet" generated by the market, in which the left-hand side consists of the sum of the present values of assets and the present values of the growth opportunities, less the present value of tax obligations. These values are "balanced" by the market values of the stock and debt, plus an organizational surplus (a budgetary slack). Now, the organization[20] (presumably, all the human resources at the disposal of the shareholders) wishes to maximize corporate wealth. This is quite different from the standard notion of maximizing shareholders' wealth.

Under these conditions, anything that is not counted in organizational surplus is out of the control of the firm. Thus, managers wish to keep as much as possible in this surplus account. Myers (1990) handles the issue of dividend policy by assuming that such policy is "sticky." In effect, Myers surmises a contractual arrangement between managers and shareholders concerning the payment of dividends. This "contract" has no justification in terms of the economic rationale that is being offered.

There are more questions left unanswered than explained in Myers's (1990) organizational theory of capital structure. A partial list of such questions includes:

How does the market generate this balance sheet? Why and how are the two present values of normal earning potential and growth opportunities decomposed? How does the market *partial out* this value of Organizational Surplus? What is the status of management in case of a negative surplus?[21] How can non-shareholding members of the organization transfer their firm-related wealth when they move? What conflicts of interest are being resolved as a function of management-ownership? How are contracts on dividends written and how and when are such contracts changed? Why does one see a set of diverse contracts?

Despite its shortcomings, Myers's (1990) organizational theory may be useful in advancing the now-decaying theoretical development of the central issue of corporation finance: capital structure—cost of capital—value. His theory may be an implicit realization that a more comprehensive and progressive theory of corporation finance should evolve from the combination of two rationalities: that of economics and that of organizational theory.

Dividend Policy

The subject of dividend policy has created a voluminous literature of its own. From the early days of the bird-in-the-hand theory[22] to Miller and Modigliani's (1961) irrelevance proposition (discussed earlier in this chapter), to dissipative/non-dissipative signaling,[23] a handful of theories have been offered to resolve the inherent paradox of dividend payments to shareholders.

The mounting empirical evidence of the positive relationship between share value and an empirical proxy for dividend policy has overshadowed the MM theory. Miller and Modigliani (1961), who constructed their model on pure economic rationale and a set of restrictive assumptions, argued that in a frictionless[24] world the dividend decision is irrelevant. Thus, firms would face only two types of financial decisions: (1) the investment decision (that hierarchically precedes everything), and (2) the financing decision. It is this argument of MM that makes the issue of dividend policy part of the capital structure—cost of capital controversy. Thus, the dividend policy problem is a residual of the financing decision (if we declare dividends how do we finance them?), because the investment decision is already based on the expected return of the project under consideration.

In a less than perfectly competitive environment (in which some frictions such as taxes and brokerage fees do exist), the payment of dividends is irrational. Financial scholars, therefore, invented models to explain the discrepancy between empirical evidence (taking for granted that such evidence was statistically meaningful and valid) and theory within the confines of a uni-dimensional rationality. Most of the meaningful[25] post-MM theories had been based, one way or another, on the prevalence of asymmetric information.

Dividend Signaling

The most prominent parts of this asymmetric information literature are the models of signaling. In the confines of theoretical development, they follow closely the dictum of a formulation that is rigorously proven in a mathematical framework. In that sense, and as a pattern, this literature resembles the work in classical theoretical physics with one exception. Although most of the work in the latter is testable, given the right instruments and methods, the bulk of the analysis in the former is untestable. This lack of verifiability originates either in the variables that are integrated in the mathematical phase or the necessary violation of the many assumptions. These violations or relaxations of the assumptions are essential for testing the models, but they make attempts of empirical scrutiny subject to criticism.

Progress in the development of this theory is achieved by moving from the mechanical to the conceptual. In contrast to what occurs in classical physics, it is the mathematical model here that moves the theory. To ensure the mathematical consistency of the model, a large set of assumptions, often unrealistic, is needed. As long as the final implications of the model remain acceptable by the economic rationale (a prescription given in Sharpe 1964), these assumptions are exculpated. What is being sacrificed is the possibility of rigorous, or even any, testing and correspondence to the facts.

Proponents of the signaling theories counter criticism by arguing that the burden of proof is on the antagonists. This appears to be the case since countless event studies show positive abnormal returns occurring concurrently with dividend announcements.

Combining the explicit signaling models of Akerlof (1970), Spence (1973),[26] and Riley (1979), with an intricate set of assumptions, Bhattacharya (1979, 1980), Miller and Rock (1985), John and Williams (1985), Ambarish, John and Williams (1987), Ofer and Thakor (1987), and Williams (1988) construct models to conclude that dividends serve to signal the true quality of the firm.

The intricacy of the structure of these models is demonstrated by the assumptions made by John and Williams (1985), as a prototype. The point we make here is that this body of assumptions is extensive and unrealistic. The assumptions and the massive labor of mathematics that follow are for one single purpose: to demonstrate that a rational (wealth maximization) explanation of the dividend mystery is possible.

In the signaling models, dividends are *credible* because they are *costly*. Nonetheless, such costs must be justified. Hence, there must be some value associated with dividends and dividend policy, that exceeds the costs. In the signaling literature, this "value" is the reduction of informational asymmetry. Still, two unresolved issues in dividend signaling are identified by Thakor (1989, p. 42):

1. less costly means of signaling than dividends are likely to be available;[27] and
2. signaling theories are incapable of explaining the dynamic aspects of dividends.

This latter point warrants elucidation. Signaling models assume a one-period "memory" of investors (both current and potential shareholders). There is no "learning curve" and no significance to a maintained, or maintainable, payment pattern. In practice, many firms preserve a dividend payment standard (inclusive of "no payment") whether they can or cannot signal something "good." Frankfurter, Lane and Darom (1989) show convincing empirical evidence that firms with seriously declining performance choose to increase dividend payments. A similar pattern is observed by Baskin (1988, p. 234) in the historical record. In a different context, Lamoureux (1990) shows that "…the selection of an E-V [mean-variance] efficient portfolio of risky assets is virtually independent of the investor's tax status." He also concludes that higher dividend yields become attractive to investors who show increasing risk aversion (p. 128).

A so-far unmentioned, but nevertheless major, problem with the signaling models is that, although they fashion human behavior, there is no effort to authenticate that indeed there is a case of signaling; that there are a signaler, signalee and a signal with an intended purpose that is verifiable by at least the signaler.

Agency Theory Explanations

Easterbrook (1984) applies the agency theory rationale to dividend policy. He argues that monitoring is too costly for individual investors, who would thus defer to an invisible hand of exogenous monitoring by the market (the avatar of God, again). Managers, on the other hand, prefer to invest in safe projects financed by earnings to minimize total risk, which has an additional wealth transfer effect (from stockholders to bondholders). Paying dividends is seen as a means to increase the firm's need for external financing and thereby to subject its management to monitoring by the capital markets (the hero that saves the damsel in distress) and to reduce the funds available from earnings.

These agency theory arguments are, however, little more than ad hoc explanations without theoretical or empirical support, and are refutable on their face. There is no mechanism to determine an optimal dividend payout, but it is explicitly large ("... increase dividends to the extent possible ...," p. 653). Risk-neutral principals would be unaffected by management's efforts to reduce investment risk. If principals in the market were risk-neutral, then no premium for risk would exist in prices and no wealth transfer would occur. Risk-averse agents would seek to avoid or minimize monitoring, not encourage it. Indeed, the principal would desire additional monitoring only if other measures of the agent's effort such as profits are suspicious (Levinthal 1988, p. 170).

The agency solution of the dividend paradox by Easterbrook (1984) propagates a 100-percent payout ratio. Very few U.S. firms follow such a practice, even occasionally, unless it is a poison pill. Jensen's (1986) free-cash-flow hypothesis is just another variation of the Easterbrook argument, advocating the syphoning away of all "free cash" from management. As a normative maxim, it stands on very shaky grounds, if it stands at all. As a positive theory, which it supposed to be, it is unobservable.

CAPITAL ASSET PRICING

Arguably, the CAPM, mentioned earlier, evolved into the strongest and perhaps the most enduring example of the paradigm of financial economics. Its choke-hold on the profession was absolute for more than two decades. It withstood repetitive attacks (on logical, theoretical, and empirical grounds) by agnostics, and of late, by its former prime promoters. It still lives in the minds and hearts of a determined group of its most orthodox supporters who cannot imagine "life" in financial economics without the model's ability to neatly tie together risk and return.

The CAPM that evolved during its reign from a single-period, bi-variate model into multi-period, multi-factor transmogrifications was the basis of thousands of event studies, other research projects, and doctoral dissertations, and was the cause of the creation of what is known as the index fund. Its influence on financial economics and its methodology is so profound that we devote the next chapter of this book, entirely, to the discussion of the CAPM.

With all its influence, it had its critics from its inception. One of the major arguments against promoting the CAPM was its dependence on a quadratic utility function, which is to be maximized by investors, or equivalently, that rates of return on capital assets were normal. Both contentions were severely criticized in the early literature that evolved at the dawn of the CAPM's rise to fame. To "fix" the problem of invalid assumptions (as if invalid/ unrealistic assumptions ever were a problem in positive economics), Ross (1976, 1978) introduced a new theory, which has come to be known as the arbitrage pricing theory [APT, subsequently]. Yet, both models exist under the aegis (Zeus' breastplate, in its strictest meaning) of the Efficient Markets Hypothesis [EMH, subsequently]. Hence, first we turn to discuss this paradigm that today practically divides the ecclesia of finance into three unequal (both in numbers as well as status) groups of "true believers," agnostics, and, God forbid, heretics.

The EMH

Question: How many financial economists does it take to change a light-bulb?
Answer: None. If the light-bulb needed to be changed, the market would have changed it already.

—Old light-bulb joke.

As we have already noted, William Jahnke (1994), writing the eulogy for the EMH, tells the story of the CRSP seminars at the University of Chicago and the existence of a "Murderers Row."

The CRSP Seminars, as they were called, provided an ideological home for those desirous of promoting an efficient market agenda.... The few brave souls venturing to the CRSP seminars with *evidence* [our italics] contradicting CAPM were met by a band of academics known as "Murderers Row," who usually made quick work of dispatching the heretic (pp. 7-8).

Indeed, the EMH became synonymous with the Chicago/Rochester School of financial economics, in general, and with Fama (1970, 1976, and 1991) in particular. The hypothesis is ingrained in the hearts and minds of those who count themselves as either the members of that school, or their imitators—so much so that a graduate-level textbook counts the EMH among the 12 principles of finance. The same textbook lists these 12 principles in the first page after the hard cover, making them look not unlike the Ten Commandments inscribed by Moses. Needless to say, there is a marked difference between a principle (a general truth) and an hypothesis (a tentative explanation that accounts for a set of facts).

There is something in the word *efficiency*, when applied to markets, that is both arrogant and misleading. The context of EMH is quite different from the context of Markowitz's "frontier of efficiency." There, efficiency is defined as a technical term, meaning that a portfolio that lies on the frontier has the highest possible return for a given level of risk.

In the context of the EMH, efficiency implies Pareto optimality, meaning that the market finds a solution that cannot be changed without hurting someone. This in turn implies both freedom of choice and decision making only with economic tenets in mind, where one selects the best among many of some "good" alternatives. Neoclassical economics does not make allowances for other considerations, and for the sad fact that many economic agents/individuals have really no favorable choices some of the time. Examples of "pessimality" abound, but perhaps the most illustrative is King Solomon's judgment relating to the child claimed by two women. For the real mother of the child both of the king's choices were terrible, yet she preferred to see her child with the other woman, and alive, than to win custody of half a corpse. In a sense, her decision was *subpessimal*.

In the world of finance, there are three versions of market efficiency:

1. informational efficiency;
2. allocational efficiency; and
3. operational efficiency.

Informational efficiency, in turn comprises three forms: the weak form, the semi-strong form, and the strong form. According to the weak form, price relatives follow some form of a random walk. This means that the best indicator of tomorrow's price is today's price, or equivalently, that there is no special knowledge to be gained from the historical study of price movements. There are practically hundreds of studies that show that price relatives do indeed follow some form of a random walk. These studies conclude that the weak form of the hypothesis holds.

This conclusion, of course, does not mean that one cannot formulate other tests, showing the existence of some method by which one can glean additional knowledge from studying historical prices. In statistical tests, the cards are always stacked in favor of the null hypothesis, as we will see later.

The semi-strong form of the hypothesis states that prices at any time reflect all publicly available information. This form is, in fact, Sir James[28] famous joke about the $20 bill lying on the ground; that is, the bill is an illusion; because otherwise, someone would have picked it up. Several empirical studies set out with some success to empirically validate the semi-strong form of the hypothesis.

The strong form of the hypothesis states that all available information, both public and private, is encapsulated in the current price of an asset. The practical meaning of this form is that the market "knows" everything, and knows it at the same time that corporate insiders know it. The authors of this book know of no study that has shown the empirical validity of this form, nor do they believe that a reasonable and convincing statistical test can be constructed that would show the validity of this hypothesis.

Allocational efficiency is the economic concept of marginal productivity. In this context, markets are allocationally efficient, if investment projects are financed at the marginal productivity of capital. Operational efficiency is concerned with the ease and speed by which capital markets make the meeting of buyers and sellers possible. It is also referred to as market liquidity.

The theological domination of the EMH was the driving force behind the development of all known capital asset pricing theories. Nevertheless, the reader should note that the refutation, or lack of empirical validity, of any of the asset pricing models we discuss here is not equal to the refutation of the EMH. The EMH was, and continues to be, a matter of religion.

The APT

The APT is no more nor less than a combination of a system of simultaneous linear equations and the notion of arbitrage, as introduced into financial economics by MM, under the fiction of market equilibrium. Mathematically,

$$R_i = E(R_i) + \beta_{i1}\, \delta_1 + \beta_{i2}\, \delta_2 + \ldots + \beta_{ik}\, \delta_k + \epsilon_i, \ i=1, N \text{ and } k=1, K \quad (3)$$

where $E(\bullet)$ is the expectation operator;
             R_i are the return on capital asset I;
             β_i are factor loadings;
             δ_i are common, orthogonal factors; and
             ϵ_i is a random error with zero mean and fixed variance.

Equation 3 is based on the assumption of homogeneous and certain expectations, factor loadings and factors. These all come about either by investors' "common" insights, or by the arbitrage mechanism that eliminates excess return from the riskless portfolio and determines the equilibrium relationship portrayed in Eqation 3.

In applications (meaning, normative use), Equation 3 must be estimated, using factor analysis [in one of its myriad forms] to estimate factor loadings. The method is not just arbitrary, but also totally dependent on the data to which is applied. Small changes in the universe of assets (exclusively stocks in empirical work), and/or the number of observations available, result in drastic changes of the coefficients of Equation 3. Shanken (1982, p. 1137) makes this point quite clear:

> The factor model can be manipulated rather arbitrarily by repackaging a given set of securities. A new set of returns and a corresponding factor model can be produced, with virtually any pre-specified random variables as the factors.

When the more stringent assumption of a system of linear regressions is made, Equation 3 turns into the well-known multi-index model of the late 1960s. Yet, Myers (1972) already has shown that there is no such thing as an equilibrium restricted regression. And Cohen and Pogue (1967) demonstrated the inferiority of multi-index models to the single index, or market model (Sharpe 1963) in the context of efficient portfolios. These "minor" distractions do not bother many who from time to time come up with "improved" versions of Equation 3.

Other Pricing Models

Commenting on the concept of rationality and its role in the efficient market hypotheses, Kenneth Arrow (1982) observed that individuals may not be precisely calculating expected-utility maximizers (as per the common assumption of financial economists). Herbert Simon (1979) showed that people seem to have difficulty in arriving at rational choices even in simple circumstances. Although cognitive psychologists have been researching the areas of perception and judgment for more than 25 years, many of their findings have not fallen on sympathetic ears of financial economists. Yet, there is now a limited, albeit promising, line of research supporting the notion that individuals and markets process information in a complex manner not at all captured and explained by the guiding principles of value maximization and the *homo economicus*. That is, the pricing of risky assets is also susceptible to behavior outside the domain of what economists consider rational.

DeBondt and Thaler (1985) use the theoretical framework of Kahneman and Tversky (1982) to develop a trading strategy of buying losers and selling winners. This framework implies that, in disharmony with Bayes' Rule, individuals tend to "overreact" to unexpected and dramatic information releases.

The overreaction hypothesis suggests that firms with low P/E ratios are thought to be undervalued (temporarily) because of excessive pessimism, and that firms with high P/E ratios are overvalued because of excessive optimism. These excessive mood swings are the result of systematic overreaction to positive or negative news released about the stock. The main point that is made is that anomalous behavior is interminably observed in the stock market (something that is totally unexplainable by the efficient market hypothesis). One can hold the belief that these anomalies are the result of faulty methods of analysis (and in some cases, this may be true) or that market participants do not always exhibit the same economic rationality that is imputed by theory.

Based on such findings, the authors then test whether such behavior can be detected in the financial markets. They construct a trading rule of buying losers and selling winners, consistent with the overreaction hypothesis. Winners and losers are classified and combined in portfolios according to their past performance. Then, cumulative average excess returns[29] are calculated for both portfolios. The results show that the losing stocks earned approximately 25 percent more than the winning stocks during a 36-month period following the formation of portfolios. This finding is especially interesting since the portfolios of winners are significantly more risky than those of the losers.

The DeBondt and Thaler (1985) study also has implications for other anomalous stock market findings. Reinganum (1981), Keim (1983), and Blume and Stambaugh (1983) redefine the small firm effect around the turn-of-the-year as largely a losing firm effect. This is consistent with DeBondt and Thaler's conclusions that losers earn exceptionally large January returns and winners do not. Their results also support the price-ratio hypothesis that high P/E ratio stocks are systematically overvalued while low P/E stocks are undervalued.

Another potential anomaly of economic rationality is the apparent excess volatility of security prices. One of the earliest observations of this phenomenon is made by John M. Keynes, who remarks that:

> "…. day-to-day fluctuations in the profits of existing investments, which are obviously of an ephemeral and nonsignificant character, tend to have an altogether excessive, and even absurd, influence on the market" (1936, p. 153).

Subsequent to this commentary, researchers such as Shiller (1981) have attempted to demonstrate this phenomenon in a more rigorous format. The basic concept, however, is that stock prices move more than can be explained by purely economic variables. To some researchers, this result is unacceptable because it implies irrationality (narrowly defined).

It is possible, however, that economic rationality is but one type of rationality and therefore, market behavior, like all aggregate human behavior, can be explained only when all other rationalities are identified and understood. The reason that economically rational and irrational behavior can coexist in the same market (i.e., irrationality is not arbitraged away) is explained by Russell and Thaler (1985). They argue that the existence of some rational agents is not sufficient to guarantee a rational expectations equilibrium in an economy composed of both rational and quasi-rational agents.

When individuals and groups do not behave according to economic models, researchers must look to other fields of study for explanations. Lichtenstein and Slovic (1971) conduct a series of stunning experiments in which individuals' choices under uncertainty are analyzed. In these experiments, the individual is offered a choice between a pair of gambles and is also asked to identify his certainty equivalence for each gamble. In total contradiction to the transitivity axiom of rationality, the preferred gamble is found to have a lower certainty equivalence much of the time. The authors call this phenomenon "preference reversal."

Grether and Plott (1979) replicate these experiments and are unable to provide an explanation of the results consistent with the usual postulates of rationality. It appears that human behavior is much more complicated than assumed by economic and financial theory; utility functions may be a powerful mathematical device, but they fail to capture the full scheme of human behavior. Also, we know very little about how individuals formulate expectations. When these two are combined, the outcomes may lie far outside of the domain of standard economic postulates.

The inadequacy of the narrowly defined rationality hypothesis is consistent with specific observations made by cognitive psychologists such as Tversky and Kahneman (1974, 1981). As noted by Arrow, "They and others have identified several heuristic devices by which individuals form cognitive judgements and note that, while each has useful properties, each can also lead to biases in judgement" (1982, p. 5).

One such bias is termed the "representativeness heuristic." In this case, it is shown that individuals tend to judge the likelihood of a future event by its similarity with present evidence and will often ignore both prior information and the quality (sample size, for example) of present information.

The results of another relevant experiment are reported by McNeill, Pauker, Sox, and Tversky (1981). The authors show that individuals' choices are significantly affected depending on trivial framing of the choice.

Although these works open a new area for financial economists, the methods of analysis remain the same as in the case of the more traditional thinking. Thus, theoretical models are eventually translated into either a multi-variate regression or an event study, or both, using the market data everyone before used. Consequently, the limited behavioral work done in finance does not represent a new *methodology*, but a *methodical variation* on the traditional paradigm.

Pricing of Contingent Claims

A major creation of the field has been a model of option pricing, first suggested by Black and Scholes (1973) [BS, subsequently], and Merton (1973). The model rests on the assumptions of:

1. equilibrium;
2. the existence of a riskless asset; and
3. the distribution of the underlying stock price being log-normal.

When these assumptions were combined with the mathematics of Brownian motion, the model opened a new vista for would-be model-builders, and of course, a literature of its own. The original model that was designed to price a European call option[30] evolved into several variants of models pricing American puts and calls and other and different contingent claims (assets whose value is derived from the price of another security, also called, for this reason, derivatives). But the intellectual opportunities offered by this new set of models opened the door for applying the logic of contingent claims to other subjects such as capital budgeting and capital structure. So important was the invention of these models of contingent claims that Merton (1995) considered this the cardinal contribution of financial economics to the world.

Indeed, today, the literature of contingent claims is vast. More importantly, the models were quickly adopted by the street—first, by traders at the Chicago Board of Option Exchange (CBOE) and then by the participants of its clones around the world. This ready acceptance can be attributed to the fact that, at the time the exchange opened, the marketing of a hand-held calculator version of the BS model started. For traders to whom the pricing of this new financial asset was cloaked in mysticism, the cheap calculator, showing a theoretical price, was a godsend.

Later, however, many investment houses hired an elite group of academics, who developed around themselves a cadre of mathematicians, statisticians and physicists, aptly named "rocket scientists." As new financial instruments, contingent on other assets, were developed, derivatives departments all across the land started doing brisk business. The academic models provided the stamp of *kashrut* (a verification of purity) for these instruments to the masses who barely or not at all understood the constructs upon which the real instruments were built.

Strangely, however, countless empirical studies have shown that (1) the option pricing model's assumption of log-normally distributed price relatives is false, and (2) that it is a good predictor only for in-the-money, short-maturity options. Also, although the model is a "new" academic invention, somehow, options priced themselves close to the model's prediction.

Alongside the original model, a whole sequence of "improved" versions, notably to make the model more realistic, especially with respect to expected dividends (which are not shared with the option buyer), and/or the riskless rate appear. Also, the model or the improved variants are used to "imply out" variables, such as the riskless rate, the volatility of the underlying stock, and so on, that the authors of these studies argue are not directly observable. The "implying out" process is to calculate one variable from the model, while assuming that all the other variables are both correct and observable. This is quite a strange logic, especially when one reads papers where what is *implied out* in one paper is *given* in an other paper and vice-versa. Regardless, a whole cottage industry has evolved around the improvements of the original model, enriching the literature of obscure mathematics and newly minted esoteric journals of financial mathematics/engineering.

With all the criticism and caveats, one must concur, nevertheless, with Merton (1995) about the importance of the option pricing models, both intellectually and as a tool for the finance practitioners. One must also concur, with sadness, that although we know relatively little about the pricing of common stocks, we "know," somehow, quite a lot about the pricing of financial assets that are derivatives of common stocks. This is both a paradox as well as an indication of the major fallacies that underlie financial model building.

MARKET MICRO-STRUCTURE

Micro-structure literature derives from the recognition that securities markets do not operate according to the assumptions of the classical economic precepts of the Walrasian auction market. It has been long recognized that security markets are not frictionless, nor is the information about securities symmetrical.

At the dawn of the micro-structure literature, the concern was with the market maker, also known as the specialist. More specifically, interest has focused on the bid-ask spread, that supposedly is not zero, to cover the real costs of the specialist, to provide "immediacy" for the market (see the EMH's operational efficiency facet, above, and Demsetz 1968). Later, a whole literature emerged focusing on the size of the bid-ask spread as it related to individual dealers (Stoll 1978). The Stoll model is a complex model in which the bid-ask spread is decomposed into three components, supposedly satisfying different needs/compensation of the specialist.

From this early literature, an immense volume of work has evolved encompassing a whole slew of issues in different security markets. This literature is the result of complex model building in the financial economist's "laboratory" and then testing, invoking newly invented methods of econometrics. The value of these works is best summed up by Black (1995), as quoted in *Euromoney*:

> Econometric studies can tell us about variances and covariances, including autocovariances. They can tell us about correlations, including partial correlations. But they can't tell us anything direct about cause or effect, impact or influence, structure or *meaning* [our italics]. We kid ourselves when we say that one variable helps to 'explain' another. This sounds like causation, but really means only correlation (*Euromoney*, January, 1966, p. 35).

In this chapter, we argued that finance built a grandly elaborate, but fundamentally quite frail, edifice upon the foundation of Friedman's instrumentalist philosophy and a limited set of unrealistic assumptions about how the world is supposed to work.

Most, if not all, theoretical developments in finance over the last four decades have been endless variants and combinations of a few simple elements. But Sharpe assures us that this is not a problem, declaring that all that matters is that the implications of our theories be consistent with an economic logic we are all supposed to espouse. Even the ever-so-important empirical validation is not important. It is no surprise that theories that evolve in this milieu are consistent with the logic that creates them. In essence, this revised *philosophy* of Friedman boils down to the formalism of complex or not so complex mathematics.

The next chapter expands upon the themes of this chapter with a detailed examination of the intellectual history of the CAPM and the statistical measurement of risk which is the critical, but usually taken-for-granted, assumption.

NOTES

1. This is, of course, not counting the time value of money, present value, duration models, widely applied in finance, which are economic models that have been around since the middle of the previous century.

2. The term *financial economics* surfaced much later, however. Although the authors have made several attempts to find the earliest use of the term, their efforts, have so far been unsuccessful. By 1972 a new journal was anchored to the name, creating the wide-spread conviction that finance is just a special branch of economics. The most plausible definition for the term is by Gordon (1994):

What I propose to do .... at this point is to examine what academics who are concerned with financial management and those concerned with financial economics have in common and how they differ with respect to their activities.

What both groups have in common is the subject matter of finance: the sources and uses of funds for individuals and firms, the financial intermediaries and other institutions that are employed in finance, and the laws that govern their activities. Financial management is concerned with a number of related pragmatic questions. What are the objectives of individuals, firms, and institutions? What should be their objectives? What do they do to realize these objectives, and what should they do? How do financial institutions operate, and how should they operate to serve better their objectives and those of their clients? Sometimes we do it well, and sometimes we do it poorly..., but I think that's a fair description.

Financial economics, it would seem, should have the same concerns as financial management and, in addition, also the consequence of finance for the functioning of the economy as a whole (p. 177).

3. The term *approach* is an indication of the nature of the two postulates, NI and NOI: there never was anything "stronger" supporting them than individual beliefs. The pivotal contribution of MM to the field was (1) transforming the NOI approach into a positive paradigm, (2) lending a scientific aura to the field, and (3) retrofitting the neo-classical theory to the [more] realistic conditions of *uncertainty*.

4. For the interest of the reader, we recap here the three propositions that constitute the MM theory of capital structure, cost-of-capital, valuation:

Proposition 1. The cost of capital is independent of the capital structure of the firm, and it is equal to the return on a pure equity stream in the risk class of the firm, or equivalently, that the average cost of capital is constant.

Proposition 2. As a result of Proposition I, the return on equity is made up of two components: the return on a pure equity stream and return due to financial risk as measured by leverage.

Proposition 3. Managers of the firm will maximize value if they invest in all opportunities with expected return equal to or higher than the average cost of capital.

Note that Propositions 1 and 2 are positive statements, whereas Proposition 3 is normative (what wealth-maximizing managers should do). Also, that the three propositions together imply that the investment decision is superior to all other financial decisions.

5. Strictly speaking, Proposition 2 recasts Proposition 1 in terms of the required rate of return, demanded by the equity holder. Consequently, there is nothing unique in Proposition 2.

6. Examples include corporate and personal taxes, the positive relation between leverage and the marginal cost of borrowing and the difference between the cost of borrowing on personal and corporate accounts.

7. This, in and of itself, did not invalidate the MM theory. By way of an analogue, the Big Bang and Big Crunch theories evolved from, and are inconsistent with, the general theory of relativity: at these two points, however, all laws of science break down. Physics supplements this shortcoming of relativity with quantum mechanics, to explain both theory and observations.

8. MM do provide an empirical test that did not prove much one way or another; otherwise, it was extremely primitive as far as econometrics is concerned.

9. Many of the opponents appeared as expert witnesses in court, or rate hearings, to argue the case of the public utility involved.

10. What is implied here is a large-scale analysis of corporate decision making regarding Proposition 3 (the only normative aspect of the theory). This would have involved research methods and techniques that economists usually do not use. Regardless, even if the validity of Proposition 3 could and would have been verified, the question of capital structure decision would have been wide open. None of these qualifications, however, lessens the value of the MM theory as a theory. They just imply that it could have been much easier to falsify it, if it would have been done.

11. Myers (1990) calls this the trade-off theory, whereas the benefits of the tax subsidy are being traded off at the margin for the risk-factored costs of bankruptcy.

12. The terms *bankruptcy-cost theory* and *trade-off theory* are freely interchanged in the discussion that follows.

13. MM did not explain observable traditional leverage ratios: why do all firms not use the tax subsidy to its fullest? The trade-off theory, strictly speaking, is at variance with observable behavior; older and more established firms opt for lower debt/equity ratios than younger, less established firms. Also, several studies (e.g., Haugen and Senbet 1978) have shown that for most firms the real costs of bankruptcy are infinitesimally small.

14. The word *pragmatic* (in the absence of a better one) is used here to appraise the benefits of progress in the development of a theory. It is acceptable to perceive a theory that holds in general equilibrium more respectable than a theory in partial equilibrium. Does this perception of reputability contribute necessarily to the enhancement of knowledge, especially if the general equilibrium model is defensible only at the expense of poor correspondence to the facts?

15. At the limit, it is possible to argue that Marxism provides a source for the origins of agency theory.

16. That is to say, one study's findings contradict the other, using different data, which are questioned by the other, and so on and so on.

17. The concept of perquisites as a theoretical tool, by itself, is a controversial one. When supplicated, it serves as a *deus ex machina*. Yet when one argues that a Mercedes Benz is a perk for the CEO of, say, a successful software firm, someone else can contend that it is an inexpensive means of advertising the competence of that firm. The same contention can be made regarding the much-invoked example of high-powered computer systems. That is, the boundaries between unnecessary perquisites and the certain costs of sales/production are unclear.

18. As argued later, this assumption of managerial labor market inefficiency is the moving force behind some of the more recent theories of dividend policy.

19. References are too numerous to cite. A partial list includes: Cyert and March (1963), Kamin and Ronen (1981), Lambert (1984), Magee (1980), Schiff and Lewin (1970), Williamson (1964) and Young (1985).

20. An important distinction should be noted here. Myers (1990) does not talk about agents anymore. His organizational theory encompasses all who work for the owners.

21. Negative surplus is both a mathematical and an empirical possibility, particularly for firms that are reaching the end of their life cycle. Since market values of debt and equity must be non-negative, it follows that the corporate surplus must be negative. What then would prevent the widespread desertion of managers of such companies?

22. See Gordon and Shapiro (1956), Gordon (1963), Solomon (1963) and Walter (1963).

23. See Bhattacharya (1979,1980), Miller and Rock (1985), John and Williams (1985) and others.

24. That is a world without taxes and transaction costs.

25. Theories put forth by King (1977), Miller and Scholes (1978), Auerbach (1979) and Bradford (1979)—all of whom argue that a dollar paid out has a higher value than a dollar retained, a twist of the bird-in-the-hand models—and by Feldstein and Green (1983) are not considered as too meaningful, since all can be criticized a priori for one reason or another.

26. It is important to remember that the signaling situations modeled by Akerlof and Spence are very specific. A one-on-one relationship between the signaler and signalee must exist and the content of the signal cannot be vague. These two points might seem trivial, but they are crucial in the extension of these two models to corporate finance and dividend policy.

27. This is the fundamental criticism in Feldstein and Green (1983) of Bhattacharya's (1979) signaling model.

28. James Tobin. The British attach the "Sir" to the first name.

29. We will return to "cumulative average excess returns" later, when we discuss the event study method of analysis. Note, however, that, although this model is a new way of thinking, the research technique remains the same as in the case of the traditional models.

30. A European option (call, or put) can be exercised only on the day of expiration. An American option, by far the more interesting and more common option in the United States, in contrast, can be exercised any time until its maturity.

Section 3

**LOGICAL INCONSISTENCIES:
THE CASE OF FINANCE AND RISK**

Chapter VI

Positive, Normative, or Useful Finance (or, is it a Plane, a Bird, a Man?): The History of the CAPM

As we have discussed in the previous chapters, the "positivism" of Bacon, Mill, Comte, and the Vienna Group became the "positive economics" of Milton Friedman, which is still with us as the orthodox methodology of finance. But what does the word *positive* really mean?[1]

> [Comte] used "positive" to refer to the actual in contrast to the merely imaginary, what can claim certainty in contrast to the undecided, the exact in contrast to the indefinite, the useful in contrast to the vain, and finally, what claims relative validity in contrast to the absolute (Habermas 1971, p. 74).

This is a rather portmanteau definition, quite different from current usage. Nowadays, we are more inclined to consider "positive" in contrast to "normative" in tune with John Neville Keynes' definition (in a work originally published in 1891).

> As regards the scope of political economy, no question is more important, or in a way more difficult, than its true relation to practical problems. Does it treat the actual or the ideal? Is it a positive science concerned exclusively with the investigation of uniformities, or is it an art having for its object the determination of practical rules of action? (Keynes 1955, p. 31).

> As the terms are here used, a *positive science* may be defined as a body of systematized knowledge concerning what is; a *normative* or *regulative science* as a body of systematized knowledge relating to criteria of what ought to be, and concerned therefore with the ideal as distinguished from the actual; an *art* as a system of rules for the attainment of a given end. The object of a positive science is the establishment of *uniformities*, of a normative science the determination of *ideals*, of an art the formulation of *precepts* (Keynes 1955, pp. 34-35).

Machlup (1969) offers a variety of synonyms and an extended discussion of "positive science," "normative science," and "art" in his essay "Positive and Normative Economics: An Analysis of the Ideas." Both of the terms in the title have been used to convey a number of ideas, not all of which are perfectly consistent with Keynes' usage. These are summarized in Table VI.1:

The "normative" column really includes two separate concepts—the specification of objectives or norms, and the means of attaining those objectives or norms. Both Keynes and Machlup apply the term *normative* to the former, whereas Keynes refers to the latter as an *art* and Machlup as an *instrument*.

But how do the terms *positive, normative,* and *art* or *instrument* apply to the current practice of finance, which has chosen to call itself "positive" and quite certainly eschew "normative?"[2]

Actually, finance finds itself in a somewhat contradictory position. In its process-of-discovery (also called research), it empirically tests theories with real data in an apparent attempt to explain what is going on; that is, what people out there are doing. This is "positive." At the same time, in its teaching and consulting, based on the normative implications, if any, of its positive models, it attempts to sell its knowledge to "the world out there" as what they ought to be doing. This is "normative."

If finance is positive, then it cannot know more than what almost everyone already knows (and presumably cannot sell it to them, at least with a clear conscience); it can only cast it in a different form. If finance is normative, then it cannot test its theories; what everyone is doing is not necessarily what they ought to be doing. While finance uses the very Cartesian, scientific-sounding term "positive" to describe itself, what it actually does is something much more complicated. The case of the CAPM points out that what a theory is (positive, normative, art or instrument, or something else entirely) is often hard to describe, and may even change over time.

THE ALTERNATIVE CAPMS

The press was quick to supply effusive expressions of praise following the award of the Nobel prize in economics to Harry Markowitz and William Sharpe for their work on portfolio theory and asset pricing. From *The Wall Street Journal,* for example, comes:

> "Widows live safer lives because their portfolios are invested according to the diversification principles developed by Markowitz and elaborated by Sharpe," said Harvard economist Lawrence Summers (Murray 1990, p. B1).

Table VI.1.

Positive	Normative
Description	Prescription
Explanation	Recommendation
Theory	Practice
Theory	Policy
Thought	Action
Laws (Uniformities)	Rules (Norms)
Science	Art
Factual Judgements	Value Judgements
Indicative Statements	Imperative Statements
Testable Facts	Non-testable Feelings

Source: Machlup (1969, pp. 102-103).

And from a writer for *The New York Times,* we read:

> To academics, they are top-shelf theoreticians whose quarter-century-old insights into
> the economics of finance still dazzle the brightest graduate students. To nuts-and bolts
> types, they are researchers whose ideas have changed Wall Street and the investment
> habits of millions of people (Passell 1990, p. D1).

But what *is* the CAPM? What does it *mean?* What can or should one *do*
with it? What *knowledge* has it brought into the world?

Algebraically, the CAPM[3] is usually expressed as:

$$E(R_i) = E(R_f) + [E(R_m) - R_f][\sigma_{Ri,Rm} / \sigma^2_{Rm}], \qquad (1)$$

where $E(\bullet)$ is the expectation operator;
R_i is the rate of return on capital asset i;
R_f is the risk-free interest rate;
R_m is the rate of return on the market, the portfolio of all assets
weighted by their respective market values;
$\sigma_{Ri,Rm}$ is the covariance of asset i rates of return with the rates of
return on the market; and
σ^2_{Rm} is the variance of the rates of return on the market.

The rightmost term in square brackets in Equation 1 is the equivalent of
the slope coefficient of a bivariate OLS regression, and, thus, many times
expressed as β_i. Also, it can be expressed in terms of correlation and standard
deviations as $\rho_{Ri,Rm} \sigma_{Ri} / \sigma_{Rm}$.

There are at least two, and possibly three, interpretations of the CAPM
that appear to offer "rational" answers to the questions posed above.

The Positive, and Normative CAPMs

The "positive" CAPM (CAPM-P) can be explicated as follows:

CAPM-P: At equilibrium, $E(R_i)$ (the expected rate of return on capital asset i) is a positive, linear function of the expected rate of return on the market $E(R_m)$, plus the fixed rate of return on the risk-free asset R_f. The higher is the slope multiplier of the return on the market, the higher is the asset's risk which is market dependent. Asset i would be priced consistent with its market-dependent risk factor. Accordingly, the slope, or β_i is often referred to as systematic risk (market dependent risk). All other aspects of risk, which are not systematic, can be diversified away through judiciously investing in a portfolio of assets.

The normative CAPM (CAPM-N) is really nothing more than the normative logic of CAPM-P (if indeed it holds):

CAPM-N: In the market portfolio all risk but systematic risk is diversified away, accordingly, one cannot do better than invest in the market as a whole, unless one is willing to bear higher risk. Randomly selected portfolio returns are highly correlated with the market, and other things being equal, non-systematic risk is reduced at the margin with the level of diversification (the number of assets in the portfolio).

The interpretation of the CAPM is not a trivial matter. As the CAPM-P holds at equilibrium, the CAPM-N is both a necessary and a sufficient condition for utility maximization. This, of course, will move the market toward equilibrium, if it is not already near or at it, which activity will make the CAPM-P hold—a scenario of the cat chasing, and eventually successfully catching, its tail.

By this reasoning, the CAPM-P is a consequence of the CAPM-N, and the CAPM in general "explains" investor behavior in the sense that the appeal of the model results in investors pricing assets according to the CAPM. This implies that assets would not or could not have been priced in accordance with the CAPM prior to the original publication of the model in 1964 except by accident.

One may alternatively reason that the CAPM-P is descriptive and predictive of asset pricing in the sense that assets have always been priced *as if* investors were behaving according to the CAPM. This implies that the CAPM-N is irrelevant, except perhaps as a new name for a prescription or norm that has always been implicit in investor behavior.[4] Thus, the interpretation of the model has empirical significance. A strictly positive model should have universal applicability and be descriptive of asset returns at any time or place. A normative model should be descriptive of asset returns only as belief in the model spreads from its time and place of origin.

CAPM-U

There might be, however, a third concept implied in the CAPM literature that is not covered by Keynes or Machlup—that of the "useful" CAPM (CAPM-U). In popular textbooks, the CAPM-U is heralded according to the following lines. "Because it provides a quantifiable measure of risk for individual assets, the CAPM is an extremely *useful* tool for valuing risky assets" (Copeland and Weston 1988, p. 202). "The CAPM framework, with its focus on market as opposed to total risk, is clearly *useful* as a way of thinking about the riskiness of assets in general" (Brigham and Gapenski 1987, p. 64).

Unlike the other interpretations, the CAPM-U makes no specific assertion; rather, it is the fact that the model expresses certain ideas in a formal language, and, in doing so, is in some way useful to theoreticians (and possibly to practitioners) for shaping their thoughts or selecting their actions. It has become very common for the term "useful" to be applied to describe theories or models, especially those that have no normative or positive value but are too endearing to abandon. But "useful" has had no philosophical explication and the term is used in often confusing ways to convey a variety of meanings.

All the uses of the term "useful" contribute something to an understanding of the different aspects of the CAPM-U. One such aspect appears in Friedman's economic methodology. His position in his instrumentalist essay, "The Methodology of Positive Economics" (Friedman 1953), is that theories are neither true nor false; rather, they are or are not useful instruments for making predictions.

> Its ('positive economics') task is to provide a system of generalizations that can be used to make correct prediction about the consequences of any change in circumstances (Friedman 1953, p. 4).

According to Friedman, a positive theory of what *is* (more accurately: what *has been*) may be instrumental in achieving what *is desired*, and it is this power as an instrument that makes it useful. In this sense, the CAPM-P becomes the CAPM-N, which here is equivalent to the CAPM-U. But the CAPM-U implied in the textbooks makes a weaker statement than the CAPM-N. Whereas the CAPM-N interpretation states that pricing according to the CAPM *will* maximize utility, the CAPM-U states only that pricing according to the CAPM will yield higher utility than some unspecified alternative. The CAPM (CAPM-U) may not get an investor where he or she wants to go, but it does have some value in setting him or her off in the right direction.

In fact, the CAPM-U often does not even take the standard mathematical form. Frequent use is made of the "market model"—a simple linear regression of the returns on an asset against the returns on some measure of the market, developed by Sharpe (1963), to simplify Markowitz (1952), upon the instructions of the latter. This form eliminates the risk-free rate and the risk premium and uses observable realizations rather than expectations. Nevertheless, it retains the basic linear relationship, and the market model's beta becomes the observable mathematical equivalent of the CAPM's beta. Authors often make it a point to note the distinction between the market model and the CAPM; however, this practice is similar to a judge's instructing a jury to ignore a remark made in court. The market model cannot help but gain a superior significance from its resemblance to the CAPM, and in a sense, it *is* the CAPM incarnate.

It is as the market model that the CAPM has had one of its strongest influences. The market model is used to estimate return expectations, which are required to compute the "abnormal returns" that indicate the response of the market to significant "events" of all sorts. Of course, the use of such a simple linear model to estimate return expectations in these "event studies" does not require the theoretical baggage of the CAPM for justification; in fact, an even simpler average of historical returns "works" just as well as the market model (Brown and Warner 1980, 1985).

Another "worthwhile" aspect of the CAPM-U is its value as a heuristic device, providing insights into asset pricing that may lead to better models. The CAPM may be neither positive, nor normative, but may still be useful if its descendants (such as arbitrage pricing theory) are. Still another aspect of the CAPM-U is its value as a rhetorical device in the manner discussed at length by McCloskey (1985). The model may be a useful expression for communicating certain concepts or principles or for convincing theoreticians or practitioners of the value of these concepts or principles. The apparent role of the CAPM in many textbooks is as a pedagogical device to illuminate portfolio diversification and the trade-off between risk and return.

The CAPM-P, the CAPM-N, and the CAPM-U all look alike. Their mathematics and literal translations are identical. However, each interpretation is fundamentally different from the others; that is, each makes its own more or less unique claim regarding knowledge of asset valuation. In a mathematical sense, there is a single CAPM in the finance literature. But in an epistemological sense, there are at least two and possibly three CAPMs, and different CAPMs have been dominant at different times in the last quarter century.

THE PREDECESSORS OF THE CAPM

The CAPM has evolved from one interpretation to another over the course of its lifetime. Its origin is in the doctoral thesis of normative portfolio theory [NPT], devised by Harry Markowitz shortly after World War II. His dissertation, written under Marschak at the University of Chicago, was declared by Friedman, a member of the dissertation committee, as neither economics, or mathematics, nor even English (Bernstein 1992).

The Expected Return-Variance Maxim

The seminal article that came out of the dissertation was Harry Markowitz' (1952) "Portfolio Selection." This article created NPT, which in many ways laid the foundation of the CAPM. The paper is decidedly normative, because it is a prescription for a risk-averse, one-period, expected utility maximizing investor whose utility function is quadratic, to select a portfolio, subject to a budget and a set of trading constraints. Markowitz is clear about being Bayesian, yet, as a matter of demonstration, he opts to choose expected rates of return and the variance-covariance matrix of the expected returns of *stocks* as measures of portfolio return and risk. In a simple three and four security setting, he demonstrates that efficient portfolios are diversified:

> Various reasons recommend the use of the expected return-variance of return rule, both as a hypothesis to *explain* well-established investment behavior and as a maxim to *guide* one's own actions (Markowitz 1952, p. 86) (Italics added).

He concludes that his maxim is a guide, which is consistent with the adage, "Don't put all your eggs in one basket," and he implies that his maxim is not inconsistent with observable behavior. Yet, his model was and still is the only one that is capable of prescribing an exact portfolio composition, and which does not include all stocks of a given stock universe.

Markowitz compared his maxim with the rule of maximum return. According to the latter, all securities traded in the market must yield the same return, in which instance, investors would have a portfolio of a single asset. This is, of course, not observable; therefore he concludes that:

> Diversification is both observed and sensible; a rule of behavior which does not imply the superiority of diversification must be rejected both as a hypothesis and as a maxim (Markowitz 1952, p. 78).

> Not only does the E-V hypothesis imply diversification, it implies the "right kind" of diversification for the "right reason." The adequacy of diversification is not thought by investors to depend on the number of different securities held. A portfolio with sixty

different railway securities for example, would not be as well diversified as the same size portfolio with some railroad, some public utility, mining, various sort of manufacturing, etc. (Markowitz 1952, p. 88).

NPT, a combination of mathematical programming and statistics is found not to be inconsistent with observable investment behavior. The difference between NPT and observed behavior is that NPT is a strict prescription: the "right kind of diversification for the right reason," whereas observable behavior is intuition. That the idea of diversification existed for some time before either NPT or the CAPM were invented is apparent from Pigou (1920):

It follows, that, if out of a hundred people, each of whom has 100 to invest, every one divides his investment among a hundred enterprises, the aggregate amount of uncertainty-bearing undertaken by the group is smaller than it would have been had every investor concentrated on a single enterprise.... The principle thus explained is fully recognised by businessmen, and has long lain at the root both of insurance and of much speculative dealing on change (Pigou 1960, p. 778).

The same idea is expressed in Makower and Marschak (1938):

As before, an asset's contribution to yield is in general not independent of other assets. This is illustrated by Investment Trusts. The object of an Investment Trust is to increase the safety of the whole property by properly mixing the risks attached to various assets. A gas share added to a holding of electricity shares has a greater marginal safety than if it is added to a holding of gas shares (1938, p. 273).

But these ideas and principles were already unequivocally expressed in an article published before the turn of the century.

From this it follows that the one least able to make a doubtful venture is the small undertaker who embarks his entire capital; abler is the rich man who supports several other enterprises in the same line of business, ablest is the man of ample resources who has many investments in widely sundered departments of activity (Ross 1896, p. 117).

Testing the Normative Hypothesis

A prescription is as good as its promise to achieve an underlying objective. Thus, the true and only test of normative theory is ex post performance. Normative theories are of two kinds: intuitive and formal. Regarding investment decisions, the first kind is individual and subjective. In this category fall such normative "models" as Joe Granville and a large number of other stock-pickers (also called investment gurus), possessors of "unfailing" crystal balls, and Madame Ludmilla, predicting the future from tea leaves. The set of intuitive normative models is very large—close to infinity for all practical purposes—and, consequently, it requires an infinite number of combinations to compare each possible pair of intuitive models with each other and with all formal models.

Formal models are quantifiable models, of differing complexities. For example, there is a school of investment that advocates the 1/5 rule. Accordingly, one should have 20 percent of one's wealth invested in each cash, CD's, stocks, bonds, and real estate. This is a formal model of relatively low complexity. The other end of this spectrum is a portfolio model, such as Markowitz,' which is a complex amalgamate of economic utility theory, statistics, and a branch of mathematical programming known as quadratic programming. This complexity may make it just as mystifying for the uninitiated as Madame Ludmilla's tea leaves reading.

Another predicament of the Markowitz model and all its "work-a-likes" is that they solve a non-existent problem—a problem in which estimates are used in place of known parameters. The combination of estimation error and selection [algorithm] error plays havoc with ex post performance (see, e.g., Frankfurter and Lamoureux 1989). That phenomenon might be a serious problem only for normative purposes, if ex post results are consistently worse than ex ante expectations, in comparison to a benchmark.

Another difficulty with performance evaluation is the availability of data. We argue elsewhere, and repeat the axiom here again, that there is no such thing as a conclusive empirical test. One reason for this postulate is that we are dealing with an infinite process from which we have only limited observations. Accordingly, all types of empiricism, performance evaluation inclusive, must be taken with a grain of salt.

There is, however, one unique aspect of the Markowitz model and its ilk (to be discussed a bit later) that no one of the other, known, formal models have: the Markowitz type models create a precise portfolio. Given the objective function and its set of constraints, and given a universe of stocks for which data are available to estimate the parameters of the model, the end result of the algorithm is a completely determined portfolio in which stocks are invested in unequal proportions, ranging from 0 percent to less than or equal to 100 percent.[5] No other formal model, known to us, has the same property.[6] For this reason, the Markowitz-type models could never have been compared, for example, with the first-, second-, and/or third-order stochastic dominance portfolio model, because the latter must have an a priori determined portfolio.

Perhaps the first step in evaluating the Markowitz model is to compare and contrast it with models that promise to accomplish the same thing: they have the same objective function and are subject to the same set of constraints.

There are three such models, each an outgrowth of the original Markowitz, full covariance model [FCM, subsequently]: Sharpe's single index model [SIM, subsequently], Elton, Gruber and Padberg's (1976), which is a simplification of SIM [SIM*, subsequently], and Elton, Gruber and Padberg's (1978), a simplification of FCM [CCM, subsequently].

SIM is the simplification of Markowitz that makes possible the application of the model to large stock universes. In fact, pentium or even 486 CPU microcomputers can select the set of efficient portfolios from universes as large as 5,000 to 6,000 stocks. This is, of course, impossible for FCM, even for mainframe supercomputers, because they cannot invert a matrix of 6,000 x 6,000, or they can do so only with extremely expensive programming efforts.

SIM's simplification is achieved at a cost of a set of additional assumptions to be layered on top of the original Markowitz assumptions. The validity of these assumptions, in contrast to a positive model, is crucial when one deals with a normative model.

SIM* is a simplification of SIM. CCM is a simplification of FCM, making the rather ambiguous, and perhaps misleading, assumption of a constant correlation coefficient prevailing for all stocks of a stock universe (that is, that each stock's correlation with each and every other stock is exactly the same).

Hammer and Phillips (1992), and Phillips (1993) studied the properties of the three "simplification" models and concluded that ex ante they are different from Markowitz. Consequently, each one of the four is a different model, yet each is a member of the set of portfolio selection methods that have the same objective functions and are subject to the same [budget and trading] constraints.

Occasional empirical evidence demonstrating the superiority of the Markowitz-type models over, say, an index portfolio, has surfaced in the literature (e.g., Frankfurter and Frecka 1979, and Frankfurter and Phillips 1982). Yet, until very recently, there was no published, large-scale, empirical study of performance. The first such attempt was made by Frankfurter, Phillips and Faulk (1996), [FPF, subsequently]. FPF use a 30-year time period, starting from January 1964 for which they compare portfolio performance, selected by FCM, SIM, SIM* and CCM in three, ten-year subperiods, for expected monthly returns ranging from 6.0 percent to 0.5 percent, based on estimation periods of 120 and 60 months, respectively.

FPF find that expected (ex ante) returns are poor predictors of realized (ex post) returns. They note, however, that the problem hinges only tangentially on the accuracy of prediction. The ultimate criterion is performance vis-a-vis an alternative. The alternative they compare performance with is the return on an index portfolio, such as the Standard & Poor's 500. They find that the return in two out of the three subperiods on the index is negative and about the same (-1.010% and -0.920%). The exception is January 1994, when the ex post return is an uncharacteristically and unusually high 3.250 percent. SIM realizes positive returns for ex ante expectations for 2.5 percent or less, with 120 months of estimation, and with the exception of the 1969-1973 subperiod, for 4.0 percent or less ex ante returns, based on 60 months of estimation. For the 1989-1993 data set, all realized returns for FCM, SIM and SIM* are positive. The exception is CCM, which seems not to be able to deliver, neither ex ante nor ex post what its inventors promised to deliver.

FPF also conclude that both ex ante predictions and ex post performance depend on the structure of the universe. They find that the 1974-1983 and the 1984-1993 subperiods' selections are much influenced by NASDAQ stocks whose return-generating process poorly fits all four models. The response of the selection algorithms is to over-diversify, a phenomenon demonstrated earlier by Frankfurter and Frecka (1979).

Of course, even a 30-year period is insufficient to scientifically prove the superiority of these models over an alternative strategy. Yet, for a Bayesian, the moral is that, with all likelihood, SIM's low expected return-risk portfolios of 30 to 40 stocks is the way to bet (with FCM and SIM* as close seconds).

Comparing these models with models of intuition is an interminable task. That does not mean that crystal balls and tea leaves are not superior to models of the Markowitz ilk. Yet, for most simple-minded folk, while access to these models might be cheap, their end results might be devastatingly costly (if past anecdotal evidence is any indication).

THE ORIGINAL CAPM

Because of the influence of a certain school of financial economics, and its unquenchable thirst for positive, equilibrium-based models, however, the normative portfolio selection of Markowitz was transformed into a bluntly positive model of asset pricing.

Tobin's Liquidity Preference Model

The transformation began with James Tobin's (1958) article, "Liquidity Preference as Behaviour Towards Risk." Tobin's objective was to explain the demand for non-interest-bearing cash in preference to interest-bearing monetary assets. He related his work to that of Markowitz in a footnote in which he implied that Markowitz was normative.

> Markowitz's main interest is prescription of rules of rational behavior for investors; the main concern of this paper is the implications for economic theory, mainly comparative statics, that can be derived from assuming that investors do in fact follow such rules (Tobin 1958, p. 85).

Tobin argued that, if investors do hold expected return-variance efficient[7] portfolios, then investors will hold portfolios of both cash and interest-bearing monetary assets. Since investors are observed to hold both cash and interest bearing monetary assets in the same portfolio, his theorem constitutes an explanation in principle; that is, if investors did hold expected return-variance efficient portfolios, then along with other assumptions, this behavior could explain their behavior with respect to cash and interest-bearing monetary assets.

To assert that investors do hold expected return-variance efficient portfolios on the strength of this evidence would be to commit the fallacy of affirming the antecedent. They may, of course, hold cash for other reasons.

There is a certain plausibility in the arguments of Tobin, but there are problems with mixing normative statements and explanations in principle. Markowitz' work was normative—in Tobin's words, he prescribed rules of rational behavior. Now, this does not mean that investors were irrational before Markowitz. While investors may always have been rational, their rationality may have been constrained by their knowledge and ability. There is nothing to preclude investors improving their techniques.

But if Markowitz is normative as Tobin claims, then Tobin has not provided an explanation of liquidity preference that could have applied before Markowitz. Unless investors follow Markowitz' rules, one cannot use Tobin to conclude that they will hold cash in their portfolios of monetary assets. Since investors did hold cash prior to Markowitz, it is necessary to abandon Tobin, or to change his interpretation of Markowitz. It may be that investors have always behaved *as if* they were following Markowitz, in which case Tobin's universality is rehabilitated. This means, however that Markowitz did not provide any superior prescription for rational behavior, but merely translated the existing unwritten rules into another, more explicit language. By this line of reasoning, modern portfolio theory [MPT, subsequently] is not normative, but positive and descriptive and potentially useful in deriving a possible explanation of observable behavior. In the CAPM, this potential explanation becomes a testable hypothesis, and the transformation to a wholly positive statement is complete.

Sharpe's Original CAPM

The positivism in Sharpe's (1964) "Capital Asset Prices: A Theory of Market Equilibrium Under Conditions of Risk" is not unequivocal. Sharpe begins and ends the article with rhetoric that is indicative of "useful."

> We will show that such an extension provides a theory with implications consistent with the assertions of traditional financial theory described above. Moreover, it sheds considerable light on the relationship between the price of an asset and the various components of overall risk (Sharpe 1964, p. 431).

> We have now shown that with regard to capital assets considered individually, it also yields implications consistent with traditional concepts: it is common practice for investment counselors to accept a lower expected return from defensive securities (those which respond little to changes in the economy) than they require from aggressive

securities (which exhibit significant response). As suggested earlier, the familiarity of the implications need not be considered a drawback. The provision of a logical framework for producing some of the major elements of traditional financial theory should be a useful contribution in its own right (Sharpe 1964, p. 442).

In these passages, the language is reminiscent of the distinctively positive element that is characteristic of Tobin (1958)—that the model is consistent with well-established practices and observable behavior.[8] This seems to be the case at another point in the article as well; however, it is quite clear that Sharpe's term "classical financial doctrine" refers to the neoclassical use of equilibrium conditions in theories, and Friedmanian positivism. In fact, as we have already noted, Sharpe goes one important step beyond Friedman:

> Needless to say, these are highly restrictive and undoubtedly unrealistic assumptions. However, since the proper test of a theory is not the realism of its assumptions but the *acceptability* of its implications, and since these assumptions imply equilibrium conditions which form a major part of classical financial doctrine, it is far from clear that this formulation should be rejected—especially in view of the dearth of alternative models leading to similar results (Sharpe 1964, p. 434) (Italics added.)

Whereas Friedman requires predictive ability from a good positive model, Sharpe is satisfied if the model's implications are acceptable. Implications are acceptable if the model is consistent with rudimentary economic wisdom, and/or its mathematics is internally consistent.

While never mentioning empirical validation of his newly found paradigm, Sharpe, nevertheless, makes a boldly declarative statement that implies that he may have had it in mind.

> If so, diversification enables the investor to escape all but the risk resulting from swings in economic activity—this type of risk remains even in efficient combinations. And, since all other types can be avoided by diversification, only the responsiveness of an asset's rate of return to the level of economic activity is relevant in assessing its risk. *Prices will adjust until there is a linear relationship between the magnitude of such responsiveness and expected return* (Sharpe 1964, p. 442) (Italics added).

Any doubt about Sharpe's positive intent is dispelled by a passage from his textbook.

> In this chapter the realm of positive economics is entered, where a descriptive model of how assets are priced is presented.... The exact manner in which expected return and beta are related is specified by the CAPM (Sharpe and Alexander 1990, p. 194).

John Lintner, whose 1965 article, "The Valuation of Risk Assets and the Selection of Risky investments in Stock Portfolios and Capital Budgets," is considered to be the other source of the CAPM, was very cautious about his claims regarding the model.

> It is emphasized that the results of this paper are not being presented as directly applicable to practical decisions, because many of the factors which matter very significantly in practice have had to be ignored or assumed away. The function of these simplifying assumptions has been to permit a rigorous development of theoretical relationships and theorems which reorient much current theory (especially on capital budgeting) and provide a basis for further work (Lintner 1965, pp. 33-34).

This is consistent with the "useful" interpretation of the model, but, at its genesis, the positive interpretation of the CAPM was clearly dominant.

The Maturing CAPM

Stephen Ross, the creator of the CAPM's major competitor, arbitrage pricing theory [APT, subsequently], begins his 1978 survey, "The Current Status of the Capital Asset Pricing Model (CAPM)," with the following statement:

> The report will also have a distinctly positive focus; the attractiveness of the CAPM is due to its potential testability. It is a paradigm, precisely because it is cast in terms of variables which are, at least in principle and with the usual exception of the *ex ante-ex post* distinction, empirically observable and statistically testable. Its positive orientation and apparently simple intuition have made it the central equilibrium model of financial economics (Ross 1978, p. 885).[9]

This passage is quite specific about the attractions of the CAPM. One attractive quality noted by Ross was considered significant by Markowitz and emphasized by Sharpe as well—the model's apparently simple intuition, which intuition is the same as the beliefs that had led to the well-established portfolio selection practices since before Markowitz. Ross goes on to articulate this intuition and expand upon the value of the CAPM:

> The CAPM theory outlined above not only "explains" asset prices, but it does so by providing an analytical basis for a brilliant, if not entirely reliable, intuition.... The CAPM substantiated the idea that, in competitive equilibrium, assets earn premia over the riskless rate that increase with their risk, by showing that the determining influence on risk premia is the covariance between the asset and the market portfolio, rather than the own or intrinsic risk of the asset (Ross 1978, pp. 886-887).

The claim that deserves closer scrutiny is the "analytical basis" that "substantiates" the intuition. By "analytical basis," Ross must mean the assumptions from which the CAPM is derived and the process of the derivation itself. That "highly restrictive and undoubtedly unrealistic" set of assumptions, in Sharpe's own view, can lend substance to an idea or convince anyone to believe in it is a peculiar notion.

It may be that the "substance" comes from the familiarity of the "analytical basis." After all, the CAPM's assumptions regarding markets and investors do involve elements that could be expected a priori to have an influence on asset pricing, and these elements along with the process of derivation are similar to those commonly used in neoclassical microeconomic theory. "Substance" also carries the connotation of empirically observable and statistically testable, and a key contribution of both modern portfolio theory and the CAPM was the transformation of intuitive concepts such as "risk" and "the right reason for diversification" into the measurable quantities of "variance" and "covariance with the market portfolio."

Restating the essence of Ross' description less effusively, the CAPM takes a somewhat plausible but otherwise unjustified measure of risk (variance of return), combines it with a standard set of highly simplified or unrealistic neoclassical microeconomic assumptions, and generates a simple formula, the implications of which agree with intuitive notions of proper principles of investment, and/or the same neoclassical logic from which it was derived at the first place. This formula that allegedly explains asset pricing forms the nucleus of one academic discipline, and plays a key role in others. This is clearly a much broader claim than Markowitz, Tobin, Sharpe, or Lintner ever made.

Testing the CAPM

By the tenets of the "scientific method," a positive theory must be verifiable by empirical evidence, and one virtue of the CAPM, as Ross pointed out, was that it was "cast in terms of variables which are, at least in principle and with the usual exception of the *ex ante-ex post* distinction, empirically observable and statistically testable." The CAPM also makes a bold prediction of linearity worthy of the physical sciences; that is, that there is a linear relationship between the measure of risk, beta, of an asset and the return on the asset.

It is beyond the scope of this book to survey the results of the early empirical tests of the CAPM; however, Fama's summary of these efforts 12 years after the model was first published was: "In truth, all we can really say at this time is that the literature has not yet produced a meaningful test of the Sharpe-Lintner hypothesis (Fama 1976, p. 370). But this apparently did not bother Fama too much, who goes on to say: "The overall view of market equilibrium is that of the Sharpe-Lintner model" (p. 370). Fama attributes the fact that there were no meaningful tests of the CAPM to the problem of choosing an appropriate proxy for the market portfolio.

In two papers, Roll (1977, 1978) dealt what should have been a devastating blow to the CAPM. The choice of an appropriate proxy for the market portfolio presents more of a problem than had been believed. The risk, as measured by beta, and return for assets will necessarily be linearly related if the market portfolio chosen for the computation of beta is mean-variance efficient. Any portfolio chosen as a proxy for the market portfolio, even what might be regarded as an inappropriate one, will support the CAPM if that portfolio is mean-variance efficient. The CAPM is essentially a mathematical artifact. According to Roll,

> The theory is not testable unless the exact composition of the true market portfolio is known and used in the tests. This implies that the theory is not testable unless *all* individual assets are included in the sample (Roll 1977, p. 130) (Italics in original).[10]

This argument is, incidentally, the centerpiece of Roll and Ross (1993), which intends to refute the devastating empirical findings of Fama and French (1992), that beta has no predictive power. What Roll (1976, 1978) and Roll and Ross (1993) conveniently forget to mention is that, if the assumptions of the CAPM do not hold, there is no market portfolio—indeed, there cannot be a market portfolio. And if there is no market portfolio, then any and all proxies that may be used as such can be useful for testing the predictive ability of the CAPM (which is what is tested by Fama and French 1992), and, thus, the validity of the CAPM-P.

Black (1993) is very explicit about the existence of a good proxy for the market portfolio:

> In the U.S., the problem of not knowing the market portfolio to use is not too severe (except, as I note later, it tends to flatten the line relating expected return and beta). In my view, all candidates for the U.S. market portfolio are highly correlated (p. 37).

As there is no realistic possibility of an empirical test, the CAPM cannot be considered as a scientific model. Accordingly, it is strange that it should be accepted for its usefulness, when common sense would suggest otherwise.

THE CAPM TODAY

Despite the seriousness of the Roll critique, which had, as Roll admitted in an introductory footnote, been anticipated in some ways by others, the CAPM-P has died hard.

The Failure of the CAPM-P

Ross, of course, had to address Roll in his 1978 survey article. He was not quite so impressed with the seriousness of the problem.

The response to Roll's critique has been largely a rejection of what is misinterpreted as a nihilistic message. "If we take Roll's objections to heart, then no theory is testable."[11] This pessimism is not wholly warranted.... It might be possible to construct tests of the efficiency of (the market portfolio) by using (a proxy). This will not be easy, but it should be possible (Ross 1978, p. 893).

And Ross concludes the article with a mixed message:

It is not impossible to test the CAPM, but it is ironic that after more than a decade of study no robust test of a supposedly testable theory exists (1978, p. 898).

Roll's critique did not terminate CAPM testing. Some authors appear to have agreed with Ross that Roll's arguments were not so decisive as he had presented them. Friend, Westerfield, and Granito (1978) and Cheng and Grauer (1980) among others attempted to devise alternative tests taking Roll's arguments into account.[12]

It is common to acknowledge empirical difficulties with the CAPM-P, but there is a strong reluctance to abandon it, and references to the model continue to use the language of testing and falsifiability. In his well-known text, *Financial Statement Analysis*, Foster (1986) comments that:

Equilibrium theories of equity security expected returns (including the CAPM) ... have been the subject of detailed empirical testing. Several severe problems arise in this testing that make it difficult to place heavy reliance on the results of any single study (Foster 1986, p. 355).

However, the "severe problems" listed by Foster include the problem with *ex ante* versus *ex post* measurements of return, the problem with the measurement of beta, and the problem with the measurement of the market portfolio. Foster does not mention Roll's "problem" at all.

Findlay and Williams (1980) have pointed out that there is in fact an implicit bias in empirical testing in finance.[13] "Tests" are of whether a model or theory has at least some validity, not of whether it has more validity than alternatives.

In sum, do we interpret Fama-MacBeth (1973) as an empirical effort 1) conducted with a CAPM prior which showed that the prior could not be rejected, or 2) conducted with a diffuse prior which found, after an investigation of several plausible alternatives, that the CAPM was (markedly?) superior? ... If it is 2), then it could have powers to persuade (or discredit) those of differing beliefs. Yet if it is 1), it may only be used to fend off those who would attempt to alter the beliefs of the CAPM (p. 13).

Even with this built-in bias to the "tests," the CAPM fares poorly. Yet some authors cling to the model so strongly that they hesitate to blame the model itself for any of its empirical deficiencies.

Both advocates and detractors of the CAPM can find support in the literature. Much of the evidence presented in this chapter will appear to refute the CAPM. Certainly, many researchers have had difficulty finding evidence of the simple relationship expressed by the CAPM. There are several reasons why this is true, prime among them the fact that our research techniques may not be up to the task (there may be so much extraneous information that the basics are obfuscated), and that we may have used the wrong data in our research (Harrington 1987, p. 54).[14]

Even those who more explicitly acknowledge that the model has probably been proven not valid (to the extent that its validity can be proven or is an issue) maintain that it has "some" validity.

The CAPM was shown to provide a useful conceptual framework for capital budgeting and the cost of capital. It is also reasonably unchanged by the relaxation of many of the unrealistic assumptions that made its derivation simpler. Finally, although the model is not perfectly validated by empirical tests, its main implications are upheld— namely, that systematic risk (beta) is a valid measure of risk, that the model is linear, and that the trade-off between return and risk is positive (Copeland and Weston 1988, p. 231).

Fama and French (1992) seem to have put the final nail in the coffin of the CAPM, at least for research purposes. Their paper contained nothing especially new, but the fact that one of the foremost "authorities" in finance, indeed one whose name was closely connected with the CAPM,[15] denounced it gave the article prominence far beyond its content. Nonetheless, the spirit of the CAPM continues to stalk classrooms and seminar rooms. It has clearly become a Kuhnian paradigm, as Ross hinted, or part of a Lakatosian hard core, effectively immunized from its obviously severe theoretical and empirical deficiencies. But the CAPM is not necessarily being retained in the forms in which it was developed (the CAPM-P, or the CAPM-N), although the descriptions of some authors seem to indicate one of these interpretations. As suggested by the quotation from Copeland and Weston, the CAPM-U seems to be more relevant.

More About the Useful CAPM

As the CAPM-P, the model has consistently failed to survive tests of verification, perhaps because of the problems with the market portfolio pointed out by Roll, or perhaps not. Specifically, the constant term and the coefficient of beta in a linear regression of realized asset returns on beta do not correspond respectively to the risk-free rate (according to the best estimate of what might reasonably be regarded as a risk-free rate) and to the market risk premium (according to the best estimate of what reasonably would be regarded as a market risk premium). But, as the quotation from Copeland and Weston states, there seems to be a positive linear relationship between asset returns and beta, and it is implied that this endows the model with some usefulness and an aura of validity.

There being a positive relationship between an asset's returns and beta is equivalent to there being a positive relationship between an asset's returns and the covariance of those returns with the returns on a large portfolio of assets including the asset itself.[16]

This is no different from the intuition described by Markowitz that there is a "right kind of diversification for a right reason." It is desirable to add assets to a portfolio that are "different" from those assets already in that portfolio, and, because it is desirable to add such assets, one must be willing to sacrifice some return in order to obtain the concomitant reduction of risk. It is also no different from Sharpe's "common practice for investment counselors to accept a lower expected return from defensive securities (those which respond little to changes in the economy) than they require from aggressive securities (which exhibit significant response)." This concept regarding the nature of risk—one reason for the "usefulness" of the CAPM— long preceded the CAPM.

Although its "useful" conception of risk may not have originated with the CAPM, a second possible reason for the "usefulness" of the CAPM is its ability to quantify risk. It is intuitive to many that risk is some measure of the dispersion of some sort of distribution of asset returns, and a linear beta is one of these measures. (This is, of course, another "intuition" that has never been substantiated and one that we challenge in Chapter VII.) Yet, the CAPM-P theoretically "explains" all the variability a portfolio should have. Numerous studies have shown that it "explains" less than half of the variability, and, when comparisons are made, often does not "explain" as much as other measures (Cooley et al. 1977; Arnott 1983).

The remaining possible reason for usefulness is the value of the CAPM as a stage in the development of a superior positive model to explain asset returns. Making the model's assumptions less restrictive and more realistic in a Cartesian process of decreasing abstraction or successive approximation has made no difference, and this process seems to have been terminated as a viable line of research. It is doubtful whether the CAPM will be a direct ancestor of some future model, although it will never be possible to discount its ending up as a distant relative. Yet, if one considers "usefulness" in the Friedmanian sense, then the CAPM-U is a creation of art, and there is no progress in art. Consequently, it does not matter whether a new paradigm, when and if it appears in the academic firmament, will or will not build on either the CAPM-P or the CAPM-U.

Since all interpretations of the CAPM are flawed, there is no rational reason for the success of the model. Its normative value for investors is demonstrated by the extent of the existence of index funds. (This is, indeed, a very weak recommendation, because many have shown that, on average, mutual funds underperform the market.) There are serious difficulties with it as a positive description of investor behavior. Finally, it is questionable just how useful the CAPM really is. The ideas for which it is valued have been around much longer than the model, and its quantification of risk has no justification and is not necessarily the best heuristic when an estimate of risk must be made. Furthermore, it seems to have become a theoretical dead end. Why then has it reputedly changed the investment habits of millions of people and won a Nobel prize?

THE NOTORIETY OF THE CAPM

The answer to this question lies outside the realm of economic "rationality." There are two explanations for the notoriety of the CAPM, one sociological and one psychological. And the current "usefulness" of the CAPM is much different in the practitioner community than it is in the academic community.

The Sociological Explanation: Academics and Practitioners

The institutional milieu within which the CAPM rose to prominence has been thoroughly documented by Whitely (1986). After Word War II, transformations in both financial research in universities and financial practice in the economy converged to create the proper environment for the CAPM. On the academic side:

> Business finance became transformed into financial economics when university business schools recruited relatively large numbers of economists and applied mathematicians as part of their attempts at developing more analytical and "scientific" approaches to management studies. This growth in employment opportunities, and the concomitant change in orientation towards intellectual goals, standards, and priorities, enabled new reputational organisations, such as financial economics, to become institutionalised around novel cognitive objects and concerns (p. 180).

The CAPM translated venerable investment heuristics into the language of theoretical neoclassical microeconomics, and the ability to master its intricacies—to fine-tune it theoretically by relaxing its assumptions or to discover new econometric subtleties in its empirical tests—was the perfect filter for selecting those intellectually superior individuals deserving of recognition in this new science of financial economics.

On the applications side, there were a number of motivations for embracing theoretical financial economics in general and the CAPM in particular. First, it enhanced the professional prestige of a rapidly expanding number of finance specialists.

The "scientific" field of finance thus became attractive to a growing number of practitioners through its combination of portfolio construction and analysis techniques and its promise of academic legitimation for a nascent profession (Whitely 1986, p. 183).

Second, it meant that performance could be measured in an economy in which risk was becoming an important consideration along with return.

ERISA's formalisation of the "prudent man" standard for the behaviour of pension fund managers further emphasized the risks attached to equity investments in a period of rising inflation and decreasing real returns, and the importance of having some "objective" indicator of the degree of risk associated with particular portfolios of investments (1986, p. 184).

Third, it may have yielded some competitive advantage.

By holding out the promise of general theories of capital markets and claiming detailed knowledge of how markets value new "contingent claims," such as options and futures contracts, the leaders of financial economics offered a means of coping with increased uncertainty and competition among financial intermediaries. As generators of intellectual innovations, they are seen as potential sources for innovations in financial services and as providers of understanding of how markets in new instruments function (1986, p. 186).

All these considerations are undeniably true, and they may indeed explain initial enthusiasm for the CAPM. However, they do not explain the durability of the CAPM, in whatever form, in light of its obvious deficiencies.

Despite the encomia that followed the Nobel prize, the CAPM has in fact not been especially durable among practitioners (Ibbottson Associates' *Beta Book* notwithstanding), and what limited influence it continues to have is not difficult to understand. Even in the midst of the early enthusiasm, there was skepticism.

These people with math and computer backgrounds who are coming into the investment business and who think they can assign precise degrees of risk to five or six decimal places are nothing but charlatans.... The real fact is that beta is nothing but a fad, a gimmick. It tells you nothing on which you can make a portfolio decision. In my opinion, these knaves must be driven from the temple (Welles 1971, p. 22).

This statement may be dismissed as a reactionary response to an innovation that many found difficult to comprehend; however, doubts about the CAPM and beta did not abate. A critical article in *Fortune* magazine, "The Strange News about Risk and Return" (Wellemeyer 1973), was followed by a defensive response in the *Financial Analysts Journal* in which the authors argued for a negative answer to the title question, "Is Beta Phlogiston?" (Fouse, Jahnke and Rosenberg 1974). The controversy about the CAPM was fully bared in a famous article in *Institutional Investor*, "Is Beta Dead?,'' in which Roll's critique was offered as strong evidence against the efficacy of "scientific' quantitative methods.

Now, the use of the CAPM and beta by practitioners appears to be severely limited. Information sources such as the Standard & Poor's Stock Reports and Value Line continue to report betas, but, out of three leading U.S. business periodicals,[17] for example, only *Business Week* includes any risk measure at all in its annual ranking of mutual fund performance, and, while *Business Week* uses a statistical measure, it is not beta. According to Robert A.G. Monks, Department of Labor pension fund administrator:

> Modern portfolio theory is absolute horse manure. I had to take a year to stop being bullied by it. I don't believe that just because I, as trustee, have a low beta in my portfolio, I should sleep better at night. Much of MPT is ratification after the fact. We do not use MPT in the regulatory process here (quoted in Cohen, Zinbarg and Zeikel 1987, p. 185).

Not unexpectedly, the failure of the CAPM to be successfully applied to real investments has not had much of an effect on the academic community, perhaps because:

> The transfer of knowledge from finance theory to investment practitioners, then, was largely a transfer of skills through the educational system and a direct transfer of a particular measuring instrument for particular purposes. It was not, I suggest, the transfer of a true theory which transformed and directed practical activities (Whitely 1986, p. 185).

Yet, the CAPM as a finance theory had to face its own empirical failures along with the apparently devastating Roll critique. Nonetheless, its current academic "usefulness" far exceeds its "usefulness" in practice. Why was it then that academics were so much more reluctant to abandon their CAPM than the practitioners, when its deficiencies with regard to finance theory were at least as great as its deficiencies in application?

The Psychological Explanation and the Academic Community

There are a number of possible answers to this question. One, of course, is that, if it is possible to falsify the CAPM, it has not been. The Duhem-Quine thesis states that it is possible to immunize any theory against falsification, given that any empirical test is necessarily a joint test of the theory, the correspondence rules linking the theoretical terms to observable data, and the econometrics used in the test. Thus, it is always possible to claim that apparent falsification does not represent a failure of the theory, but a failure of one or more auxiliary assumptions. This appears to be the argument used by Harrington above. Unfortunately, the evidence against the CAPM, inclusive of the Roll critique, is so substantial that it should convince the most resolute defender. The invocation of the Duhem-Quine thesis must be less a legitimate conviction that it applies than an excuse to defend a more deeply held belief.

A second possible answer is that reputations have been built upon work associated with the CAPM; in fact, the entire reputational system within finance and a significant component of that within accounting rests upon CAPM-like theorization. Those at the top will not recant the beliefs that placed them there (Fama excepted), and those who aspire to the top embrace the beliefs that can place them there. It may indeed be that virtually all the members of an entire profession profess for professional reasons beliefs they do not hold to be true; however, this is a profoundly cynical view. It is doubtful that the intellectual integrity of so many financial economists could not only be so low, but also remain so low for so long.

A third possible answer is that the CAPM is retained solely for lack of an alternative. The obvious candidate from finance theory, the APT, is insufficiently specific regarding the identity of factors that generate systematic risk. If it is true that no theory may be abandoned without a successor, then the CAPM remains, with its deficiencies fully acknowledged, until one is discovered. However, there is no dearth of asset-pricing schemes and risk measures in the historical literature, yet none are taken seriously enough to be subjected to the same empirical scrutiny that the CAPM has. Nor does there seem to be much of an effort to seek other alternatives.

There is a widespread belief in something about the CAPM that is sincere and deep and impervious to "rational" analysis. The CAPM embodies the idealization that the complexities of asset pricing can be reduced to a simple intuitive expression and that there is an easily obtainable measure of risk that is suitable for a wide variety of purposes in accounting and finance. This reflects a need or belief that has been around at least since the 19th century (Hacking 1990). As Lord Kelvin declared in a familiar quotation:

> When you can measure what you are talking about and express it in numbers, you know something about it; but when you cannot measure it, when you cannot express it in numbers, your knowledge is of a meager and unsatisfactory kind, it may be the beginning of knowledge but you have scarcely in your thoughts advanced to the stage of science whatever the matter may be (quoted in Hogben 1957, p. 254).[18]

It is possible that this belief or need is an aspect or manifestation of the "Cartesian anxiety" that began in the Enlightenment and strengthened with the Industrial Revolution. However, it may be a quite different phenomenon that borders on the mystical. As a belief or fulfillment of a need rather than an empirically testable scientific theory, the CAPM is little different from the more arcane forms of technical analysis—the technique of inferring future prices from the patterns of past price movements. Although this approach to asset pricing was popularized in the United States in the writings of Charles Dow around the turn of the century (Hamilton 1922), there is evidence that it was practiced in Japan as early as the Seventeenth century (Shaw 1988).

The CAPM may be more an effect of a Pythagorean numerological impulse than of anything that might be regarded as "rational." Lord Kelvin's quotation above was long preceded by one by Plato which is less well-known: "He who never looks for numbers in anything will not himself be looked for in the numbers of famous men" (quoted in Georgescu-Roegen 1971, p. 79). In chapters 9, and 10 we will explore these issues in greater detail, but we now turn to a more in-depth discussion of the statistical measurement of risk upon which all so-called "uncertainty" models such as the CAPM are based.

NOTES

1. We will try not to fall prey to Hutchison's observation that "the term 'positivism' has become a 'kind of dustbin into which anything considered objectionable is summarily swept'" (Blaug 1994, p. 133, footnote 16, quoting Terrence *Hutchison, Changing Aims in Economics*).

2. "Art" and "instrument" are hardly the adjectives to which a science ought to aspire, and are quite beyond the pale.

3. Fama and French (1992) refer to the CAPM as the Sharpe (1964), Lintner (1965), Black (1965), or SLB model. Somehow, this acronym "sticks" in later writings (see, e.g., Roll and Ross 1994).

4. The implication is that Markowitz more or less stumbled on an area of application for his quantitative techniques that investors already knew about.

5. The highest-risk, highest-return portfolio will include just one stock.

6. The normative implication of CAPM-P, of course, will be an exception. But, even in this case, the opinions are divided between equal weighting and market value weighting, how many stocks to include to represent the market, and what might be the best proxy for the market.

7. Efficiency in this context means quadratic stochastic dominance.

8. Not to mention such adages as "Don't put all your eggs in one basket," and "No pain, no gain."

9. Many versions of the APT do in fact resemble what would once have been disparagingly called *ad hoc* asset-pricing models. As Fama remarks:

> In contrast, the multifactor models are licenses to search the data for variables that, *ex post*, describe the cross-section of average returns. It is perhaps no surprise, then, that these variables do well in competitions on the data used to identify them (Fama 1991, p. 1598).

10. The Roll critique does not prevent a measurement of the "explanatory power" of beta in regard to return variability. Roll himself made this measurement in a 1988 article "R^2." Such measurements are not strictly "tests" of the CAPM, and what the measurement actually

measures is problematic. Of course, these measurements look like tests of the CAPM, and the R^2 looks a lot like a measure of the explanatory power of the CAPM.

11. The quotation within the quotation is attributed to "a learned economist."

12. These authors misinterpret Roll. "It would appear that this recent study has rediscovered the fact that the testing of a theory is a joint test of the validity of the empirical constructs used in testing it" (Friend et al. 1978, p. 905) Roll's critique is far more serious.

13. Findlay and Williams also use a paper by Foster (1978) to illustrate this bias in CAPM tests.

14. Harrington (1987) provides a comprehensive, albeit sympathetic, summary of the empirical tests of the CAPM.

15. People with memories a bit longer than what event studies presuppose still remember that Fama (1968) reconciled the difference between Sharpe's (1964) and Lintner's (1965) CAPMs. Also, Fama, a self-proclaimed inventor of event studies, and his many students used the model for empirical studies to estimate "abnormal returns." An indication of academic jockeying is the fact that, in Fama and French (1992), the model was re-christened the SLB model, where the acronym stands for Sharpe, Lintner and Black, distancing Fama as much as possible from a "fallen angel."

16. In all empirical work, "assets" are really common stocks and not any other capital asset. In Fama and French (1992), even the universe of common stock is screened, because of a certain logic.

17. *Business Week, Fortune* and *Forbes*.

18. According to McCloskey:

> An approximation to this version is inscribed on the front of the Social Sciences Research Building at the University of Chicago. Jacob Viner, a famous University of Chicago economist is said to have remarked on it one day: "Yes, and when you can express it in numbers, your knowledge is of a meager and unsatisfactory kind." Frank Knight, the famous University of Iowa economist, wrote, "Yes, and when you can't measure, measure anyway."

Knight was also a famous critic of statistical measurement of risk, as discussed in Chapter VIII.

Chapter VII

Risk, Uncertainty, and Probability: Language and Concepts

In earlier chapters, we discussed in general terms the problems associated with building theories on simplifying assumptions. Such assumptions are not only unproven, but also never even tested. In fact, it is not considered necessary to test them. If the theories built on the assumptions fail to predict adequately, then they are abandoned and replaced by new theories built on new (and equally simplifying) assumptions. Had the assumptions of the failed theory been thoughtfully considered in advance and their inherent limitations and contradictions recognized, the failure might have been anticipated.

As we have seen in the previous chapter, one of the premier theories of finance, the CAPM, has been a notoriously dismal failure at prediction. The model was obviously built with a cavalier disregard for the realities of risk and uncertainty, which disregard led to their wholly inappropriate translation into the language of mathematical probability. The failure of the CAPM makes an excellent case study of the belief that greater attention to assumptions—especially assumptions concerning the different "languages" in which problems are suggested, theories constructed, and theories tested—might have prevented decades of futile effort.

Improper treatment of risk has been one of the more subtle, yet also more egregious, failures of finance, and, ultimately, a cause of many problems. In this chapter we discuss what these problems are; and in the next chapter, how they came to be ignored.

FINANCE, LANGUAGE, AND TRANSLATION

Scientific thought takes its ultimate point of departure from problems suggested by observing things and events encountered in common experience; it aims to understand these observable things by discovering some systematic order in them; and its final test for the laws that serve as instruments of explanation and prediction is their concordance with such observations (Nagel 1961, p. 79).

99

Economic activity, like all other human endeavor, is fraught with uncertainty. Individuals and firms gamble, take chances, place bets, make wagers, face risks, and expose themselves to hazards. Some outcomes are probable, likely, to be expected, plausible, reasonable, credible, believable, or imaginable; others are improbable, unlikely, not to be expected, implausible, unreasonable, incredible, unbelievable, or unimaginable. These are the things and events encountered in common experience, and these are the common language terms in which they are described. But to solve the problems suggested by observations of these things and events, the common language will not do. The terms need to be translated into a formal language or theoretical language to formulate laws—a language in which terms are well-defined and logical operations are well-specified. And to test the laws that serve as instruments of explanation and prediction, the terms need to be translated into yet another language in which their concordance with observations can be determined.[1]

Marschak (1946) affirms this process of translation in his review of von Neumann and Morganstern's (1947, originally published in 1944) *Theory of Games and Economic Behavior*.

> 'Intuitive' or 'heuristic' considerations generated in the authors' minds by experience [in the common language] are formalized into concepts and propositions [in the formal language] which, once stated, are detached from experience until the final conclusions are reached.... The formal conclusions thus obtained are then materialized: they are translated into the language of the concrete field [the observation language] ... and are thus prepared for empirical test (Marschak 1946, p. 115).

It is not a simple matter, however, to make the successive translations from the common language in which things and events are usually described into the formal language in which they are modeled and then into the observation language in which they are recorded or measured. Unfortunately, the difficulties are often masked by use of the same terms in all three languages. The words *uncertainty* and *risk* have meanings in the common language of individuals and firms, meanings in the formal language of the theories of finance, and meanings in the observation language of statistics. There is no perfect correspondence between one language and another; therefore, every translation from one language to another has unintended consequences. Some shades of meaning attached to a word in the original language are lost; others attached to the word in the new language are picked up. This should not be a special problem for a science. If theories or models predict successfully, then any changes in meaning during the translations are likely to have been slight (predictions are not consistently accurate by accident) and are essentially irrelevant. But if theories or models predict unsuccessfully, then the translations must be examined.

Finance, however, pays insufficient attention to the possibility of translation error. "Debt" and "equity," "capital" and "labor," "supply" and "demand," and "savings" and "investment" are things and events discussed in these common language terms, both personally and professionally. These become the "D"s, "E"s, "K"s, "L"s, "S"s, and "I"s that appear in the formal language of theory and the quantities that appear in the observation language of accounting information and national economic statistics. But it is often mistakenly taken for granted that the "debt" in the minds of corporate treasurers or boards of directors in a corporate financing decision is identical to the "debt" on the balance sheet or that the "savings" that someone sets aside for their future is the same as the personal "savings" that appears in the national accounts.

There are undoubtedly similarities, which may be great or which may be slight; nonetheless, the same terms in the different languages do not have the same meanings. The failures of finance theories, however, are rarely if ever attributed to the changes in meaning that occur during the translations.

This chapter considers the case of "uncertainty" and "risk," an excellent example of theory failure that may well be attributable to translation error. Since the early Twentieth century, a mathematical probability calculus has been used as the formal language to model these concepts (Fisher 1906), and has been the basis of the statistics that have been used to test models incorporating them. The reason that models such as the CAPM have met with such limited predictive success is that the things and events encountered in common experience that suggested the original problems are quite different from the things and events modeled and measured. Investors face "uncertainties" or "risks" as they price assets, for example, and financial economists measure the "dispersions of relative frequency distributions" of asset returns. The two are not the same thing.

That they are not absolutely identical will come as a surprise to no one, but, on the surface, the assumption that they are virtually identical has some plausibility and seems no more heroic than any number of other assumptions in neoclassical economics. Beneath the surface, however, the standard translation of "uncertainty" or "risk" from the common language into a formal language and then into an observation language results in contradictions and confusions that essentially preclude investors and economists from speaking of the same thing. Yet even this deeper perspective is not unfamiliar—"uncertainty" or "risk" has not always been the "dispersion of a relative frequency distribution." When such a translation was first suggested, it was studied and soundly rejected (Knight 1921; Fisher 1930), and the subsequent drift toward acceptance did not occur unexamined and unopposed, as Chapter VIII chronicles this story. Nonetheless, these problematic translations have today become the unquestioned standard in research in economics, finance, and accounting.

The next section describes the four probability theories that represent the alternative translations of the common language concepts of "uncertainty" and "risk" into the formal language of the probability calculus and into the statistical observation language. Only one of these theories is suitable for the economic sciences, and the use of this particular theory places severe restrictions on the modeling of economic activity. More serious issues are introduced in the last section. Just how severely restrictive the conditions must be in order for "uncertainty" or "risk" to be able to exist in the form of probability becomes fully apparent when three basic concepts from the probability calculus are considered.

PROBABILITY THEORIES

The Theories Defined

A probability theory is a dictionary that translates or interprets the formal language of the mathematical probability calculus into the common language. In the formal language, probability is a real number between 0 and 1 that obeys certain operational rules; in the common language, this number expresses something about a thing or event. There is no standard set of probability theories, and several alternatives have been proposed. Weatherford's (1982) list is a good foundation scheme that is more thoroughly specified than others and that was explicitly devised considering the alternatives in Carnap (1962), Nagel (1939), Kyburg and Smokler (1964), Good (1962), Von Wright (1957), Black (1967), and Fine (1973). According to Weatherford, there are four probability theories:

P_0. (Classical Probability): The probability of an event is the ratio of the number of ways the event can occur to the total number of equipossible outcomes.

P_1. (Relative Frequency Probability): The probability of an event is the limit, as the number of trials increases, of the ratio of the number of times the event has occurred to the total number of trials.

P_2. (Logical Probability)[2]: The probability of an event is the degree of rational belief, relative to given information, in the event's occurrence.

P_3. (Subjective Probability): The probability of an event is the quantitative degree of individual belief in the event's occurrence.

Probability in all of these theories is numeric—a real number between 0 and 1. This fact makes for straightforward consistency with the formal language, but inappropriately distances the *notion* of probability from the common language. After all, the notion of probability preceded the probability calculus by thousands of years and must therefore have some meaning independent of it. It is useful to add an additional definition (not truly a theory) to label the common language sense of probability that exists independent of any numeric representation.

P_4. (Behavioral Probability): The probability of an event is the non-quantitative degree of individual belief in the event's occurrence.

The Theories Explained

Classical probability (P_0) applies to games of chance in which something about the structure of a game (in the usual examples, the shape of a die, the contents of an urn, or the design of a deck of cards) suggests that it is possible to list all equipossible alternative outcomes of a trial and to identify those that represent the event of interest. In the simplest case of a single throw of a fair die (the trial), there are six equipossible numbers that can appear on the uppermost face (the outcomes), and one of these is a five (the event). The probability of a five is 1/6. Though it is certainly possible to replicate a trial an indefinite number of times, the probability of an event is an attribute of the structure of the game; therefore, the probability for each trial is the same regardless of the number of trials that have occurred or will occur.

Relative frequency probability (P_1) associated with Von Mises (1957) and Reichenbach (1949), is deceptively similar to P_0. Both appear to be objective attributes of the real world and not simply subjective knowledge of it. P_1 has a larger domain than P_0, though, including in addition those "games" too complex for the specification of equipossible alternative outcomes. There is a set (deck?) of hypothetical universes "out there" (on the faces of a celestial die or in a cosmic urn, perhaps?) from which "draws" are made. Because the universe of equipossible alternatives is not observable, it is necessary to infer it from the real events that have been observed. The probability of an event is the limit approached by the relative frequency of the event as history unfolds, and the current relative frequency of the event is the best estimate of that limit or probability. Replications are necessary to obtain a probability, and the value of the probability is a function of the outcomes of the trials that have occurred.

One problem with P_0 is the definition of "equipossible." Equipossible alternatives must be those that occur with equal probability or in the limit with equal relative frequency—a circularity that uses probability to define itself. P_0 presumes equipossibility as an attribute of the structure of the game, but it is only possible to guarantee this apparent equipossibility (whether the die is fair, the urn well-shaken, or the deck well-shuffled) by repeating the elemental trial and observing the relative frequency of the outcomes to see whether the relative frequency of a five, for example, converges on 1/6. P_0 is contingent upon knowledge of the die's being fair, the urn's being well-shaken, or the deck's being well-shuffled, which knowledge can only be obtained through observation of a number of trials. P_0, in effect, cannot exist without P_1.

But observations, whether of a simple game or of a complex one, may not be "representative" of the set of hypothetical outcomes of the game. If the number of trials or observations were to increase, the relative frequencies of events could change considerably. Although P_1 appears to be an attribute of the real world because relative frequencies are observable, its reality is limited to what it is that has been observed. One can never conclude with certainty what the "real" probability (or from statistics, the "true" distribution or "underlying" parameter) upon which observed relative frequencies must converge is, or even if such a "real" probability exists at all.

P_0 and P_1 are contingent not only upon the outcomes of the trials that have occurred, but also upon circumstances surrounding the trials. Suppose the game is to draw one die from an urn full of what are believed to be fair dice and throw the one die. The probability P_0 of a five is 1/6. If all the dice were known to be loaded, but the urn was known to contain equal numbers of dice that were loaded in such a way as to be biased, by the same amount, toward each of the six faces,[3] the probability P_0 of a five would still be 1/6. But if it were possible to know the bias of a die after it was drawn but before it was thrown, the probability P_0 of a five would be greater than 1/6 (say 7/12 for example) if it were a five-biased die and less than 1/6 (1/12) if not. P_0 is contingent upon the presence or absence of knowledge of which die was selected from the urn.

For P_1, this is referred to as the problem of reference class. Suppose the game is now to draw a die from an urn full of what are known to be loaded dice and throw it. If the dice are loaded as described in the previous example, the relative frequency of a five would approach 1/6 as more and more throws are made. The best estimate of the probability P_1 of a five, conditional on the reference class of all dice in the urn, is 1/6. But if it were possible to know whether a die were five-biased before the throw, the reference class of all dice is irrelevant. Now, after a number of throws, the relative frequency or probability of a five is 7/12 with respect to the reference class of five-biased dice and 1/12 with respect to the reference class of not-five-biased dice. As these examples show, P_0 and P_1 both have a marked epistemic nature, being dependent upon the knowledge of something about the world other than simply the structure of a game or the historical relative frequency with which an event has occurred. Just as P_0 cannot be verified without reference to P_1, P_1 itself is dependent on "something else."

The logical probability P_2 of Keynes (1921) and Carnap (1962) captures this relationship between probability and knowledge—this "something else." The probability of a future event is the strength with which the event can be logically asserted on the basis of the information available, which may include the structure of the game of which the event is an outcome, the historical relative frequency with which the event has occurred in the past, the circumstances (reference classes) under which the event has occurred more or less frequently in the past, or any other relevant information. Computation or estimation of P_2 in effect requires an inductive logic with which to link the truth of a statement with its evidence.

Whereas P_0 and P_1 at least appear to be objective in that something about them is observable, P_2 is much less tangible in that the probability of an event is not "out there" somewhere, but depends explicitly upon what is known regarding the event. It is not truly subjective, however, for everyone confronted with the same information would assess the same probability, given the same rationality.

This is not true of the subjective probability P_3 of Ramsey (1931), de Finetti (1972), and Savage (1972). Here, probability is the personal quantitative degree of belief that an event will occur. Each person is free to set his or her own probability of an event, and whatever value he or she comes up with is perfectly correct. All information taken into account to arrive at P_2 also goes into P_3, but there is no unique logic by which a probability is derived from the information. Individual beliefs, emotions, hopes, fears, preferences, prejudices, and so on, enter into the probability estimate. The only limitation on subjective probabilities is that they be logically consistent.

All of the probability theories P_0 through P_3 are numeric—expressible as real numbers between 0 and 1 that obey the operational rules of the standard probability calculus. In fact, the requirement that subjective probabilities P_3 be logically consistent essentially means that the probabilities fulfill these criteria. This, of course, presupposes a specific formal language. But forming beliefs regarding the occurrence of an event and taking action on those beliefs are things that do happen and can be described in a common language with or without the existence of a formal language. The notion of "probability" is meaningful without mathematics. This is behavioral probability P_4, the "probability" that is encountered in common experience. Probability is the personal non-quantitative degree of individual belief in an event's occurrence.

Even for a single throw of a die, then, the question, "What is the probability of a five?", is difficult to answer. If it is a fair die, the probability (P_0) is $1/6$. But what if the die might be loaded? Then, throw it a large number of times and observe the relative frequency of a five to get an unbiased estimate of the probability (P_1). But what if it is a die that wears unevenly as it is thrown? Then, take this information into account in inferring the probability (P_2). But what if there are no accepted equations or procedures for doing so? Then, make some sort of educated guess at the numerical probability (P_3). But what if it is necessary to just do something about the situation (such as deciding whether to place a bet) without explaining the action on the basis of a number? Then, just act on the basis of your sense of probability (P_4). Depending on the nature or complexity of this or any other "game," either P_0, P_1, P_2, P_3 or P_4 could apply, with the term "apply" meaning that all important attributes of the situation describable in the common language can be captured by a translation in accordance with the theory.

The Theories and the Languages

The five theories of probability are subsets of each other. P_0 is a translation or interpretation of probability that only applies to very simple events. P_1, P_2, P_3, and P_4 apply to more and more complex events. Whenever an event or activity is within the domain of one probability theory, it is also within the domains of all the broader theories. As the theory that expresses the common language concept, P_4 must apply to the probability, uncertainty, or risk in any economic activity. As noted in the introduction to this chapter, P_4 probabilities are associated with beliefs regarding the everyday probable or improbable, likely or unlikely, to be expected or not to be expected, plausible or implausible, reasonable or unreasonable, credible or incredible, believable or unbelievable, and imaginable or unimaginable consequences that may occur when individuals and firms gamble, take chances, place bets, make wagers, face risks, and expose themselves to hazards.

Unfortunately, all the matters expressible in the common language are not necessarily translatable into the formal language. In order to "scientifically" model an activity or event, it must be translated into the formal language of mathematics. It may be necessary to circumscribe or simplify an activity or situation as follows so that it falls within the domain of P_0, P_1, P_2, or P_3:

P_3. Assume that individual beliefs regarding the activity may be represented by a numeric probability.

P_2. P_3 assumption plus assume that individuals have homogeneous beliefs given an information set.

P_1. P_2 assumptions plus assume that the information set consists only of historical relative frequencies.

P_0. P_2 assumptions plus assume that the information set consists of probabilities determinable from the structure of the activity.

In other words, in order to "squeeze" the everyday matters encompassed by the P_4 theory of probability into a form that can fit within one of the more formal theories, it is necessary to make simplifying assumptions. When any simplifying assumptions are made, however, the *meanings* of "risk" and "uncertainty" change.

Probability theories are also involved in the translations of the formal language into (or interpretations of the formal language in) the observation language. Each theory implies that a different observation or measurement is to be made in order to obtain values for the probabilistic concepts referred to in the formal language.

P_4. Simply record actions which occur.
P_3. Infer probabilities from observations of individual actions.
P_2. Infer probabilities from information using inductive logic.
P_1. Determine probabilities from the historical relative frequencies.
P_0. Determine probabilities from the structure of the activity.

The task of economic enquiry begins with an activity expressed in terms of the common language of P_4. For example, one might be undertaking research into the question of how university professors incorporate "risk" into their decisions regarding the allocation of their retirement income between TIAA and CREF. One way to approach an answer might be to avoid the use of a formal language altogether and employ what is effectively a P_4 observation language; that is, to simply interview or survey university professors regarding their approaches toward making their decisions.

The more economically conventional way to approach an answer is to first construct a formal model by making certain simplifying assumptions: a P_3 model in which each professor is assumed to make a numerical assessment of probable returns in some way; a P_2 model in which a representative professor is assumed to make a numerical assessment of probable returns using some available information; a P_1 model in which a representative professor is assumed to make a numerical assessment of probable returns based on some past returns; or a P_0 model in which a representative professor is assumed to make a numerical assessment of probable returns based on some characteristics of the structure and function of TIAA and CREF.

Then, it is necessary to make formal observations to acquire the empirical data required to test the model: a P_3 observation of individual probability distributions; a P_2 observation of the information required for the computation of the representative probability distribution; a P_1 observation of the historical probability distribution; or a P_0 observation of the attributes required to construct a probability distribution.

What is occurring in those inquiries involving a formal language is that a model incorporating a probability distribution is constructed and a value for that probability distribution is obtained through observation. For both the theoretical probability distribution in the model and the empirical probability distribution that is observed, it is necessary to have an underlying probability theory, which makes some general statements about what it is that the probability distribution can and cannot represent. The distributions mathematically *work* the same regardless of the probability theory, but they do not *mean* the same thing. This fact is important, as finance presumably interested in meaning and not simply manipulation.[4]

Problems may arise, however, when the domain encompassing the real thing or event of interest is not equal to or not a subset of the domain of the observation language. If the domain of the observation language were a subset of the domain of the thing or event, then some meanings or characteristics or attributes of the activity would not be captured. For example, it is not effective to use classical probabilities P_0 for loaded dice, which are within the domain of P_1, nor to use relative frequency probabilities P_1 with dice that wear unevenly, which are within the domains of P_2 or P_3. A P_0 observation language only captures all the important attributes of a P_0 situation; a P_1 observation language only of a P_0 or P_1 situation; and so on. So if P_1 is the only observation language, it is necessary that whatever thing or event is being considered is sufficiently simplified by assumption to be encompassed by a P_1 domain.

P_1 is indeed the only significant observation language in finance; that is, historical relative frequencies are the overwhelmingly dominant source of numerical probabilities with which to test theories. P_0 probabilities apply only to activities too simple to be of interest. For no economically interesting activity is it possible to specify equipossible alternatives solely on the basis of the nature of that activity. P_2 requires an inductive logic that does not yet exist. There is no way to compute "rational" degrees of belief incorporating information other than historical relative frequencies. It is possible to infer P_3 probabilities in simple laboratory experiments; however, testing of more complex theories requires that these probabilities be aggregated in some way, which cannot be done. P_4 is non-quantitative, which to most economists puts it beyond the pale. This means that economic events or activities must be explicitly assumed to lie within the domain of P_1; that is, there must be no information outside of the historical relative frequency of an event that is relevant to the estimation of the probability of the event.

Finance must "squeeze" all inquiries regarding risk and uncertainty into theoretical models and observations using probability distributions derived from the historical outcomes of trials. This is very difficult to do without losing the essence of an economic activity. Relative frequencies are dependent on the choice of a reference class, and it is far from necessary that the reference class a researcher chooses to test a theory of economic activity bear any resemblance to the reference classes (i.e., other information) used by economic actors in the performance of the economic activity. Relative frequency probabilities are dependent on the existence of some "real" distribution, and without one of these problematic "real" distributions, relative frequencies exist but probabilities do not. But how severely restrictive the conditions imposed by the P_1 theory must be in order for "uncertainty" or "risk" to be able to exist in the form of probability does not become fully apparent until three basic concepts from the probability calculus are considered.

THE PROBABILITY CALCULUS AND ECONOMIC RISK

The Concepts

The three concepts of mathematical probability that are essential to an understanding of economic uncertainty and risk are Christian Huygens' mathematical expectation, James Bernoulli's law of large numbers, and Daniel Bernoulli's expected utility. It is something of a misstatement to attribute the discovery of mathematical expectation to Christian Huygens. His contribution in the 1657 *De Ratiociniis in Ludo Aleae* was three theorems for the calculation of the "value" of a game.

1. If I have equal chances of getting a or b, this is so much worth for me as $(a+b)/2$.
2. If I have equal chances of getting a, b or c, this is so much worth for me as if I had $(a+b+c)/3$.
3. If the number of chances of getting a is p, and the number of chances of getting b is q, assuming always that any chance occurs equally easy, then this is worth $(pa+qb)/(p+q)$ to me (quoted in Hald 1990, p. 69).

This is, of course, the mathematical equivalent of the modern concept of mathematical expectation. But as Hacking (1975) points out, Huygens' proof indicates that he was interested in computing the value of a single trial and not the average for multiple trials. Since "average" was an uncommon concept at the time, Huygens would not have interpreted the "value" he computed in the modern sense as the "average value" one would expect to receive after a large number of trials.

In the 1713 *Ars Conjectandi*, James Bernoulli acknowledged the limits of classical probability in its restrictive domain:

We have now reached the point where it seems that, to make a correct conjecture about any event whatever, it is necessary only to calculate exactly the number of possible cases, and then to determine how much more likely it is that one case will occur than another. But here at once our main difficulty arises, for this procedure is applicable to only a very few phenomena, indeed almost exclusively to those connected with games of chance (quoted in Maistrov 1974, p. 68).

When dealing with more complex "games," probabilities are not so easy to "calculate."

There is, however, another way that will lead us to what we are looking for and enable us at least to ascertain it from the results observed in numerous similar circumstances. It must be assumed in this connection that, under similar conditions, the occurrence (or non-occurrence) of an event in the future will follow the same pattern as was observed for like events in the past (quoted in Maistrov 1974, p. 69).

Under such conditions, Bernoulli's law of large numbers[5] applies. But:

Lest this matter be imperfectly understood, it should be noted that the ratio reflecting the actual relationship between the numbers of the cases—the ratio we are seeking to determine through observation—can never be obtained with absolute accuracy; ... The ratio we arrive at is only approximate: it must be defined by two limits, but these limits can be made to approach each other as closely as we wish (quoted in Maistrov 1974, p. 69).

Bernoulli was not just making a convenient assumption that the future would follow the past; rather, as a true Cartesian, he believed that this was the fundamental principle of a deterministic world. "Real" distributions did indeed exist "somewhere." This belief is reflected in his use of the phrase "actual relationship" in the preceding quotation and expressed more explicitly in the following:

If all events from now through eternity were continually observed (whereby probability would ultimately become certainty), it would be found that everything in the world occurs for definite reasons and in definite conformity with law, and that hence we are constrained, even for things that may seem quite accidental, to assume a certain necessity and as it were, fatefulness (quoted in Maistrov 1974, p. 75).

Daniel Bernoulli's 1738 "Exposition of a New Theory on the Measurement of Risk" considers that decisions based on Huygens' mathematical expectation violate common sense.

Somehow a very poor fellow obtains a lottery ticket that will yield with equal probability either nothing or twenty thousand ducats. Will this man evaluate his chance of winning at ten thousand ducats? Would he not be ill-advised to sell this lottery ticket for nine thousand ducats? To me it seems that the answer is in the negative. On the other hand

I am inclined to believe that a rich man would be ill-advised to refuse to buy the lottery ticket for nine thousand ducats. If I am not wrong then it seems clear that all men cannot use the same rule to evaluate the gamble (Bernoulli 1954, p. 24).

Bernoulli's alternative decision rule, maximization of expected utility, is simple, at least in principle.

To do this the determination of the value of an item must not be based on its price, but rather on the utility it yields. The price of the item is dependent only on the thing itself and is equal for everyone; the utility, however, is dependent on the particular circumstances of the person making the estimate. Thus there is no doubt that a gain of one thousand ducats is more significant to a pauper than to a rich man though both gain the same amount (Bernoulli 1954, p. 24).

The Concepts, the Theories, and the Languages

Huygens' probability lies in the P_0 domain as does *his* version of mathematical expectation, the "value" of a game. James Bernoulli's law of large numbers lies in the P_1 domain, and it is in this domain that mathematical expectation has its familiar interpretation as a long-run average. Daniel Bernoulli's expected utility is problematic. In one sense, the concept of utility is independent of the theories of probability.

Although utility is "subjective" (a very P_3-sounding term), Bernoulli's example illustrates that it is compatible with "objective" P_0. In another sense, however, the concept of utility at least presupposes a theory of probability that is meaningful for a single event. If Bernoulli's "poor fellow" had found a thousand lottery tickets, then mathematical expectation would have been an appropriate decision criterion. He would have been ill-advised to sell any of the tickets for nine thousand ducats. He would also have been ill-advised to sell any ticket for nine ducats if the tickets he had found had entitled him to one each of one thousand separate lotteries with equal chances in each of winning either nothing or twenty ducats.

Expected utility is an appropriate decision rule in P_0, P_2 and P_3 domains in which single events have probabilities, but it is a highly problematic decision rule in a P_1 domain. In this domain, historical relative frequencies can be interpreted as the probabilities of future single events; however, these future single events cannot be isolated events as in P_0, P_2, and P_3, but must be part of a series of past and future events in order to have a numerical value. Under these conditions, mathematical expectation is the appropriate decision rule as a consequence of the law of large numbers. As discussed at the conclusion of the previous section, a P_1 observation language domain dominates finance, and it is necessary that whatever thing or event is being considered is sufficiently simplified by assumption to be encompassed by the P_1 theory. Yet risk cannot be translated as probability in the P_1 domain, in which a mathematical expectation decision rule is appropriate.

The explanation of this begins with the subtleties of expected utility. Daniel Bernoulli compared a gain of one thousand ducats for a pauper to a gain of one thousand ducats for a rich man. He conceived utility as a function of a monetary amount and personal circumstances (wealth). Another way to view the same example is as separate comparisons between nine thousand ducats and the gamble between zero and twenty thousand ducats for both the pauper and the rich man. They each compare nine thousand ducats with certainty to a risky expected value of ten thousand ducats. Here, utility is a function of the monetary amount and some measure of the uncertainty of receipt of that amount (or risk). Utility is a function of personal circumstances—Bernoulli assumes that the pauper and the rich man rank the alternatives differently in this example—but it need not be. The pauper could be less risk averse than the rich man. (Perhaps that is how he became poor.) It was well-established by the Ninteenth century that total utility of investment in an asset is a function of both a good (return) and a bad (risk).[6]

The problem is that, for multiple events in a P_1 domain where a mathematical expectation decision rule is appropriate, probability and risk cannot be the same thing. Probability is a characteristic of the gamble used in the computation of the mathematical expectation, and risk is the possible deviation of the realized value from the mathematical expectation. As the number of trials grows, probability converges to a limit, and by the law of large numbers, risk (the uncertainty of receipt of an amount *on average*) shrinks to nothing. If the pauper were to have found a thousand lottery tickets, each would still have represented an equal probability of twenty thousand ducats and nothing. But the risk of receiving *on average* an amount different from ten thousand ducats for each becomes very small. Only for single events can probability provide an accurate measure of risk.

The assumption that there must be no information outside of the historical relative frequency of an event that is relevant to the estimation of the *probability* of the event—the assumption that is required to place the event within a P_1 domain—must be more restrictive than it appears. There must be no information outside of the historical relative frequency of an event that is relevant to the estimation of the *riskiness* of the event, including the fact that the event must be repeatable.

For example, investors whose behavior is modeled in conventional economic terms must believe that each return on an asset is a sample from a distribution of returns that will reveal itself as returns for different periods are observed, but are constrained to behave as if there will be only one future sample, for which some measure of the dispersion of the distribution of returns is the risk.

Assume that investors are offered two investments, one of which earns a mean twenty percent per year with a standard deviation of fifteen percent, and the other of which earns a mean ten percent per year with a standard deviation of two percent. Economists believe that the choice between the two depends on an investor's risk aversion. But by the law of large numbers, the term "mean" means that that is what the investment will earn on average over several years.

Investors must know this but ignore that they will almost certainly earn twenty percent per year on average if they repeat the first investment year after year. Something is permitting a replication of the investments, or there would be no distribution of returns, but investors are prevented from taking advantage of the fact. It is as if the pauper found a thousand lottery tickets, all of which he should certainly keep, but is forced to behave for each as if he found only one, which, according to Daniel Bernoulli, he should sell.

In finance, "uncertainty" and "risk" are translated in terms of relative frequency probabilities for purposes of creating theoretical models (such as the CAPM) and testing those models. The use of this particular probability theory is not a consequence of its being the best for the purpose, but that it is the only one that yields the quantitative reproducibility that "science" reputedly demands. Just what it is that is reproducible, however, is another matter. Finance pays insufficient attention to the difficulties inherent in translating the things and events of everyday experience into formal modeling languages and observation languages. Without a thorough understanding of what is happening during the process of translation, it is difficult to know why theories that failed did so. It is perhaps even more difficult to know why a theory that has succeeded has succeeded at all.

Had finance thought more about its assumptions concerning probability, it might not be used so cavalierly. In fact, the historical record shows that quite a bit of thought did indeed go into the applications of probability theory to economic decision making; however, the problems were eventually just swept under the rug. We continue this case study in the next chapter with a history of what it was that occurred.

NOTES

1. This is not unlike a fourth-generation programming language, say, FORTRAN. FORTRAN is a collection of instructions resembling a primitive, limited-vocabulary human language. In order to "work," it has to be translated to assembler language, and that translation, in turn, has to be translated to machine language (a binary code, really).

2. Weatherford refers to this as "a priori probability."

3. That is, there are the same number of one-biased dice, two-biased dice, three-biased dice, eand so on. A one-biased die increases the probability of a one by the same amount that a two-biased die increases the probability of a two, a three-biased die increases the probability of a three, and so forth.

4. Of course, we consider "meaning" to be very important, as it appears in the title of this book. We more fully consider its definition in Chapter XIII.

5. This appellation was coined later by Poisson.

6. "Payment for risk, nearly all economists agree, enters into gross interest" (Haynes 1895, p. 419).

Chapter VIII

The History Of Risk "Measurement"

A brief summary of the previous chapter would be useful at this juncture. The relative frequency probabilities used in financial models are subject to a number of severe problems that make their use as measures of risk very questionable. The first problem is the reference-class problem. There is no simple way to determine which historical conditions, *if any*, are sufficiently similar to current conditions in order to use the relative frequencies of an event under *those* conditions as an appropriate "measure" of the "rational" probability with which to expect the event to occur under *these* conditions.

For example, if A percent of all firms historically go bankrupt, it would seem as if A is the risk of bankruptcy. But if the current ratio of firm X, whose risk of bankruptcy is of interest, is less than 1, and B percent of all firms having a current ratio less than 1 historically go bankrupt, then it would seem as if B is the risk of bankruptcy of firm X, and B may be much different than A. But, in addition, the debt ratio of firm X may be less than 20 percent. Historically, C percent of all firms having a debt ratio less than 20 percent go bankrupt, although D percent of all firms having a current ratio less than 1 *and* a debt ratio less than 20 percent go bankrupt. D, C, B, and A may all be much different from each other, so it is unclear what the "risk" of bankruptcy of firm X is.

The second problem is the law-of-large-numbers problem. The "mean" or "expected value" of a distribution is the value that will be realized on average in the long run. Recall that, if investors are offered two investments, one of which has historically earned a mean 20 percent per year with a standard deviation of 15 percent and the other of which has earned a mean 10 percent per year with a standard deviation of 2 percent, economists believe that the choice between the two depends on an investor's risk aversion. Some investors may accept more risk to earn a higher return; others may be willing to accept a lower return for less risk. An investment having a standard deviation of 15 percent is much "riskier" than one having a standard deviation of only 2 percent.

But, by the law of large numbers, the term *mean* means that that is what the investment will earn on average over several years. If the relative frequency distribution is stable enough to use its standard deviation as a "measurement" of risk, it is also stable enough to ensure that investors will almost certainly earn the mean 20 percent per year on average if they repeat the first investment year after year. By holding the investment long enough, investors can earn however close to the expected 20 percent they are comfortable with, as the standard deviation of the distribution of the expected long-term average return shrinks with repetition. Through willingness to ignore short-term fluctuations in return, patience can eliminate the "risk" of earnings different from expectations.

The third is the estimation problem. The dispersion of a real relative frequency distribution of historical events is used to estimate the dispersion of a hypothetical relative frequency distribution of possible future events, existing in the mind of a decision-maker prior to the decision; therefore, the "measurement" of risk is itself risky, and so on *ad infinitum*. Investors may be offered two investments, both of which have historically earned a mean 20 percent per year with a standard deviation of 15 percent, but may be much more confident that this 15 percent is a better "measurement" of the riskiness of one for the future than for the other.

From the current literature in finance, one would never know that these problems existed. The historical record, however, is quite different. Risk did not come to be "measured" probabilistically without considerable thought. The next section describes the period up to 1930, during which early enthusiasm with the potential applications of probability to economic issues was extinguished as economists acknowledged the insurmountable problems. The last section describes the much different period between 1930 and 1950, during which mathematicians who had crossed over into economics began sidestepping the problems, but not without the expectation of eventually returning to them. By 1950, however, it was clear that the problems would never be addressed within the current research program.[1] To admit the problems now would mean abandoning modern portfolio theory and the asset valuation models that have come to form the core of much of finance despite their dismal empirical record. So risk continues to be "measured" in a "common sense" way it was once known made no sense.

PROBABILITY AND RISK IN ECONOMICS UNTIL 1930

Interest Before 1900

Just before the turn of the century, research programs in economics and mathematics came together. In economics, work on the theory of distribution had taken up the question of profit—specifically, whether profit is the return to the entrepreneur for bearing risk in the same manner as wages, interest, and rent are the returns to the laborer, capitalist, and landlord, respectively (Clark 1893). It was natural for this discussion of risk and risk-bearing in economics to include consideration of the economic role of insurance, which had used descriptive statistics for a number of years. At the same time, in applied mathematics, advances in inferential statistics were generating an interest in the subject that lead some to seek other economic applications of statistics.[2]

In one of the earliest articles, Edgeworth (1888)[3] applied probability to historical cash flows in order to estimate cash reserve requirements. As expected in a pioneering effort that is over a century old, his methods now appear quaint, but his comments on the modest role of the use of a formal mathematical language in this context provide an interesting counterpoint to the aggressive position that many were to take over one-half century later.

> The theorist must not pretend to wisdom, if he knows so little what he is about as to mistake his abstract formulae for rules immediately applicable to practice (Edgeworth 1888, p. 127).

Edgeworth clearly has a *normative* view of quantification. It is a way to sharpen intuition or to make heuristics more precise. As we have shown in Chapter VI, Markowitz (1952), who was largely responsible for the institutionalization of probabilistic measurement of risk in finance and won a Nobel prize for his efforts in modern portfolio theory [MPT], shared this view, at least in his early work. It is more common nowadays for Edgeworth's "abstract formulae" to be viewed as a necessary step in the scientific process of the construction of *positive* theories.

Before the century was out, some authors had begun to explore the relationship between probability and risk, usually in the context of insurance. For insurance purposes, the usual "measure" of the risk of an event was the relative frequency with which the event had occurred in the past. A recurring theme in Haynes (1895) was that, for many risks, such statistics are either unreliable or non-existent. Since risk is present even when statistics are not, risk and relative frequency probabilities must not be the same. Other authors struggled with this difference in different terms. Ross (1896) used "variation" and "uncertainty." "Variation" is descriptive of the possible outcomes, for which there are no historical relative frequencies or statistics, and "uncertainty," the equivalent of "risk," is a consequence of this variation.

By 1900, risk had become an important topic in economics. There appeared to be opportunities for the use of new probabilistic methods to understand risk, but no specific steps had been taken in this direction. From a historical standpoint, the legacy of the pre-1900 period is the point made by both Haynes (1895) and Ross (1896) that reverberates throughout later work—Haynes that there are risks for which there are reliable statistics and those for which there are not; and Ross, that it is unquantifiable variation that creates uncertainty. This is the reference-class problem—that there are economically important circumstances that are perceived as risky, but that are also perceived as being without relevant historical precedent.

Excitement from 1900 to 1920

The new century opened with several confusing attempts to be more precise regarding probability and risk. Willett's (1901) monograph makes a distinction between probability or chance and uncertainty and risk. Initially, "uncertainty" is defined as the degree of rational ambivalence between two alternatives, which is greatest when both are equally probable and declines as one or the other becomes more likely. "Risk" is said to be commonly associated with both probability and uncertainty, although the risk premium is more closely related to uncertainty. Then, Willett confuses the issue by defining "uncertainty" as the deviation of a probability from its normal value and "risk" as the quantification of this in the form of mean absolute deviation. Later, he introduces still another set of definitions of "uncertainty" and "risk."

> Risk and uncertainty are the objective and subjective aspects of apparent variability in the course of natural events. Whatever effect risk may have on economic activity is brought about through the psychological influence of uncertainty" (Willett 1901, p. 50).

Despite this confusion, or perhaps because of it, one can conclude from Willett (and from Haynes and Ross) that there is a difference between probability or chance and risk or uncertainty and that this difference is very difficult to specify.

Norton's (1904) article a few years later is also confusing regarding the specific application of probability to risk, but his enthusiasm over the possibilities contrasts with Edgeworth's restraint.

> ... great development is possible for theoretical economics, since, by positing these frequency distributions severe thinking will be able, step by step, to work out the various cases (Norton 1904, pp. 42-43).

> This entire field is capable of exact statistical study, and it is in this world of probability and interest that financiers work (Norton 1904, p. 54).

The paper's discussant, however, points out that the transformation of "risk" into statistics is not such a simple matter.

As to the diagrammatic representation of thought presented, there are few people who are accustomed to think in terms of 'skew curves,' etc.; to most readers no idea is conveyed by such a device (Norton 1904, p. 60).[4]

Fisher's (1906) underlying philosophy is that probability is a measure of ignorance. His words reflect a subjective theory of probability rather than a relative frequency theory.

Chance exists only so far as ignorance exists; varies with different persons according to their comparative ignorance of the matter under consideration; and is in fact a measure of ignorance. Of course the actual statistical record may afford an important and sometimes the only basis for our degree of knowledge and ignorance.... But while statistics supply data for the forming of subjective estimates of chances, they do not, themselves, constitute chances (Fisher 1906, p. 268).

Probability is thus not merely an affair of pure mathematics, as is so often imagined. It is, first of all, a matter of concrete human estimate (Fisher 1906, p. 270).

Fisher does not really make a recommendation on the use of relative frequencies. At one point, his concern is the same as that of Haynes and Ross with reference to classes.

Usually, however, the chances involved are so indefinite that the reckoning is made only by rule of thumb. Any further attempt to apply the theory of probability would therefore outrun the exigencies of practice (Fisher 1906, p. 283).

Other passages indicate greater optimism regarding the use of relative frequencies.

Nevertheless it is more than conceivable that the time may come when practical brokers will make use of probability computations in the same way that they now make use of bond tables (Fisher 1906, p. 283).

In this and other ways business men could, as Professor Norton has shown, make better use of their past experience than they do. Merely to glance over past earnings and receive an impression is not a very scientific mode of utilizing the facts which those earnings display. To average them is not of much more value. While it is important to know the mean, it is also important to know the dispersion about the mean. This dispersion is shown by the standard deviation (Fisher 1906, p. 409).

Given Fisher's belief in subjective probability, perhaps the best way to summarize his position regarding probability and risk is that the dispersion of a relative frequency distribution is an important piece of information in *assessing* risk, but it is not a *measure* of risk.

Between 1906 and 1920, the idea of risk as the dispersion of a relative frequency distribution was at least made explicit, if not fully accepted. Lavington (1912) wrote:

This condition may be represented by a curve of prospective net returns, which range, perhaps, from a large positive to a large negative amount. The 'spread' of this curve represents the amount of Uncertainty (Lavington 1912, pp. 398-399).

He attributes this idea to Pigou, but it does not appear in writing under Pigou's name until eight years later.

A scheme of prospective returns can be represented diagrammatically in the following manner. Along a base-line OX mark off all possible yields that may result from the exposure of a £ to the scheme in question; and, through each point on OX, draw an ordinate proportionate to the probability, on the evidence, of the corresponding return. Join the tops of all these ordinates (Pigou 1960, p. 773, originally published in 1920).

Pigou is somewhat vague, however, about the relationship between the dispersion of the distribution and risk.

Within the symmetrical group we may distinguish curves which are spread out, like open umbrellas, and curves which are narrow, like closed umbrellas. The former sort represent schemes in which a wide divergence, the latter schemes in which only a small divergence, of the actual from the most probable return, is preferable (Pigou 1960, p. 774).

Pigou does admit some skepticism regarding the use of a relative frequency distribution for the measurement of risk, as subjective probabilities are probably more appropriate, but is able to rationalize it in the end.

It would seem, therefore, at first sight that the amount of uncertainty-bearing involved in carrying through any operation must depend, not only on the nature of the operation, but also on the temperament and knowledge of the people who bear the uncertainty. Such a conception, however, is fatal to the symmetry of our analysis.... We must define uncertainty-bearing objectively.... There is, it must be admitted, an arbitrary and artificial appearance about this method of defining our key term; but there appears to be no way in which this can be avoided (Pigou 1960, p. 773).

By 1920, therefore, the dispersion of a relative frequency distribution had been clearly identified as risk. Terminology was still somewhat vague, and the philosophical considerations were not fully understood, but risk could be "measured." It is peculiar, though, that despite the unrestrained optimism of Norton and the more cautious optimism of Fisher, no one actually attempted to measure risk and relate it to returns. Data was available, and there was no reluctance to make lengthy computations in other contexts—computations that were tedious without computers but not technically difficult (see Norton 1902, for examples). Yet specific measurements of risk were never made. Perhaps this was because the apparent enthusiasm for the measurement of risk as the dispersion of a relative frequency distribution was tempered by the concern regarding the reference class problem raised over twenty years earlier. Risk was indeed something different or something more.

Caution from 1920 to 1930

That statistics could not be used to measure risk was certainly Knight's (1921) belief. His distinction between "risk" and "uncertainty" is the one idea from this period that is at least referenced (although not accepted) in the current literature. Although his definitions were not the same as those of earlier authors, he was concerned with the familiar reference-class problem that had been around for many years. His statement of the problem is nonetheless worth quoting in full for its unambiguous expression of the issue.

> It will appear that a measurable uncertainty, or 'risk' proper, as we shall use the term, is so far different from an unmeasurable one that it is not in effect an uncertainty at all. We shall accordingly restrict the term "uncertainty" to cases of the non-quantitative type.... The economic relations of risk in the narrower sense of a measurable probability have been extensively dealt with in the literature of the subject[5] and do not call for elaborate treatment here. Our main concern will be with the contrast between Risk as a known chance and true Uncertainty, and treatment of the former is incidental to this purpose (Knight 1921, pp. 20-21).

> Business decisions, for example, deal with situations which are far too unique, generally speaking, for any sort of statistical tabulation to have any value for guidance. The conception of an objectively measurable probability or chance is simply inapplicable (Knight 1921, p. 231).

It is clear from these quotations that, according to Knight, relative frequency probability (risk) is uninteresting and that logical or subjective probability (uncertainty) is the only one that has real economic interest. Knight also recognized the law-of-large-numbers problem, and he noted the estimation problem as well.

> Fidelity to the actual psychology of the situation requires, we must insist, recognition of these two separate exercises of judgment, the formation of an estimate and the estimation of its value.... A man may act upon an estimate of the chance that his estimate of the chance of an event is a correct estimate (Knight 1921, p. 227).

The remainder of the decade echoes Knight's caution and skepticism. Even in a book with the title *Risk and Risk Bearing* (Hardy 1923), there is little regarding quantification. Hardy goes so far as to point out in an appendix that with the usual exception of insurance, "Calculations of mathematical probability are seldom of much importance in actual business" (Hardy 1923, p. 29). This fact is explicitly attributed to the reference-class problem.

Cases of uncertainty where neither the mathematical nor the statistical basis of determining probability is available call for the exercise of what we call"judgement.' These are cases where the events to be feared are so rare, or the difficulty of forming homogeneous classes among them as a basis for statistical generalization is so great, that there is no adequate basis of experience for judging whether they will take place, or what is the probability of their taking place (Hardy 1923, p. 46).

Judging from the extended discussion of "judgement" that follows, the author clearly believes it to dominate quantitative techniques in business.

Knight did not, however, provide the final word on terminology. Lavington's (1925) interpretation was that "risk" is the probability of a loss (however determined) and "uncertainty" is the confidence in that probability. In 1929, Florence was still struggling with making some sense of all the terms that had been associated with the concepts of uncertainty and risk. He managed to capture the problem quite elegantly in terms of contending probability theories, but did not come up with a definitive solution. He believed that there were really three values associated with uncertainty or risk—the value of the probability itself, the theory of probability (the source or meaning of that value,) and the precision of that value (the quality of the information on which it is based.) Precision may be interpreted in two ways—in an objective statistical sense using sample values to estimate the hypothetical distribution, or in a subjective sense of the confidence an individual has in his or her estimate.

Florence made a real contribution elucidating the issue of different theories of probability and emphasizing the difference between probabilities and the confidence in those probabilities; however, he failed to standardize the definitions of "risk" and "uncertainty." Knight's (1921) distinction was that "risk" applied to relative frequency probabilities and "uncertainty" to subjective probabilities. Lavington's (1925) attitude was that "risk" is the probability and "uncertainty" is the confidence in it, regardless of the theory. Both of these interpretations were to reappear later in the literature.

The early history concludes with a key work published by Fisher in 1930 in which his position regarding the statistical measurement of risk was unambiguous.

While it is possible to calculate mathematically risks of a certain type like those in games of chance [classical probability] or in property and life insurance where the chances are capable of accurate measurement [relative frequency probability], most economic risks are not so readily measured. To attempt to formulate mathematically in any useful, complete manner the laws determining the rate of interest under the sway of chance would be like attempting to express completely the laws which determine the path of a projectile when affected by random gusts of wind. Such formulas would need to be either too general or too empirical to be of much value (Fisher 1930, p. 316).

This rejection of a probabilistic measure of risk was not because Fisher was unwilling to make simplifying assumptions in general, for elsewhere in the book he makes it clear that he regards hypothetical conditions and approximations to be essential in science. His real basis for this conclusion is not as thoroughly specified as Knight's, but addresses the same, by now familiar, reference-class and law-of-large-numbers problems.

> It seems likely that in ordinary communities, realization justifies the average expectation. But in an individual case this is not always true; otherwise there would be no such thing as risk. Risk is synonymous with uncertainty—lack of knowledge. Our present behavior can only be affected by the expected future,—not the future as it will turn out but the future as it appears to us beforehand through the veil of the unknown (Fisher 1930, p. 222).[6]

The Rejection of Probabilistic Measurement of Risk

Probabilistic measurement of risk had been soundly and unambiguously rejected by 1930. There are a number of possible explanations of why this occurred. It might have been because there was insufficient pressure for, or insufficient interest in, measuring risk, yet, there was considerable interest in the stock exchange, an obvious target of statistical analysis, and volumes of data were readily available. Before computerization, the computations would have been tedious, but the mathematical techniques were well known, and the possibility of beating the market was a strong incentive to apply them.

It might have been that an intuitive sense of risk was thought to be sufficient, but both Edgeworth (1888) and Norton (1904) spoke of the benefits of quantification. It might have been that the concept of probabilistic measurement of risk was not as well-developed then as it appears to have been in retrospect, but authors from Fisher (1906) on are too explicit to be significantly misinterpreted, and there is ample evidence that the idea had been in gestation for a number of years before then.

It also might have been that the accepted economic methodology of the time was antithetical to a probabilistic measurement of risk. This was, after all, the era of non-mathematical American institutionalism. However, Willett (1901) and Fisher (1906) seem to have been willing in principle to make the simplifying assumptions common in neoclassical economics, and Weintraub (1985) notes Fisher's difficulties establishing an econometric society in light of the math-phobia of *others*.

The only realistic explanation for the rejection was the consensus that a probabilistic measure of risk was inapplicable to economic activity. There were too many theoretical problems that would have to be ignored in making such a foolish simplification. There was no way to specify reference classes; in fact, reference classes did not even exist for the unique situations that were regarded as typical. Even if there were reference classes, the law of large numbers eliminates risk when there are stable relative frequencies. And risk lies not just in the dispersion of a relative frequency distribution of possibilities, but in the dispersion of the dispersion as well. It simply made no sense, even to those who might have been most inclined to do so, to measure risk with probabilities.

THE RESTORATION OF THE PROBABILISTIC MEASUREMENT OF RISK

Hicks' Initial Reaction

Since the late nineteenth century, risk in economics was associated with the theory of distribution. It was in this context that Hicks (1931) began the restoration of a statistical measure of risk. In this paper, he is clearly critical of Knight.

> It is because I feel a conviction that an economic theory of profit should be based on economics and not on metaphysics and psychology that I here venture to suggest a line of approach alternative to that followed by Professor Knight in the latter part of his book (Hicks 1931, p. 171).

The reasoning behind his criticism is interesting. Hicks seems to be saying that there is something "uneconomic" about Knight's subjective "uncertainty." In doing so, Hicks is forcing the methods to shape the subject matter rather than the subject matter to determine, or at least to suggest, the methods. Of course, it still remains for Hicks to deal with the technical problems that Knight pointed out. First, he tackles the reference class problem.

> And most operations which do not form part of a class of this sort, are nevertheless separable into partial operations which do; or if not, they form part of a class of nearly similar operations, in which we cannot speak of chances with the same perfect accuracy, but still our error is not large. Those "unmeasurable risks" or "true uncertainties" which escape any such classification, and which bulk so large in Professor Knight's theory, must justify their claim to a large measure of our attention by showing that a satisfactory theory of profit cannot be constructed without paying special attention to them. I believe it can (Hicks 1931, p. 171).

Hicks claims that the error in assuming reference classes is not large, and it is up to those who challenge reference classes to prove that the error *is* large by showing that theories based on reference classes are unsatisfactory. This position hardly provides a decisive solution to the reference-class problem, yet it is difficult not to be sympathetic with such a bold attempt at theory construction. If the simplification works, so much the better; if not, nothing is lost but a little time. Hicks' claim to the intellectual high ground is not as brazen as it appears; after all, he is the one preserving neoclassical economic orthodoxy and not the one challenging it.

Although Hicks believed that there was potential for a satisfactory theory of profit based on a probabilistic measure of risk, the 1931 article provides no evidence of a practical commitment to it. He repeats Pigou's description of a relative frequency distribution, but does not make use of it. He also mentions the law-of-large-numbers problem,[7] but he says nothing about what this implies for a probabilistic measure of risk.

This paper by Hicks was one of the last in which the primary importance of risk was its association with profit. Earlier, in 1930, Fisher had begun to associate risk with money, and it was as an element in research on the theory of money that a probabilistic measure of risk returned. Ironically, one of the first papers in this new research program was also by Hicks, in which he largely continued where his earlier paper left off.

> Where risk is present, the particular expectation of a riskless situation is replaced by a band of possibilities, each of which is considered more or less probable. It is convenient to represent these probabilities to oneself, in statistical fashion, by a mean value, and some appropriate measure of dispersion. (No single measure will be wholly satisfactory, but here this difficulty may be overlooked.) Increased dispersion means increased uncertainty (Hicks 1935, p. 8).

This is not a wholehearted return to the use of relative frequencies; in fact, it seems much more consistent with subjective probabilities, as the distribution is a personal representation of possibilities rather than anything objective. Yet Hicks does not share some of Knight's concerns. He does not make any sort of distinction between "uncertainty" and "risk" that would acknowledge the reference-class problem and he "overlooks" the estimation problem. It is difficult to assess what Hicks believes about this distribution. On the one hand, he regards it as is a convenient representation of risk that unfortunately may not be able to be measured. On the other hand, he holds out the possibility that in the future it might be measured. The following passage expresses his difficulties.

> It needs judgment and knowledge of business psychology much more than sustained logical reasoning.... When once the connection between objective facts and anticipations has been made, theory comes again into its rights.... Nevertheless, it does seem to me most important that, when considering these further questions, we should be well aware of the gap which lies behind us, and that we should bring out very clearly the assumptions which we are making about the genesis of anticipations (Hicks 1935, pp. 13-14).

One would think that if Hicks thought that it were possible to use objective distributions to measure expectations, he would have more explicitly said so. At least he recommends being explicit about the assumptions that need to be made.

The First Austrian Assault

Weintraub (1985) and Craver (1986) describe a virtual exodus of German and Austrian economists to the United States in the late 1930s. Many of these emigré economists had been mathematicians before they turned to economics, and they played a major role in the pre-war explosion in the collection and analysis of economic statistics. Among them were Jacob Marschak, Gerhard Tintner, Paul Rosenstein-Rodan, and Oscar Lange, whose names are all associated with the probabilistic measurement of risk. They first appear in the literature in 1938.

Two articles in that year by Marschak (the first co-authored with Helen Makower) continued the movement away from Knight's and Fisher's skepticism toward an objective probabilistic measure of risk. In the first article, the terms used by the authors are defined in a footnote. It is worth quoting in full to illustrate how Knight's position was being misconstrued.

> We appreciate the importance of Professor Knight's distinction between risk and uncertainty. It seems that we may interpret Professor Knight's 'risk' as the dispersion of the frequency distribution of alternative future events, and his 'uncertainty' as the degree of ignorance about this frequency distribution. For the first concept we too shall use the term risk; as to the second, we find it more convenient to call it degree of ignorance. This enables us to reserve the term uncertainty to denote the fact that risk exists, i.e., that no event is assigned the probability 1 (and therefore the dispersion is greater than zero). This seems consistent with the ordinary use of the word 'uncertainty.' In the roulette room we are not ignorant about the probabilities which are to be assigned to the various alternative events; yet there is uncertainty even there about each single event. On the other hand, the fact that in ordinary life outside games of chance the frequency distributions are not exactly known, we denote as ignorance. A discussion of how, in the light of the Theory of Inference, we may measure the degree of ignorance, and how it affects the prices and holdings of assets, must be left for another occasion (Makower and Marschak 1938, p. 271).

Continuing in the text,

> The yields must be expressed as an array of more or less probable quantities, that is as a frequency distribution, or more strictly a system of yields must be expressed by a joint frequency distribution (p. 271).

These quotations are indeed indicative of a drift, rather than a change, in the concept of risk. In the latter quotation, it is not clear what the word *must* means—whether individuals "must" form the expectations in that way or whether expectations "must" be regarded in that way in order to be measured. Makower and Marschak's interpretation of "risk" and "uncertainty" is not Knight's, but is actually Lavington's (1925). Their interpretation is not what Knight had in mind. Knight gave no reason for subjective probabilities not to be expressed in the form of a distribution, but he was very reluctant to do so as a distribution is unable to capture the complexities of the concept of uncertainty.

There is an implication in this quotation that risk, as some measure of dispersion, can be measured in some way, and later in the article the authors state that "... the yield expectations of the various persons are based partly on the same objective facts and are therefore to some extent similar" (Makower and Marschak 1938, p. 277). Just as Hicks "overlooked" it, Makower and Marschak are "leaving for another occasion" the estimation problem.

In fact, in the second article, Marschak does take up the matter, observing that the parameters of a distribution are estimated on the basis of the information available. This is an ambiguous solution. He could be referring to subjective probabilities, but it is clear from a later article that he was referring to relative frequency probabilities in which the parameters of the hypothetical distribution are estimated from a sample distribution.

> To [the objection that the individual, except in games of chance, has no knowledge of probabilities involved]; this objection is perhaps the one made also by F.H. Knight in his Risk, Uncertainty and Profit: it must be recognized that an individual may estimate two assets as having the same expected value, yet be aware that the two estimates have different degrees of reliability according to the different types of information at his disposal. Thus the objection calls for the use of additional concepts (reliability), analogous to those developed by the modern theory of statistical inference (Marschak 1941, p. 52).

Again, this is not the major objection raised by Knight, which was the reference-class problem; rather, it is the estimation problem emphasized by Lavington.

Elsewhere in the second 1938 article, Marschak leaves little doubt that he is firmly wedded to a probabilistic measure of risk by making an *ad hoc* assertion of the parameters that are important.

> ... to each combination of assets there corresponds, in his mind, an n-dimensional joint frequency distribution of the yields.... It is sufficiently realistic, however, to confine ourselves, for each yield, to two parameters only: the mathematical expectation ('lucrativity') and the coefficient of variation ('risk'); while it would be definitely unrealistic... to confine ourselves to the mathematical expectation only (Marschak 1938, p. 320).

What cannot be "overlooked," "left for another occasion," or deemed "sufficiently realistic" must be dealt with by an appeal to the peculiar nature of economic theory with its necessity for simplifications.

> To [the objection that the acting man does not and cannot make exact calculations] I would answer that we know well that investors are not actuaries; nor are housewives accountants. Any chapter of economic theory starts from simplified and idealized behavior patterns and treats the results as mere approximations (Marschak 1941, p. 52).

Why the return to the use of relative frequencies occurred at all is the critical question. There was no empirical evidence suggesting that it was appropriate. None of the fundamental problems had been dealt with in any way other than to cavalierly dismiss them. Without attempting to sort out the various methodological currents swirling about at the time, it appears as if Hicks and Marschak viewed economic research from a much different perspective than Knight and Fisher. At least in the case of Marschak, this may have been an outcome of his close association with mathematics and mathematicians. Instead of attempting to devise an original, effective way to model the risk present in most economic activities, Hicks and Marschak simply borrowed the mathematical probability calculus, about which Knight and Fisher had already expressed serious doubts.

Snooks (1993) also believes that there may have been a shift in the perception of economic research at this time, contending that somewhere between the 1930s and 1940s there was a decline in concern for the reality content of econometric models. He quotes Morgan (1990) to the effect that data was no longer regarded as a creative source of ideas for building new models but simply as a means of testing *a priori* models. It mattered to Knight and Fisher whether people would have assessed risk probabilistically; otherwise, their theories could not have been explanatory. It did not matter to Hicks and Marschak, as long as probabilities provided data. Had their theories worked, then their simplifications would have been considered appropriate. Theirs was a sound, albeit optimistic, approach, if the attachment to relative frequency probabilities had not been so strong as to preclude its abandonment when it proved to be ineffective.

The Brief Skeptical Backlash

Because of the technical problems, not everyone was convinced of the efficacy of what was rapidly becoming the standard probabilistic measure of risk. One of the most notable critics was Shackle, who introduced his concept of "surprise" in an exchange of notes with Hart in 1940 (Shackle 1940a, 1940b; Hart 1940). Although it is not necessary to go into the details of Shackle's theory,[8] his was essentially an attempt to devise a quantitative formal language more consistent with behavior (or at least Shackle's perception of behavior). It is not, however, consistent with the standard probability calculus. Hart's response to Shackle insists on what was now the conventional approach.

> The assumption of cardinal probability estimates is clearly more satisfactory in terms of conclusions, leading to determinate valuations without arbitrary selection..... While admitting that the economist should be 'surprised' to find documents in business files in which definite probability estimates are made, the writer still finds it reasonable to set up the assumption of quantified probability estimates as an 'idealisation' of actual business practice (Hart 1940, pp. 51-52).

In spite of the problems that deterred Knight and Fisher, the rationale here is the "reasonableness" of the assumptions. Shackle responds by echoing Knight's concern with the reference-class problem.

> What is the sense or logical justification of probability estimates when the proposed experiment (investment in a plant of specific design and location, to operate in a specific historical period) is virtually unique? (Shackle 1940b, p. 56).

Hart's opposition continues in his book, *Anticipations, Uncertainty, and Dynamic Planning* (Hart 1965; originally published in 1940).

> It is uncertainty rather than risk (properly so called) which will be of primary interest to us; but a definition of the latter concept is called for, if only to delimit the problem. Estimates about any future event which is not regarded as certain may involve either uncertainty or risk. The event viewed in isolation is always uncertain. But viewed as a member of a group of events so related that their joint outcome is more certain than the individual events in the group, it is a risk (Hart 1965, p. 51).

This reflects yet another misunderstanding of Knight. Knight had used the terms *risk* and *uncertainty* in regard to the reference-class problem. Marschak claimed that he had used them in regard to the estimation problem. Now Hart is claiming that they were used in regard to the law-of-large-numbers problem.

Along with Shackle, Steindl (1941) suggests an alternative quantitative measure of risk. First, he states his version of the conventional view.

> In dealing with uncertainty of price it is usually assumed that the entrepreneur who tries to predict a price has in mind several possible magnitudes of the price in question and various chances are attributed to these magnitudes. A distribution of the chances of various possible prices is drawn up, and the dispersion of this distribution is used to measure uncertainty (Steindl 1941, p. 43).

An interesting word in this quotation is "usually." Steindl attributes the use of distributions to Pigou (1962), Hicks (1931), Makower and Marschak (1938), and Marschak (1938). Since distributions seem to have been essentially discredited in the literature by 1930, only ten years must have been required to reestablish them as "usual." Steindl claims to come up with a more objective approach, based on the assumptions that:

> ... an entrepreneur must use one and the same method of prediction consistently in predicting a certain variable repeatedly; and the same method or type of prediction must be used fairly generally, i.e. by most people who predict the particular variable in question (Steindl 1941, p. 43).

This is an early appearance (or reappearance) of the assumption of homogeneous expectations. In Steindl's method, uncertainty is a measure of the unpredictability of a variable. It is the dispersion of the distribution of prediction errors. He claims that:

> The preceding treatment of uncertainty runs contrary to the tendency of Knight's exposition on the subject. According to him, in most cases the decision of an entrepreneur is more or less unique, and decisions cannot be classified into 'groups of homogeneous cases' which would permit the calculation of frequencies. Thus 'uncertainty' in Knight's sense is fundamentally different from insurable 'risk,' because it is not measurable. In a sense, an entrepreneur's decision, like the establishment of a new plant, is unique: but in another sense, if the decision is based on a series of predictions which have more or less a routine character, it is not unique at all (Steindl 1941, p. 48).

Unlike Hart and others, Steindl correctly interprets Knight—risk and uncertainty are indeed fundamentally different. But his assumption that unique decisions are based on a set of routine predictions is heroic indeed.

Although Shackle managed to claim attention for nearly a decade and is still occasionally referred to by unorthodox economists, neither he nor Steindl had any lasting impact on preventing the establishment of a relative frequency-based probabilistic measure of risk as the reigning orthodoxy. Their work is now no more than a historical curiosity, and the skepticism that flickered for a brief period was quickly extinguished.

The Triumph of Statistical Measurement of Risk

For a brief time during the early 1940s, the subject of risk was very important, and interpretations, restatements, and clarifications appeared with unprecedented frequency. Tintner (1942a) echoes Lavington's (1925) distinction between "risk" and "uncertainty" in regard to the estimation problem:

If the probability distribution of the expectations is considered to be known with certainty (probability one), we will talk of subjective risk. If the probability distribution of the anticipations is not itself known definitely but only anticipated again with a certain likelihood, we will talk about subjective uncertainty. We add the word 'subjective' since these notions are related to, but by no means identical with, Knight's ideas about risk and uncertainty. We do not here consider any 'objective' risk, but only the subjective estimate and opinion of the individual. Hence our concept of probability is here the same as Keynes, and different from, for example, the frequency definition of von Mises (Tintner 1942a, p. 92).

What he appears to be saying is that risk is classical probability (distribution known with certainty). Uncertainty is relative frequency probability. These notions are nowhere near Knight's and much different from Keynes.' Tintner uses the terms *objective* and *subjective* to refer to whether the numbers are some observable property of the world or an intangible inference. His link between objective and subjective is that objective distributions are used to form subjective estimates of the (and he is very clear about this) "a priori" distribution via some Bayesian process. This is the first explicit use of this rationale for the equality of objective and subjective.

Hart reappears in 1942, making reference to the estimation problem.

Both risk and uncertainty, in the terminology which now tends to become standard, are subjective matters—attributes of anticipation and (by extension) of plans for action. 'Risk' is taken to denote the holding of anticipations which are not 'single valued' but constitute a probability distribution having known parameters. Uncertainty' is taken to denote the holding of anticipations under which the parameters of the probability distribution are themselves not single valued.... 'Uncertainty' implies that he has a probability distribution of probability distributions (Hart 1942, pp. 110-111).

Hart is correct when he later states that uncertain probabilities cannot be collapsed into a single distribution, an error to which subsequent authors are prone. But he makes the same mistake as others when he uses the term *likelihood*, for it applies only to an estimate of a distribution when there is a real distribution. It does not solve the reference-class problem, where there is a subjective distribution of possibilities for a unique event for which there is no "real" distribution.

In 1942 as well, Fellner (1942) addresses the reference-class problem.

The main difficulty inherent in the problem of the entrepreneur is a consequence of the fact that they are neither single valued nor a frequency distribution in the ordinary sense. Consequently, the probability calculus, as defined in statistics, is inapplicable to the problem. As is always the case in conditions like these, the difficulty leaves one a choice between one of two procedures. One may refrain from using the exact (or quantifying) method, recognizing that the problem, as it presents itself in reality, is not capable of being solved by this procedure. Or, alternatively, one may simplify the problem in such manner as to render the 'exact' method applicable, in which case the difference existing between one's simplified model and the real world has to be taken into account (Fellner 1942, p. 196).

His rationalization is that people must use some idea of reference classes in order to make a decision—that is, they always generalize from what they perceive to be the relevant past experience. Then, people modify their conclusions to take into account the "peculiarities" of the current situation. Apparently, this latter step is either insignificant or diversifiable—it is not clear how Fellner does away with it.

Fellner also is concerned with the estimation problem.

> Not much is gained by postulating a second set of probability judgements relating to the validity of the original judgments and by carrying this procedure further back. The fact remains that all probability judgments of this character relate to hypothetical homogeneous universes and not to observed ones. Consequently there always remains a residual that is not accessible to probability analysis: it is necessary to appraise the effects of deviations from homogeneity on observed results, in order to translate 'experience' into homogeneous universes. If a chain of probability judgments is postulated, the residual is carried further back, but it does not thereby become smaller. The final judgment can never be interpreted as a probability judgment alone; it always contains another constituent, too (Fellner 1942, pp. 197-198).

Fellner is correct in lumping the residuals from the homogeneous reference class into the confidence in the probabilities. They are effectively the same. He is also correct in admitting that no one knows how small they are and that they need to be investigated. But this has never been done.

The Final Solution

Two years later, in an article by Domar and Musgrave (1944), the attitude toward probabilistic measurement of risk is best characterized as acquiescent. The authors acknowledge skepticism, but move ahead.

> To handle our problem, quantitative values for the yield and the degree of risk of an investment are needed; and in the absence of a better approach, they are obtained by means of a probability distribution... [continuing in a footnote]. Objections may be raised to this assumption, as in fact they may be raised against most any feature of the 'homo economicus.' For purposes of this paper, which does not discuss risk theory as such, the probability method is adopted, because no satisfactory alternative approach to the subject of risk theory has been developed (pp. 393-394).

Of course, quantification is the only thing special about the probability method that would make *it* satisfactory. With regard to the estimation problem:

No investor is sure that his estimated probability distribution is entirely correct, but the degree of uncertainty will vary with different investors and different investments. It will be a factor in the investment decision. Yet it is extremely difficult to express the degree of uncertainty involved in workable terms… [continuing in a footnote] .. This paper being a first step in the analysis of our subject, these complications, which hardly affect the major results, are avoided here (1944, p. 394).

By 1944, it had become all too common that anything that is "extremely difficult" is "avoided" as "hardly affecting the results." Arrow's 1951 survey article, "Alternative Approaches to the Theory of Choice in Risk-Taking Situations," effectively signaled the end of the old era and the undisputed beginning of the new. He describes the alternative views of risk and the technical problems that are associated with probabilistic measurement, and then subtly dismisses each of them. First he tackles the reference-class problem.

While it may seem hard to give a justification for using probability statements when the event occurs only once, except on the interpretation of probability as degree-of-belief, the contrary position also seems difficult to defend. If an individual were told to predict whether or not two heads would come up in successive throws of a fair coin and further informed that he would lose his life if he guessed wrong, I find it very hard to believe that he would disregard the evidence of the calculus of probabilities….An extension of this suggests that in almost any reasonable view of probability theory the probability of a single event must still be the basis of action where there are genuine probabilities (Arrow 1951, p. 415).

Arrow's use of an example from the domain of classical probability is misleading. No one would suggest that classical probabilities or relative frequencies are irrelevant. What is in dispute is whether they exist in a given economic situation, and, even if they do, whether they provide the only information it is necessary to assume.

Knight appears to be worried about the seemingly mechanical nature of the probability calculus and its consequent failure to reflect the tentative, creative nature of the human mind in the face of the unknown. In a fundamental sense, this is probably correct, though it seems to lead only to the conclusion that no theory can be formulated for this case, at least not to the type of theory of choice discussed here (p. 417).

Without the assumption of a relative frequency theory of probability, a "scientific" theory of choice under uncertainty is not possible. So, in order to preserve the possibility of a "scientific" theory, and for no other apparent reason, it is necessary to make the assumption and ignore the reference-class problem.

The behavior postulates appear to be reasonable even under the frequency or any other definition of probability. The von Neumann-Morgenstern theorem then leads to the conclusion that the probability distribution is relevant when only one event is observed;

i.e., any definition of probability leads to a degree-of-belief interpretation. The objections, therefore, to the use of the probability concept in the absence of indefinite repetition seem to fall to the ground (p. 425).

Arrow is mistaking a subjective distribution of possibilities for an objective distribution of occurrences. Whereas the language of the probability calculus may be a convenient way of visualizing expectations, it has nothing to do with measuring them. There is no necessary connection between the two. Then, he turns to the law-of-large-numbers problem.

The argument is that, in that case, the law of large numbers would permit the wiping out of all risks through insurance or some other form of consolidation of cases. This proposition, if true, would appear to be of greatest importance (p. 427).

His response is:

A somewhat more obvious criticism of Knight's result is the argument that in fact, the risks occurring are mutually correlated, so that the law of large numbers may not operate (p. 427).

But a relative frequency distribution must be made up of independent events; so, if there are mutual correlations, a true relative frequency distribution is not possible. He never does "solve" the estimation problem.

Several years later, Paul Samuelson (1963) claims to have dealt with the law-of-large-numbers problem in a slightly different way. He tells the story of a colleague who would not accept a single bet (in which the colleague would win $200 but lose only $100 on a coin toss), but would accept a series of such bets. Samuelson's response to this was:

If you will not accept one toss, you cannot accept two—since the latter could be thought of as consisting of the (unwise) decision to accept one plus the open decision to accept a second. Even if you were stuck with the first outcome, you would cut your further (utility) losses and refuse the terminal throw. By extending the reasoning from 2 to $3 = 2 + 1$, ..., and from n-1 to n, we rule out any sequence at all.

Samuelson is the unwitting victim of a "sorites" paradox (Poundstone 1988). To see the fallacy, consider a specific example known as Wang's paradox. If x is a small number, then x+1 is also small. By this reasoning, every number can be reasoned to be small, even though there are obviously large numbers. Just as 1 is a small number and 100 is not, Samuelson's colleague can reasonably refuse one bet and accept 100.

It is not hard to understand why those undertaking research in economics and finance desperately want to have a way to measure risk. For this reason, it is difficult to be too critical of the cavalier attitude to the probabilistic measure that was adopted between 1930 and 1950. Mathematics had worked wonders in the physical sciences during the first half of the century, and whether it was a rational belief or wishful thinking that it would also do so in economics, it was worth the attempt. If it worked, then it was appropriate, and by 1950, it was not yet clear that it did not work.[9] Yet it is difficult not to wonder at the way the technical problems were so easily dismissed after they had led a probabilistic measurement of risk to be rejected by 1930. Phrases such as "I feel a conviction" (Hicks 1931), "this difficulty may be overlooked" (Hicks 1935), "must be left for another occasion" (Makower and Marschak 1938), "sufficiently realistic" (Marschak 1938), "finds it reasonable" (Hart 1942), "not be too great an abstraction" (Tintner 1942b), and "in the absence of a better approach" (Domar and Musgrave 1944) seem to indicate that severe problems were being dismissed entirely too easily.

As we said in our introduction to this section, the positivist way of viewing this is just that one makes simplifying assumptions, and if the subsequent theories are successful, so much the better. If they are not successful, then the assumptions can be discarded with no regrets. But these assumptions have rarely been challenged since, despite deficiencies in theories in finance. The problems that were so important to Knight and Fisher and that were at least acknowledged by Hicks, Marschak, and the others are still there. Yet no one in the mainstream of research is concerned with them any longer, although serious doubts seep into the layman literature (see e.g., Bernstein 1996). Later in the book, we will consider some sociological reasons why such obvious problems, which had once captivated the attention of economists, are now ignored.

NOTES

1. This is not to say that the problems are not being addressed somewhere by mathematicians, psychologists, or eccentric economists, for example; but within the mainstream research programs in finance, the problems are no longer admitted.

2. It is difficult to clearly differentiate "probability" and "statistics." As the purpose of 'statistics" nowadays is to make statements regarding probabilities, "probability" is effectively the more primitive concept. Ultimately, it is "probability" that underlies the 'measure" of risk that is the subject of this chapter. "Statistics" is used here to refer to the historical data from which probabilities are obtained, which is more or less the term's original use (Porter 1986).

3. Hacking (1990) refers to Edgeworth as a mathematician rather than an economist. The distinction between mathematicians and economists, or rather the lack thereof during certain periods, plays an important role in the history of the measurement of risk.

4. Edgeworth (1888) had, in fact, recounted an anecdote that seemed to indicate that the transformation *is* straightforward.

On the occasion when this paper was read before the British Association, the President of Section F, Mr J.B. Martin, speaking in the capacity of a practical banker, remarked with reference to the 'law of error' (law of the dispersion of a normal distribution) that he felt like Mr. Jourdain, who had been speaking prose all his life without knowing it" (Edgeworth 1888, p. 123).

5. Here, Knight must be referring to insurance and actuarial computations. Outside of these, the literature regarding statistics and risk was not at all extensive.

6. Crockett (1980) regards Fisher as the intellectual source of the treatment of risk that appears in the financial economics of the 1950s and 1960s. Not only does Crockett fail to consider the work of others preceding Fisher's 1906 *Nature of Capital and Income*, but he also ignores Fisher's rejection here in the 1930 *Theory of Interest* of his earlier optimism.

7. "But I find it difficult to believe that there will not be some grouping and some setting off" (Hicks 1931, p. 172).

8. A complete explanation is in Shackle (1952).

9. This is apt to be a controversial point, but many, if not most, of the accomplishments of finance theory are limited to having created a useful way of thinking about something. When the thoughts themselves become useful along with the way of thinking, then something will have been accomplished.

Section 4

PRACTICE AND LANGUAGE

Chapter IX

The Language of Mathematics

The case of finance and risk presented in the preceding chapters illustrates how the failure to carefully consider the assumptions of a theory can result in inherent contradictions within the theory that ultimately lead to failure to empirically validate the theory. In that particular case, the assumptions concerned the translation of ordinary language into mathematics so that theories concerning risk and uncertainty could be formally expressed and empirically tested. In the following section, we expand on that theme of how mathematics in general in finance is less a tool with which to make our scientific work more precise than a rhetorical device to give it a scientific appearance or a competitive device with which to demonstrate our intellectual authority.

SCIENCE AND MATHEMATICS

From Numerology to Science

Although its use is not specifically required by the tenets of positivism, mathematics plays an important role in modernity, scientism, and positivism. Indeed, the demise of scholasticism was accompanied not only with a separation of science from philosophy, but also, with regard to the use of mathematics, with a separation of science from numerology.

At the time of Pythagoras in the sixth century B.C., philosophy, science, and numerology were not separated by vast institutional chasms. It was quite easy and natural to be engaged in all three, and it was not always clear in which one was engaged. Taken with the miraculous connection between aesthetics and number he had discovered in the form of musical intervals, Pythagoras:

> ... proceeded to indulge in an orgy of mathematical speculations on the nature of the universe as a whole, got numerologically drunk, and died scientifically of intellectual delirium tremens (Bell 1933, p. 59).

Bell's contention that Pythagoras turned, most likely quite unknowingly, from science to numerology is based on what Bell believes are methodical differences between the two. Scientific mathematization is testable and tested; numerology is not.

It was not until Galileo and Newton that the scientific and numerological identities of mathematics became explicitly detached from each other.

> The Pythagorean-Platonic philosophy that number relations are the key to the universe, that all things are known through number, is an essential element in the Galilean scheme of relating quantitative aspects of phenomena through formulas. This philosophy was kept alive throughout the Middle Ages though most often, as with the Pythagoreans themselves, it was part of some larger mystical theory of creation, with number as the form and cause of all created objects. Galileo and Newton divested the Pythagorean doctrine of all mystical associations and re-clothed it in a style that set the fashion for modern science (Kline 1953, p. 213).

Thus, mathematization had its roots in metaphysics and mysticism and remained close to those roots until well into the sixteenth century.

According to Galileo, what ultimately distinguishes the mathematics of science from the mathematics of numerology is the Cartesian notion that in the former it expresses fundamental laws that are unquestionably true. These laws are part of a formal system built on a set of axiomatic principles according to which the universe "works." Indeed, "the ideal pursued (by positivism) is knowledge in the form of a mathematically formulated universal science deducible from the smallest number of axioms" (Held 1980, p. 164).

Descartes himself admired the simplicity and logical rigor of the process.

> These long chains composed of very simple and easy reasonings which geometers customarily use to arrive at their most difficult demonstrations gave me occasion to suppose that all the things which can fall under human knowledge are interconnected in the same way (Descartes, quoted in Cottingham 1986, p. 90).

In the same vein, Leibniz in *De Arte Combinatoria* outlined

> ... an ideographic system of signs that [could] be manipulated to produce logical deductions without recourse to natural language. The signs [represented] primitive ideas gleaned from prior analysis. Once broken down into primitives and represented by stipulated signs, the component ideas [could] be paired and recombined to fashion novel configurations. In this way, Leibniz sought to mechanize the production of new ideas (Heim 1993, p. 92).

What was a scientific ideal seems, at least according to some, to have turned back again into a form of conjuring.

In fact, the subsequent success of mathematics in the natural sciences is itself a matter of wonder, as evidenced by the title of a well-known article in 1960 by the famous physicist Eugene Wigner: "The Unreasonable Effectiveness of Mathematics in the Natural Sciences." It may not be so unreasonable, however, when we consider that even in the natural sciences, we may be forcing the world into a mathematical language in which it was not necessarily originally written.[1]

From Science to Numerology

Because the mathematization of the universe in a scientific manner begun by Galileo and Newton had such success, it was to be expected that mathematics would be enthusiastically applied to the social as well as to the physical sciences. Out of Jeremy Bentham's efforts to construct a rational, axiomatic basis for human behavior came the efforts of his protegé James Mill to do the same for economics, and out of these efforts came the efforts of his disciple, David Ricardo, to mathematicize economics.

There is a long history of criticism of the use of mathematics in economics,[2] and by extension, such criticism is also applicable to finance. Bell (1933) believes that much of mathematics in the social sciences as a whole is more numerology than science.

> Is it unfair to say that anyone who vigorously applies mathematical formulas to human affairs, without a critical insight into the meanings and limitations of the mathematical methods used in deriving the formulas, or without a precise understanding of the assumptions on which their derivations are based, is a numerologist? (Bell 1933, p. 114)

And as Dostoyevsky sarcastically put it:

> These laws of nature have only to be discovered, and man will no longer be responsible for his actions, and it will become extremely easy for him to live his life...A new political economy will come into existence, all complete, and also calculated with mathematical accuracy, so that all problems will vanish in the twinkling of an eye, simply because all possible answers to them will have been supplied. Then the Palace of Crystal will arise. Well, in short, the golden age will come again (Dostoyevsky, quoted in Gane 1991, p. 69).

Heim (1993) suggests how logic and mathematics can break down in certain applications such as the social sciences.

> Logic, like mathematics, operates outside the intuitive wisdom of experience and common sense. Hence the mathematical idiot savant. Like math, logic can hover above particular facts and circumstances, linking chains of statements trailing from some phantom first premise. We can be perfectly logical yet float completely adrift from reality (Heim 1993, p. 20).[3]

It is characteristic of financial research that large data bases are relentlessly processed with no regard for the particulars and peculiarities of individual entries. It is casually assumed that the very things that make the data real will be submerged by the law of large numbers and some sort of meta-reality will remain afloat.

Although it is a provocative issue, this chapter is not about whether mathematics is useful in finance however the word "useful" might be defined.[4] It is about mathematics as a rhetorical attribute. Whether it is useful in finance, mathematics has not lost a cachet it has had for thousands of years. That mathematics is taken to be a superior form of expression in finance and economics is often attributed to an attempt to emulate the physical sciences. "All science is either physics or stamp collecting. Qualitative is nothing but poor quantitative" (Lord Rutherford, quoted in West 1990, p. 260).

Those capable of mastering the most difficult mathematics of finance are as deserving of their *academic* credentials as physicists. But the mystique of mathematics goes far beyond the scientism that emerged during the Enlightenment; it at least goes back to the ancient Greeks. Legend has it that the following statement was posted over the entrance to Plato's Academy: "Let no one who is ignorant of geometry enter here" (Bell 1933, p. 34).

Mathematics in Theory Creation

There is something within everyone who practices finance as a science that believes, beyond reason, that mathematics is the key to knowledge. It is because of this numerological impulse that mathematics is such a powerful rhetorical device that its use in academic papers is mandatory. Consider theory development. It would appear from the literature that theoreticians venture forth on a bold mathematical quest and pursue it to its inevitable conclusion. What really happens, of course, is that theories are derived with full knowledge of the intended outcome—an outcome supported only by anecdotal evidence. Because theoretical finance does not require any justification for its simplifications, it is possible to "prove" that virtually anything that a theoretician may learn through limited casual observations is the result of maximization, the *raison d'être* of economic man and woman. If one sees it (happening out there), then one knows it (must have been the result of maximization).

One especially flagrant example of this process is Jack Treynor and Robert Ferguson's (1985) "In Defense of Technical Analysis." The authors begin with a set of twelve unintuitive simplified assumptions[5] and end with a daunting equation twenty-four centimeters long. Without having begun the process with full, informal knowledge that technical analysis exists, there is no way that anyone would ever have chosen that set of assumptions, produced that equation from those assumptions, or interpreted that equation to mean that technical analysis exists. In fact, the same process can be used for a much shorter "proof" that technical analysis doesn't exist.

Although there is nothing subjective about the rules of logic and mathematics used in theoretical finance, the task to which the mathematics is set—that is, the starting point, the ending point, and the path between the two—is wholly subjective. Finance makes a few limited observations and concocts a mathematical explanation using a set of *ad hoc* assumptions. The mathematics does not make the whole process any less *ad hoc* in the same way that the rules of grammar and syntax do not make any verbal statement less *ad hoc*. A scientific medium need not convey a scientific message.

As Einstein said: "Pure logical thinking cannot yield us any knowledge of the empirical world; all knowledge of reality starts from experience and ends in it (quoted in Oldershaw 1990, p. 140).

FINANCE AND STATISTICS[6]

Although it certainly has its harmful effects in terms of the inherent limitations and contradictions it introduces, as we have seen in the preceding chapters, the formulation of finance theories in the language of mathematics is not nearly as bad as the abusive use of mathematical statistics in empirical testing. Theory makes no claims to truth; in fact, it is usually quite scrupulous in insisting that it is making only provisional falsifiable statements. Empirical tests, however, claim to tell us what is and what is not true. More often, however, empirical tests are manipulated to confirm our preconceptions of the truth. This is readily apparent in the event study, the most widely used method in finance.

Hypothesis Testing in Event Studies

Before closely examining the structures of hypothesis testing in event studies, however, it is useful to consider in general some characteristics of the universal statements event studies are intended to test.

Most of what is generally thought of as science concerns deterministic universal statements of the logical form: X implies Y. Such statements *predict* Y if X were to occur and *explain* Y if both X and Y have occurred. To test a statement of this form, one conducts a controlled experiment to detect Y under sets of conditions differing only in X. If X occurs but Y does not, then the statement has been falsified. Should the statement survive repeated attempts at falsification, it comes to be regarded as a law.

Some universal statements are statistical; that is, X implies Y Z percent of the time.[7] Tests of statistical universal statements are tests of the stability of the Z percent.

What impressed early scientists about many statistical statements—indeed, what it was then that made the statements laws—was their stability under repeated measurement. Regardless of the X under consideration, Y always occurred Z percent of the time (Porter 1986; Stigler 1986). Such statements in quantum physics are known to be a consequence of irreducible chance; however, in other sciences, such statements are still regarded as a consequence of temporary ignorance of variables—hidden variables that will be discovered with further effort that can explain why the result does or does not occur.

An archetypical universal statement in finance is that event X implies a change in value Y, and the event study is clearly an archetypical empirical test in finance. The event X can be virtually anything. The outcome Y, however, is restricted to the market response as indicated by the return on publicly traded common equity, and the responses are limited to higher than, lower than, or no different than the return would have been had the event not occurred. But are event studies really rigorous scientific tests of deterministic universal statements or even of statistical universal statements? In their traditional form, they are not.

The traditional event study tests a hypothesis of the form:

> Hypothesis 1(Traditional):   Event X causes an unexpected change in the firm's value.

An unexpected change in the firm's value is indicated by a return on publicly traded common equity over the period during which the event occurred that is different than the return predicted by a simple forecasting model. The latter is a surrogate for what the return would have been had the event not occurred. The implicit assumption is that the forecasting model reflects equilibrium conditions.

Since a conservative scientist ought to be more concerned with Type I errors (rejecting a true hypothesis)[8] than Type II errors (failing to reject a false hypothesis), the standard approach is to recast the empirical test of Hypothesis 1 in the form of a test of the null hypothesis H0 of the form:

> Hypothesis 0(Traditional):   The event X does not cause an unexpected change in the firm's value.

It is simpler to compute the probability of the test results given that Hypothesis 0 is true (committing a Type I error with regard to Hypothesis 0) than to compute the probability of the test results given that Hypothesis

1 is false (committing a Type II error with regard to Hypothesis 1). Of course, this standard approach requires that H0 be the negation of Hypothesis 1, which is true of the hypotheses as stated for this traditional event study.

The test results from a traditional event study might easily be that out of 100 firms, the returns of 60 are higher than expected and the returns of 40 are lower than expected. Suppose that the null hypothesis predicts that the returns of 50 or fewer firms will be higher than expected. Using a non-parametric sign test, the test statistic z is 2.00. The probability of these test results being observed if the null hypothesis Hypothesis 0 is true (the probability of committing a Type I error with regard to Hypothesis 0) is only 2.28 percent. It is unlikely that the event X *does not* cause an increase in the value of the firm, thereby "confirming" that the event X *does* cause an increase in the value of the firm.

But laws are regarded as laws because they are well-supported, not because their negations are not well-supported. The traditional event study is not concerned with strong evidence in support of the deterministic universal statement Hypothesis 1(Traditional) of the form X implies Y; rather, it is concerned with the absence of strong evidence in support of the deterministic universal statement Hypothesis 0(Traditional) of the form X implies not-Y. In the traditional event study, there is a marked difference between what epistemology demands and the logic of statistical inference supplies. This difference, however, is not unavoidable.

A skeptical scientist might view the test quite differently and take an alternative approach—denying that the event has any effect. Now, the hypothesis to be tested is:

Hypothesis 1(Skeptical): The event X does not cause an unexpected increase in the firm's value.

And the null hypothesis is:

Hypothesis 0(Skeptical): The event X causes an unexpected increase in the firm's value.

This null hypothesis predicts that the returns of all 100 firms will be higher than expected, which is exactly what a deterministic universal statement would assert. Obviously, though, there is no probability that the returns of 40 firms will be lower than expected if Hypothesis 0 is true; therefore, it must be resoundingly rejected and Hypothesis 1 confirmed.

Because event studies are not controlled experiments, the skeptical scientist may be willing to acknowledge that there are numerous uncontrolled factors that have an influence on the test results. Thus, he or she may be willing to restate the hypotheses as:

Hypothesis 1$_{(Skeptical)}$':   The event X does not cause an unexpected increase in the firm's value, 70 percent or more of the time.

Hypothesis 0$_{(Skeptical)}$':   The event X causes an unexpected increase in the firm's value 70 percent or more of the time.

Using a non-parametric sign test as before, the test statistic z is now -2.18. The probability of these test results being observed if the null hypothesis Hypothesis 0 is true is less than before—1.46 percent. It is now more unlikely that the event X *does* cause an increase in the value of the firm often enough, thereby "confirming" more strongly that the event X *does not* cause an increase in the value of the firm. The chance of publishing these results, however, is vanishingly small, and they are retired to a file with a rejection notice attached—an example of what Stephen Jay Gould (1993) calls "Cordelia's Dilemma."

In the skeptical form of the event study, strong evidence in support of the deterministic universal statement Hypothesis 1$_{(Traditional)}$, which is the universal statement of epistemological interest, is the same as strong evidence against the deterministic universal statement Hypothesis 0$_{(Skeptical)}$, which is the formulation consistent with the logic of statistical inference. Note that neither form of the event study tests a statistical universal statement. Event studies always try to consider the universe of events for which sufficient data is available; thus, the event study is a measurement of the Z percent of the time that X causes Y, not a test of a statement that Z percent is a specific value. The authors know of no event studies claiming any special importance for the actual Z percent of Ys that follow Xs.

The obvious conflict between the two forms of event study is that two logically equivalent empirical tests yield diametrically opposite epistemological results. The traditional event study has "confirmed" that the event X *does* cause an increase in the value of the firm. The skeptical event study has "confirmed" somewhat more strongly that the event X *does not* cause an increase in the value of the firm.

It is not entirely true that the same test on the same data with the same results "confirms" conflicting conclusions. The difference is that the believer using the traditional event study will settle for a theory that does not predict too badly, while the skeptic using the alternative event study demands a theory that predicts very well. It is possible to have statistically significant results that satisfy the criterion of one but not the other. Which position, however, makes the most sense in terms of epistemological significance?

With regard to the traditional tasks of science, perhaps neither does. The limited range of possibilities for Y poses what might be regarded as an insurmountable epistemological constraint. The sorts of deterministic universal statements that event studies test have no predictive value, since there is always an infinite number of Xs contending to cause Y to be higher or lower than expected. They also have nearly no explanatory value, since there is always an infinite number of Xs that could have caused Y to be higher or lower than expected. After decades of quantitative research in finance, we are still unable to predict large movements in a stock market or to explain them when they do occur.

It is also necessary to consider that epistemological significance is different from economic significance, which is a function of the magnitude of the unexpectedly different returns that might be found in an event study. Though the returns of *all* firms might be unexpectedly different following an event, which might be regarded as epistemologically significant, the event can still be economically insignificant. The amount by which the returns are unexpectedly different is not large enough for anyone but the scientist to care. Wang (1993) argues that statistical inference can be put to three uses: scientific justification, decision-making, and intellectual exploration. The first requires epistemological significance; the second, economic significance; and the third no significance at all—the intellectual value comes from the act of inquiry. Perhaps the real value of event studies lies in personal gratification or career enhancement, as we contend in Chapter XI. Unless event studies can yield epistemological or economic significance in some way, however, there is no direct public value to them.

Considering only the task of scientific justification, it may be epistemologically desirable to know that X implies Y, even though one might not know in a practical sense exactly when it will or won't or did or didn't or whether Y is a large enough effect to matter. If so, which form of the event study makes the most sense? Both positions have their weaknesses. The weakness with the skeptics' approach is that there is no definite criteria for theory confirmation. Must a theory make an accurate prediction 60 percent, 70 percent, 80 percent, 90 percent, or 100 percent of the time in order not to be rejected?[9] Too low a percentage results in the failure to reject useless theories; too high a percentage results in the inappropriate rejection of useful theories. There is no way to specify the point at which epistemological significance appears.

With the believers' approach, which dominates the literature, the weakness is that a rejection of the null hypothesis is virtually assured with a sufficiently large sample. Eventually, a very slight bias in favor of unexpectedly different returns is sufficient to reject the null hypothesis that the event has no impact. This is a familiar phenomenon, but its importance is not fully appreciated.[10] Theory "confirmation" is disturbingly easy, and "confirmed" theories" grow strong and multiply along with the journals in which they are published and the careers of their champions.

If one agrees with Karl Popper that science should strive for falsification and that the best theories are those that have survived the most rigorous attempts to do so, the choice is clear. Finance ought to be testing theories to find those that say something meaningful about what actually occurs, not about what doesn't occur. Well-supported theories are useful; theories supported only by the strength of evidence against their negations are usually useless, considering that such evidence is pitifully easy to obtain by accumulating more data. Unfortunately, financial research has been playing tennis with the net down for so long (in the form of traditional event studies) that raising the net now by imposing meaningful epistemological standards seems next to impossible.

A term that has turned up repeatedly in the discussion thus far has been *significance*. Epistemological "significance" implies scientific value; economic "significance" implies practical value. But whether the results of an event study have scientific or practical value is a secondary consideration. The primary consideration is whether the results are *statistically* "significant." Statistical significance is technically simple to measure with great precision; however, there are a number of very common pitfalls that can seriously compromise the measurement. Event studies are highly susceptible to these pitfalls; yet, finance research neglects them.

Problems with Statistical Significance

Event studies rely on statistical inference for their scientific legitimacy, but measurement of the statistical significance that effectively determines the outcome of the event study is subject to gross distortion. It is one thing to compute impressively precise numbers, but it is another thing entirely to understand what they *mean*. And if enough numbers are computed, of course, one will eventually end up with the number one wants.

All tests of statistical significance answer the same question: what is the probability that the difference between the data predicted by the null hypothesis and the actual data is a consequence of chance? In other words, how likely is it that a sample represented by the actual data was drawn from a universe described by the null hypothesis? For example, in event studies, what is the chance that a sample of 100 firms in which the returns of 60 are higher than expected and the returns of 40 are lower than expected was drawn at random from a universe of firms in which expectations are unbiased and the returns of equal numbers of firms are higher and lower than expected? All these formulations of the underlying question of statistical inference require that the actual data be a randomly drawn sample. In the absence of a chance process, tests of statistical significance have no meaning.

It is customary for event studies to consider *all* occurrences of the event under consideration for a period during which it is possible to both identify when and to which firms the event occurred and to measure the market return for the firm when the event occurred. Thus, the "abnormal returns" of the event study are not samples from a universe of abnormal returns; they are the universe itself. Event studies are not *estimating* the effect of the event at issue; they are *measuring* it. Consequently, statistical significance has no meaning. The effect of the event indicated by the mean abnormal return is what it is measured to be; it is not possible for it to be anything different. Whatever it is, there is no chance that it could have been equal to whatever is specified by the null hypothesis.[11]

Still, there are three ways in which event studies might possibly be considered to be samples. The first way is to redefine the universe to include all occurrences of the event. In addition to the events actually used in the study, this includes all other events that occurred in the past that might not be identified and/or for which no adequate quantitative data for testing are available and those that will occur in the future for which no data whatsoever are available. By no stretch of the imagination, however, could the sample of events actually used in the study be considered *random*. These events were all of those that occurred within a limited period of time to firms having characteristics that caused information regarding them to be a part of a select automated data base.[12] This would not be a problem if these events were truly representative of all events, past and future; however, if there were enough information available about the excluded events to satisfactorily determine whether they sufficiently resembled the included events, then they would not have been excluded from the event study.

The second way in which event studies might possibly be considered to be samples is to redefine the universe to include all the impacts of the event that might have occurred but didn't. The observed impacts of the event on the firms to which the event occurred are themselves samples drawn from a universe of impacts that might have occurred to those same firms or would have occurred to other firms had the event occurred to them. This is indeed a complex metaphysical assumption, but it is quite common in finance as it is necessary in order to define risk as a distribution of alternative future values and subsequently measure it as a distribution of realized historical values.[13]

Nonetheless, the assumption is unsatisfactory. Just because one might imagine that something else might have happened does not mean that those imaginary alternatives are real enough to make significance tests meaningful. For example, one might imagine that an election could have turned out differently—the actual outcome having been the result of the infinite number of variable factors that could easily have been quite different. Nonetheless, there is no way of knowing anything at all about this distribution of alternative election results. Again because the sample of events in an event study is not random, there is no way to guarantee that the observed impacts of the event on the selected firms are in any way indicative of this hypothetical universe of alternatives. Even if one were to assume that a distribution of potential impacts is meaningful, the distribution of observed impacts bears no necessary relation to it.

The third way in which event studies might possibly be considered to be samples is to redefine the universe to include all of the impacts as they might have been measured. In event studies the fundamental problem of causal inference is that the event either does or does not occur to some firm at some time, and for those firms to which the event did occur, it is not possible to know what would have happened had the event not occurred. It is necessary to estimate what would have occurred by using a simple linear forecasting model, which in turn is an estimate of a hypothetical "true" model. Event studies estimate a functional relationship between firm returns and market returns, use this to estimate what a firm return would have been had the event not occurred, and then use this to estimate the impact of the event on the firm. It is therefore possible to consider all of the estimated impacts as random samples drawn from a universe of possible estimates of the same impacts.

Much of the voluminous literature on event studies attempts to deal with issues associated with this sequence of estimates. It is far beyond the scope of this chapter to critique these arcane matters; it is sufficient to make the point that the *best* possible outcome of the debate would be the ability to measure precisely what the probability is that the impact of one event at one time on one firm is what it is estimated to be if the real impact of that one event at the same time on the same firm is zero. But even though the logic of statistical inference can be perfectly applied to such a sample, it still cannot be applied to the universe.[14]

In short, the tests of statistical significance in event studies are meaningful only if there is some sort of chance process involved by which a random sample is drawn from a universe. This is true only if all events that occurred within a limited period to firms having characteristics that caused information regarding them to be a part of a select automated data base are representative of all the same category of events that have ever occurred or that will ever occur. Every event study implicitly makes this doubtful assumption, but the mere computation of statistical significance does not mean that the numbers computed are being correctly interpreted.

Statistical significance has a very precise meaning: the probability that the difference between the data predicted by the null hypothesis and the actual data is a consequence of chance, given that the data were obtained from a single sample drawn at random. For example, in event studies, there might be a 5 percent chance that a sample of 100 firms in which the returns of 60 are higher than expected and the returns of 40 are lower than expected was drawn at random from a universe of firms in which expectations are unbiased and the returns of equal numbers of firms are higher and lower than expected.

Although one may be well aware of the correct formal interpretation of statistical significance, it is informally interpreted in a quite different way. The example in the preceding paragraph is taken to mean that there is a 95 percent chance that the theory being tested is a good theory—a good theory being one that both explains why the event has the impact that it does and predicts what the impact will be if the event should occur in the future. This interpretation confounds statistical significance and epistemological significance.[15] Whether a theory is a good theory or not depends on all information bearing on that theory and on the alternatives to that theory; and, in the absence of a logic of induction, there is no single number that can measure the strength of the evidence one way or another. The result of a single event study is merely one piece of information in a larger epistemological puzzle, and the single result is hardly conclusive.[16]

Other Problems with Statistical Significance

Criticism of significance tests has a long history, but the literature is not vast. It is as if the users of these tests are loathe to admit their fallibility. One common theme in all of these criticisms is that there is usually quite a bit of relevant information regarding a theory that is not made public, either inadvertently or deliberately. Although this information cannot affect significance in a very narrow statistical sense, it can affect it very profoundly in a broader epistemological sense.

For event studies, this missing information is of three types. The first is what it was that originally suggested the study (Selvin 1957). Significance is complicated by the use of the same data to discover a theory and to test it. Researchers obtain their theories directly or indirectly from observations of stock market performance and then conduct event studies on the automated records of that same performance. Event studies test the theory that there are more returns that are higher or lower than expected against the null hypothesis that there are equal numbers of returns higher and lower. But the "samples" for many if not most event studies are drawn from the same records of stock market performance in which the researcher or someone else had already "casually" observed that there appeared to be a preponderance of unusually high or unusually low returns. Earlier we referred to this as "data snooping."

The second missing information is results that are not reported (Lovell 1983; Denton 1985). This is the infamous "data mining." In its classical form, it might consist of using a number of different estimates of forecasting models to obtain the "best" estimate of what would have occurred had the event not occurred. Often, forecasting models estimated using data before the event, after the event, and both before and after the event differ considerably in their estimates of the impact.

A variation on data mining peculiar to event studies is using the data to determine when the event occurred. If significance appears prior to the proposed time interval, then it is assumed to mean that the information release that constitutes the event must have happened early. That this was how the event was identified may or may not be reported, but the more places one has to look for significance, the more likely one is to find it.[17] Instead of the event causing significance, significance causes the event.

Still another form of data mining is not documenting nor submitting negative results from an event study. Although such negative results are epistemologically important, they are not worth the effort to explain possible anomalies that contradict the hypothesis one purports to prove to be true.

The third source of missing information is the "publication filter" (Sterling 1959; Tullock 1959; Feige 1975). Negative results are less likely to be published than positive results, although they also provide valuable information regarding a theory—perhaps even more if one is striving for Popperian falsification. Such papers disappear into files when they should become part of the debate. This is the aforementioned "Cordelia's dilemma."

In addition to these data omissions, certain fundamental assumptions of statistical inference are often violated in event studies. First, event studies measure the reactions of markets during periods when certain events are believed to occur. Since firms themselves determine the occurrence of most events, they are the cause and source for selecting themselves into the event study. The impact of the event is a consequence of the event itself and what it was that caused the event to occur when it did. Event studies that question the timing of events are rare and the possibility that the market may be reacting to the same cause that the firm was reacting to when it initiated the event is never considered in sufficient depth.

Second, and more serious, is sample dependence. The reaction of the market to later events must be strongly affected by knowledge of how the market reacted to earlier occurrences of the same events. An event study is like a political poll in which every respondent is told about the responses of earlier respondents before they are asked for their own response. Given that it is the market reaction that is being measured in an event study and there is obvious continuity in important market participants, a more apt analogy would be with a political poll that repeatedly queries the same person.[18] What may have been a more or less random response to an event at some time in the past could quickly have built itself into a self-fulfilling prophesy. Though this feedback effect has no influence on statistical significance, it certainly has an effect on theory justification.

The interpretation of significance tests calls for extreme caution. What appear to be very precise numbers that say a great deal about the theory being tested by an event study are really no such thing. This is recognized by the Newtonian "giants" of statistics, but not by those teetering on their shoulders.[19]

The purpose of any empirical test, event studies included, is to make some definitive statement regarding a theory which in turn, says something about the "real world." But even if one accepts that there are indeed "abnormal returns" and that the hypothesis tests are structured to yield statistics that accurately measure something "real" about the abnormal returns, so many other assumptions underlie event studies that their epistemological contribution is doubtful.

Thus, mathematics as a language is used less in finance to discover the truth than to create the truth. In fact, this is true for language as a whole. In the next chapter, we show how finance has used language in the form of metaphors not to describe reality, but to create reality, and that perhaps, rhetoric is more important in finance than substance.

NOTES

1. More than one commentator has noted that Meyerson's thesis dispels the Platonic mysticism that marvels at the 'unreasonable effectiveness of mathematics in the natural sciences.' The reason mathematics 'works' so well in science is that it is the result of a long and arduous process of adjustment of the formalism to our contingent experience. Meyerson's story goes roughly as follows: Someone proposes some hypothesis, and then a mathematical savant constructs an 'equivalent' statement $H^*(x)$ of the hypothesis, highlighting some mathematical entity x. The Meyersonian tendency then exerts its sway, and x begins to be treated analogously to the general philosophical category of substance: Namely, it is thought to obey some conservation laws. These conservation laws, in turn, provide the accounting framework that enables quantitative manipulation. Somewhere along the line, entity x gets conflated with object x, which becomes associated with all sorts of metaphorical overtones, such as the permanence of natural law, the bedrock of phenomenological reality, the identity of mind and body, and so forth. Then as is frequently the case, some troublesome class of phenomena violates those laws. The repertoire of responses includes the usual range of methods of neutralization of empirical results, generally summarized under the rubric of the Duhem/Quine thesis, but also a more fruitful tactic, which is to modify the mathematical formalisms expressing the hypothesis say to $H'(x)$, which preserves the conservation law while subtly redefining the entity x and perhaps even the object x, but concurrently presenting a new set of formalisms to recast existing theoretical statements. Thus, mathematics does not come to us written indelibly on Nature's Tablets, but rather is the product of a controlled search governed by metaphorical considerations, the premier instance being the heuristics of the conservation principles (Mirowski 1989, p. 6).

2. For example, see Charlesworth (1963). Mirowski (1989) began an entirely new round with his path-breaking historical study of economics' dubious importation of the mathematics of energy in the late nineteenth century.

3. This was discussed in Chapter VII, and is essentially the same idea expressed by Mary Hesse:

> A formal, symbolic language can never be the substitute for thought, because the application of a symbolic method to any empirical matter presupposes very careful analysis of the subject matter…that the essentials have been grasped and properly expressed in language. In other words, it presupposes that work of clarification has already been done…some necessary overtones of meaning are lost when a word is precisely and uniquely symbolized. The vagueness of living languages as compared with mathematics is the price they pay for growth (Klamer and Leonard,p. 10, quoting Mary Hesse, *Science and the Human Imagination*).

4. That mathematics in finance is not science does not preclude it from being useful.

5. The assumptions are mercifully enumerated in a discussion by Eric H. Sorenson (1985).

6. Although this section concerns the unique problems of statistics, we should not forget that it shares the Pythagorean legacy of mathematics.

It is part of our Pythagorean creed to believe that quantification is merely description, but the reverberations of the applications of statistics show how far this claim strays from the mark. These applications have called new objects into being, coined new values, and established new standards of rationality and new claims to authority, It is also part of the Pythagorean creed to believe that with numbers comes certainty" (Gigerenzer et al. 1989, p. 270).

7. One might regard a deterministic universal statement as a statistical universal statement in which X implies Y 100 percent of the time.

8. As a single falsification is logically sufficient for the abandonment of a theory and true theories are more difficult to come by than false ones, it is better for an empirical test to fail to reject a false hypotheses than to reject a true one.

9. As event studies are limited to predicting the direction of unexpected returns, 50 percent accuracy is the absolute minimum.

10. For example, Bakan (1966) divided a large sample of 60,000 subjects by such arbitrary criteria as east versus west of the Mississippi River, and Maine versus the rest of the United States, and obtained in all cases significant differences (although the actual differences in the measurements, the effect sizes, were minimal). As Nunnally (1960, p. 643) put it: "If the null hypothesis is not rejected, it usually is because the N [sample size] is too small. If enough data is gathered, the hypothesis will generally be rejected. If rejection of the null hypothesis were the real intention in psychological experiments, there usually would be no need to gather data" (Gigerenzer et al. 1989, p. 210).

11. Political polling is analogous to event studies. Although the results of a pre-election poll have meaningful *statistical* significance, the results of the election itself do not. The results are the results. The effect is intuitive—as the size of a sample approaches the size of the universe, the sample estimate of an attribute of the universe approaches the true value of the attribute. This is precisely the phenomenon that makes theory confirmation so easy in a traditional event study using a large "sample."

12. It is even rare for event studies to consider how the impact of the event might have changed over the period of time during which all the events in the study occurred.

13. Of the thousands who have made this assumption, the authors know of no one who has acknowledged in writing having done so.

14. For example, consider a very large number of political polls, so large, in fact, that everyone in the population is called once. Even though every one of these polls may be statistically sound and forecast with a confidence interval that means what it appears to mean, the aggregate of these polls is equivalent to the election, for which statistical significance is meaningless.

15. It also stalls the scientific process. Once a theory has been certified as good with 95 percent certainty, it is less likely to be rigorously tested in the future.

16. The extended debate over technical methodological details regarding event studies offers a strong argument in support of the refutability of any study on methodological grounds. As the Duhem-Quine thesis asserts, one can always immunize a theory against refutation with the claim that there were errors in the study and that these errors invalidate it as an empirical test.

17. If significance tests are performed on the "abnormal returns" for each day for 30 days before and 30 days after an event, it is a virtual certainty that the abnormal returns for several days will be statistically significant. There have been truly creative economic explanations for these "random" events.

18. In defense of event studies, one might draw an analogy between them and a political pollster's confronting a person who mumbles. It may be necessary to ask this person the same question over and over in order to form an accurate impression of his or her answer. Of course, like event studies, this is very limited information not necessarily indicative of the entire electorate.

19. In the hands of the experimenters and editors, the hybrid theory often degenerated into a mechanical ritual, although Fisher, Gosset, Neyman, and Pearson had all warned against drawing inferences from tests without judgement. In some fields, a strikingly narrow understanding of statistical significance made a significant result seem to be the ultimate purpose of research, and non-significance the sign of a badly conducted experiment—hence with almost no chance of publication (Gigerenzer et al. 1989, p. 107).

Some refer to this "process" of finding significance, come hell or high water, as "hostage taking;" that is a process in which the editor and reviewer(s) force the author(s) to make changes in their tests, until significance is obtained.

Chapter X

The Language of Finance:
A Duality of Culture

Philosophy Master:	*Quite so, sir. All that is not prose is poetry; and all that is not poetry is prose.*
M. Jourdain:	*And when a man talks what's that?*
Philosophy Master:	*Prose.*
M. Jourdain:	*What? When I say "Nicole, bring me my slippers and give me my nightcap," that's prose?*
Philosophy Master:	*Yes, sir.*
M. Jourdain:	*Well, I'll be hanged. For more than forty years I've been talking prose without any idea of it; I am very much obliged to you for telling me that.*

—Moliére, Le Bourgeois Gentilhomme, Act II.

"Language is the most potent tool of a lawyer," a well-known attorney once remarked. It seems that this declaration holds true for the cadres of practitioners in the many branches of social sciences, as well. It is true that we have high-speed computers, capable of "digesting" massive volumes of data (evaluating millions of mathematical expressions in a second),[1] and that we have "models" to funnel these data through, as well as other tools of the trade. These "instruments" notwithstanding, what is said and how it is said remain the critical tools by which opinions are influenced and with which elites perpetuate their power and control the field.

In this chapter, we discuss the deceptiveness and duplicity of such language, the rigid confines of its application, and how it is being used for the self-preservation of those who invent, embrace, and uphold a leading paradigm. We begin with some basic definitions.

FIGURES OF SPEECH

Figures of speech extend the meaning of a word or phrase beyond its ordinary, literal sense in order to make a striking point or a vivid image.

In essence, figures of speech can be succinctly defined as word imagery that makes a direct appeal to the reader's senses. Used appropriately, figures of speech can contribute to the effectiveness of the writing in which it appears. Used inappropriately, they create an impression of artificiality or deceptiveness.

Briefly, the most common figures of speech can be grouped in three categories: figures of comparison, figures of contrast, and figures of association.

The figures of comparison are *simile, metaphor,* and *personification.* A *simile,* the simplest of the three, states the comparison explicitly, without extended reference; for example, "He is like a bear." In this example, the bear is still just a bear, and we understand that the man is simply like the bear in certain respects, such as temperament, power, ferocity, and so forth. In a *metaphor,* the comparison is not stated explicitly, but implied; for example, "Oh, he is a rat!" Here, the reference is a deeper, more extended one, implying more than just a passing similarity. If the metaphorical comparison is extended, it must be carried out consistently. Otherwise, the result is likely to be what is called a *mixed metaphor,* as in "The sacred cows have come home to roost."

A special kind of metaphor is *personification,* in which a non-human thing is compared by implication to a human being. Personification is frequently used, for example in describing the work of the computer. We say, for example, that a computer reads, writes, and searches its memory. There are no such things! Computers do not read, or write, or remember things in the sense human beings do. Computers make magnetic marks in media and retrieve those marks from media to display by means understandable by humans. Other things equal, the more mythical is the work of the machine, the more humans personify what it does.

Another example in finance is the personification of the ever-powerful market, the avatar of God in neoclassical economics. We are told, for example, that the market "rewards'" "favorably reacts," "punishes," and "disciplines." Markets, of course, do no such things. They are personified to cleverly reinforce beliefs in the superiority of the market as a mechanism for controlling life as we know it in finance.

The figures of contrast, used less frequently in finance, are *irony* (extension of meaning in a direction opposite to the normal one), *hyperbole* (overstatement), and *litotes* (understatement).

The figures of association are *metonymy* and *synecdoche.* In *metonymy,* the meaning of the word is extended from its ordinary referent to something associated with the referent, and it is often used to symbolize an entire situation or concept. "The pen is mightier than the sword" is a metonymic proverb, meaning that the written word can accomplish more than physical fighting; or, extending the reference one step further, that ideas are more influential than physical violence. Other examples include "Washington" for the U.S. government; "Moscow" for Russia; "the law" for the legal system (the police, the courts, etc.).

In *synecdoche*, the association is of a more particular kind: a part of something is made to stand for the whole, or the whole for the part. Examples may include "a talking head," a person who appears in talk-shows; "threads," meaning garment, or suit; and a "hand," as in a farm worker.

The language of finance is rife with figures of speech, but there is a distinct and observable dichotomy: the finance academician's language is full of metaphors, whereas the finance practitioner's language is full of other types of figures of speech.

How and why these two languages developed and what is distinct about them is the subject of discussion later in this chapter. First, we will survey the jargon of the "Street";[2] then, because of their importance and ideological significance, consider the use of metaphors in academic finance.

THE JARGON OF THE STREET

Every profession, without exception, creates its own jargon; that is, a vocabulary of technical terms and acronyms peculiar to that profession.[3] In addition of expediting communication among the practitioners of the profession, jargon creates an aura of mystery incomprehensible to the outsiders. This mystification clearly has a wealth-maximization objective. Through the use of complex and indecipherable terminology, practitioners—whether in finance, law, automotive repair, or plumbing—can charge outsiders an inflated fee for services that, plainly stated, might not fetch so high a remuneration.

Finance practitioners, like other professionals, have developed their own jargon, rich in figures of speech. Two factors contribute to the increasing richness of the finance jargon: the evolution of new financial products and activities, and the diverse background of the practitioners themselves.[4] Financial jargon borrows its "flowers" from several walks of life. The following expressions, for example, are derived from house or home:

House	Investment firm, bank, or hospitality establishment such as a hotel, pub, or bar
Bank	From Italian *banco*, bench, the furniture on which money-changers used to conduct business
Seat	Exchange membership
Off-the-shelf	From shelf registration/preregistration
Junk	Very risky security
Garage	One of the NYSE's trading arenas

Curb	AMEX
Chinese wall	A partition that creates a separated area of a brokerage house on the exchange floor
Out the window	A lost deal
Goes through the roof	Price is increasing beyond expectations
Glass ceiling	A barrier, usually in front of women put up to prevent them from reaching top positions, showing them all the while what they could have been
Hit bottom	Reach the lowest price
Pipeline	Deals waiting to be marketed
Over-the-counter	Stocks not traded on a physically locatable exchange
Find a home	To find a buyer for something
Get out	Waiting to sell
Take a bath	Lose a great deal

Other expressions, derived from hunting and gathering; for instance:

Lame duck	One who cannot escape demise
Sitting duck	One who is incapable to act, because of constraints put on him/her
Play dead	Pretend to disregard the issue or problem
Bullish	A person who is optimistic about the market
Bearish	A person who is pessimistic about the market[5]
Killer bee	Banker or lawyer who sets out to make a firm an easy target for takeover
Cats and dogs	Firms with bad fundamentals
Paper tiger	Not a real threat
Taking the bait	Falling for a trick

Others come from the tradition of a seafaring and fishing heritage:

Come on board	Join the ranks of top executives of the firm
Loose cannon	A person out of control; one capable of inflicting damage on innocent bystanders
Sharks	Corporate raiders
Shark repellent	A tactic devised to thwart "sharks"

Others come from such diverse sources as fairy tales, sports, or superstition:

Blue chip	The highest value chips in poker; hence a high quality stock

Out of the blue	Something unexpected
Pink sheet	Issues over the counter
Gilt-edged	Covered with gold, of the highest value
Greenmail	Stock offered for a favorable price to selected holders
Red herring	Preliminary prospectus of a security[6]
Black ink	Making profits
Red ink	Losing money
Golden Parachute[7]	Clause in executive contract to compensate them in case of a takeover
Painting the tape	Performing fake trades in order to increase the price of a stock
Corporate raiders	Takeover artists
Fallen angel	Once highly acclaimed, now out of grace
White knight	A third party who is sought out by incumbent management to make a bid for the firm, to prevent the hostile takeover group from carrying out its plan
Sleeping beauty	A firm with good fundamentals that is not recognized by the market
Poison pill	Very costly tactics used by a firm to derail a hostile takeover already in progress
Crown jewels	The firm's most desirable assets
Triple witching hour	The time at each quarter when options, index options, and future contracts expire
Fill or kill orders	Orders that are canceled if they cannot be executed
Hit	An accepted bid
Tombstone adds	Announcement of completed investment banking deals
Dog and pony show	Introduction of new products/stocks
Cash cow	A firm with lots of idle cash, or one that generates a lot of cash regularly

Some even have a slight sexual overtone, such as:

Naked option	An option not covered by a long position
Stripping bonds	Separating the interest from the principal of a bond
Hot issues	A new issue with a great deal of oversubscription

Clearly, some of the terms reflect the dynamics of the times. For example, most of the metaphors of corporate takeovers entered the jargon during the 1980's. The word *curb*, on the other hand is from another era and is rarely used today to describe the AMEX.[8] In brief, then, Wall Street's figures of speech are food for the imagination—sustenance to fuel vivid images, depicting the concepts they proxy for. Wall Street jargon is not ideological; that is, it is not used to support a theory or logic, or to take sides in a debate. The ideological metaphors are the ones used in the academic language of finance.

METAPHORS IN FINANCE

Metaphors in the natural and social sciences are a means by which complex ideas and subjects can be visually and succinctly communicated. Anne Eisenberg (1992) provides an excellent discussion of how metaphors have proliferated in the sciences and the apparent reasons for this proliferation. But, as Eisenberg points out, there are problems with metaphors—problems that were recognized quite early by philosophers such as Hobbes and Locke.

According to Hobbes, "Such [inconstant] names can never be true grounds of any ratiocination" (1992). Unfortunately, in financial economics metaphors not only become "... true grounds for ratiocination," but in some instances, also take on a life of their own. In this section, we review the misuse of metaphors and discuss how this misuse fuels misinterpretation of event studies in particular.

Catch-All Metaphors in Finance

Metaphors in the social sciences can be useful imports of concepts from other sciences, but they also have the power and ability to reduce the problem one intends to solve or to illustrate to a level that becomes a precarious simplification. For example, George Lakoff (1991), in an essay titled "Metaphor and War," writes:

> The Metaphorical understanding of a situation functions in two parts .... First, there is a widespread, relatively fixed set of metaphors that structure how we think. For example, the decision to go to war might be seen as a form of cost-benefit analysis, where war is justified when the costs of going to war are less than the costs of not going to war. Second, there is a set of metaphorical definitions that allow one to apply such a metaphor to a particular situation (Lakoff 1991).

It is the second part, as will be shown later, that makes the first part so hazardous.

A worst-case misuse of metaphors in financial economics[9] can be found in Miller's (1977) presidential address to the American Finance Association.

Miller calls phenomena that are unexplainable by prevailing theory or broadly held beliefs "neutral mutations." Miller's motivation is clear. If he called the unexplainable an anomaly, the term that is most fitting, albeit unmetaphorical, he would have exposed the weakness of a theory that was first posited by him and was widely held by many in academe at the time. The theory had been accepted in spite of the fact that no empirical verification could be found and that simple observation of firms' leverage indicated the opposite of the theory's prediction.

Use of the metaphor "neutral mutation," a misapplied concept borrowed from biology, gave the aura of scientific credibility to a fallacious abstraction. As a consequence, the principle of wealth maximization was not compromised, the Miller (1977) modification of the original Modigliani and Miller (1958) theory was justified, and an easy way out of the conflict between observation and theory was invented.

The reader should not infer from the critical tone of this argument that the authors of this book do not recognize the great intellectual contribution of Miller to the development of the field of finance. Issue is taken here not with the defensibility of the original theory and its subsequent modification, but with the use of a device to cover up for what is unexplained or unexplainable. Fortunately, this particular metaphor did not create its own clientele. Perhaps the reader should be satisfied by Hobbes' remark that it could not be looked upon by other writers as "... true grounds for ratiocination."

Another example of an equally misleading and a much more arrogant metaphor is "the market for corporate control." Markets are first and foremost physical places. If there is not always a one-on-one physical correspondence between a market and the commodity (be it potatoes or labor), it is because of the development of communication and other electronic devices that do not require buyers and sellers to be in a certain place at a given time. Nevertheless, the ways and means by which exchange (and whatever is connected with it) takes place are well defined and known to all market participants.

A physical "market for corporate control" *per se* is nowhere to be found. There is no place where exchange would take place, no indication that those who vie for such control perceive it as a market and no two-sided transactions, the existence of which is one of the fundamental principles of theories of financial activities. The metaphor of a "market for corporate control" is the creation of those who subscribe to a certain theory of efficiency that in their minds pervades anything people do, including the struggle for corporate control. The use of the metaphor is tantamount to subscribing to the theory that underlies it.

Consequently, the "market for corporate control" metaphor becomes a necessary fiction to the true believers of the paradigm. It is the logical consequence of the underlying theory according to which value cannot exist without a market. And if there is a market that sets value, then there must exist a price. In order to justify valuing corporate control, it is necessary to hypothesize a market for it. Once one starts calling something a market, one must importune a number of other attributes of a real market that are either inapplicable or meaningless. This is precisely the functioning of the second part of Lakoff's definition.

A more pervasive metaphor in the financial economics literature is "signaling." This is a case where the word itself has taken on its own life and created its own literature. Thus, the second function of the metaphorical situation *á la* Lakoff's definition is more predominant. The origin of the word is in a seminal paper by Spence (1973), who develops a model for a very specific, well-defined and constrained situation in which signals are exchanged between an interviewer (the signalee) and a job-seeker (the signaler).

Later, Spence's idea, along with some additional mathematical fortification (Nash equilibrium) and a whole set of unrealistic assumptions, is transplanted into the corporation finance literature by Ross (1977), Bhattacharya (1979), Miller and Rock (1985), John and Williams (1985) and many others, too numerous to mention. Since then, signaling has become an end in itself, rather than what it was originally intended to be: the explanation of a phenomenon that otherwise cannot be explained by prevailing economic rationality (i.e., why firms select higher leverage than others, why they pay dividends, etc.).

In today's financial economics jargon (both written and spoken), whatever management does is "signaling."[10] Managers do not make decisions because of economic, institutional, and/or (corporate) cultural considerations. They do so because their intention is to "signal" something to the market—usually outsiders, but, in many instances, to their own shareholders. To the best of the knowledge of the authors, there is not a single study that attempts to verify that signaling was management's original intention and that it was clear both to management, and to the best of their understanding, to the signalees that the signalees decoded the signal properly. By conjuring up signaling, financial economists can preserve the value-maximization principle and deny the existence of another rationality. If managers were really signaling, at least one manager would have told someone about it somewhere along the line and there would be nothing special about it. Financial economics has a vested interest in creating metaphors such as signaling to preserve the illusion of scientific progress.

Event studies are routinely used to verify that indeed signaling took place; yet, there is never the slightest effort at an alternative or parallel verification through the simple expedient of asking at least some of the parties involved about signaling. This prohibition on direct inquiry occurs even when there are no incentives for the parties to lie or to conceal the fact that the true intention was to signal rather than to communicate more explicitly

Furthermore, there might exist a set of alternative hypotheses that could explain the results of the event study as well as the signaling hypothesis. Needless to say, no attempt is made to enumerate all or even most of the competing explanations (in essence, other *ad hoc* hypotheses).

The propensity of academic elites to create jargon of their own is well observed. Jargon is widely used to enhance the importance of the profession in the eyes of the layman, usually in face-to-face communication. In financial economics, however, the jargon is used in written communication just as often as it is in oral communication, and it is used among the intellectual elite even when the need to enhance the importance of the profession in the eyes of the layman is neither existent nor justified.

"Abnormal Returns—A Possible Mumpsimus?"[11]

> ... *on a cloth untrue, with a twisted cue and elliptical billiard balls."*— From the Mikado's song *"Let the Punishment Fit the Crime,"* Gilbert and Sullivan.

The core metaphor in event studies is the "abnormal return"; however, the metaphor seems to have drifted into common usage rather than having been explicitly created. Although they performed the first event study, Fama, Fisher, Jensen, and Roll (1969) cannot be unequivocally credited with (nor blamed for) the "abnormal return" metaphor. Although these authors do not expressly refer to "abnormal returns" *per se*, they do lay the foundation for others to create the metaphor. They write, "The average residual can be interpreted as the average deviation... of the returns of split stocks from their normal relationships with the market" (p. 8). Later, they add "... there are a few months for which the residuals are abnormally large and positive" (p. 20). Generally, however, they refer to the market model parameters as "... reflect(ing) the 'normal' relation between that stock and the market."

Around the same time in the accounting literature, Ball and Brown (1968) refer to an "abnormal performance index" that resembles, but is not exactly, "cumulative abnormal returns." There appears to be a contradiction here with Fama's (1991) attributing the origin of the event study method to his coauthored 1969 paper. In all likelihood, however, Ball and Brown were familiar with an earlier draft of the 1969 work. The Ball and Brown (1968) study appeared first as a result of a shorter time span between submission and publication.

Benston's (1967) supports this argument. Benston (1967) is fully aware of the "forthcoming" paper by Fama et al., quotes their relevant and supportive conclusions, and uses their "market" model to calculate some of his variables.

The first event study, to the best of our knowledge, is by Ashley (1962), however. Ashley develops the idea of "good" and "bad" events, the market's reaction to these events and tests of a null hypothesis of no difference between average rates of return for the "good" and "bad" sample of firms. However statistically "primitive," the Ashley paper has all the conspicuous elements of an event study. Ashley is quoted, in a different context, by Benston (1967), but not by Fama et al.

Nonetheless, the true promoters of the idea of event studies were, according to mavens of the inner workings of the University of Chicago, Harry Roberts and Lawrence Fisher. Fisher was the primary driving force behind the development of the CRSP data bank, creating another example of the workings of supply-side economics. As insider information has it, the original suggestion of using residual returns as the dependent variable came from Roberts, an amazingly creative statistician. Fama et al. were just shrewd middle-men, who, as usually happens, make the bulk of the profit on a successful product.

How it is possible that Ball and Brown (1968) do not mention either Benston (1967) or Fama et al. is a question left for those who are more interested in academic politics than historical evolution. By 1972, however, the metaphor is clearly being used. Scholes (1972) prefers "prediction errors" to "residuals" (p. 189), but specifically defines his cumulative measure as an "Abnormal Performance Index" and refers to it as a measure of "abnormal return" (p. 190).

The important question, however, is what difference does it make that "CARs" stood for "cumulative average residuals" in the earliest event studies and now stand for "cumulative abnormal returns?"[12] Consider the structure of the bivariate ordinary least squares (OLS) model as described by Johnston (1963). In figure 1-2 of the chapter titled "The Two-Variable Linear Model," he labels the line that meets the OLS requirements as $\alpha + \beta X$. Then he explains:

> The practical situation then is that we have n pairs of sample observations on X, Y, which can be represented on a scatter diagram as in Figure 1-2 above. The essential difference from that figure is that in practice the line $\alpha + \beta X$ is unknown. Instead we have a set of *hypotheses* (our emphasis).

$$Y_i = \alpha + \beta X_i + \mu_i \qquad i = 1,2, \ldots\ldots, n$$
$$E(\mu_i) = 0 \qquad \text{for all } i$$

$$E(\mu_i \mu_j) = \begin{cases} 0 & \text{for } i \neq j; \ i,j = 1,2,\ldots\ldots, n \\ \\ \\ \sigma^2 \mu & \text{for } i = j; \ i,j = 1,2,\ldots\ldots, n \end{cases} \qquad (1\text{-}5)^{[13]}$$

In (1-5) μ_i is called *disturbance term* (or stochastic term) in the true but unobservable relation $\alpha + \beta X_i$ which is based on all the assumptions of (1-5).

The shift from disturbance term to residuals is not simple. Residuals exist only in sample space, if and only if all the assumptions made in (1-5) hold and when the unknown parameters α, and β, in (1-5) are estimable as $\hat{\alpha}$, and $\hat{\beta}$. To do so, the principles of OLS are invoked and, as a consequence a residual term, e_i, is defined. This residual term is the vertical difference between the observed value of the dependent variable and its expected value as prescribed by the corresponding value of the independent variable and the parameter estimates: $\hat{\alpha}$, and $\hat{\beta}$.

The innocuous technical term *residual* has nothing to do with abnormality. On the contrary, it is a very normal part of the two layers of assumptions that are necessary for its conceptualization. The first layer is the estimate of the "true" relationship; the second layer is the use of this estimated relationship to estimate the value of interest. This is the parlance used in the first event studies article, but, at the same time, the authors of that article imply that, by aggregating these terms in a certain way for a certain subset of economic units, one can infer something about the economic relationship "... of the returns of split stocks from their normal relationships with the market."

The objective of event studies is to measure the difference between the actual returns and the returns that would have been observed had the event not occurred. To do so requires a set of assumptions paralleling the two layers: first that it is possible to estimate the "true" relationship between stock returns and the returns on the market; second, that the difference between the actual returns and the returns predicted by the "true" relationship measures the "true" impact of the event (the "disturbance term" or "abnormal return"); and third, that it is possible to estimate the "true" impact (the "disturbance term" or the "abnormal return") using the difference between the actual return and the return predicted by the estimated relationship (the "residual term").

There is nothing "abnormal" about a "disturbance term"; in fact, the 'disturbance term" can be quite large even when the event has no predictable impact. Furthermore, it is well known that the probability of an observed value in OLS to be exactly equal to the expected value is zero, with the exception of the trivial case when the number of observations equals the number of parameters to be estimated. There is nothing abnormal about "residual terms" either. Why, then, has there been such a hasty shift from "residuals" to "abnormal returns"? When the metaphor is used thus, it implies that the theory on which it builds is true and that there is something that is indeed different or peculiar or *abnormal* about returns as a result of the event.

The Dangerous Metaphor—The Implicit Equilibrium Assumption

Event studies are supposed to measure the deviation in return caused by the event from what would have been realized as return *sans* event. This deviation is called an "abnormal return." In reality, what one can observe is the actual return. The assumption that the abnormal return is the difference between what one observes and what the expected value is (without the event, given the model and its parameter estimates) constitutes an implicit assumption of equilibrium.[14] This is so because only at equilibrium would one expect to obtain exactly the expected value. The fact that deviations from the observed are calculated based on an expected value goes beyond the already questionable assumption of homogeneous expectations, a necessary but not sufficient condition for equilibrium.[15]

It is well known that the probability of an observed value being exactly equal to the expected value of a forecasting model is zero. If one presupposes that such probability is unity, one must assume that the market is in total and perfect harmony. An example may clarify this point. Say one uses the Markowitz-Sharpe portfolio model. One estimates alpha, beta and variance values for each stock of one's universe and the expected value and variance for a market index (the common underlying factor). Portfolio decisions will be based on these expected values. But these are used as forecasts and any deviation ex-post from these forecasts is not only accepted but also considered as an inevitable result of two sources of bias built into the model: (1) estimation bias, and (2) selection bias. The former is due to the nature of the estimator function and the latter is due to the selection algorithm. Both biases are by-products of model deficiency.

In event studies, any deviation from the expected value is termed "abnormal." Thus, it is out of the ordinary (where "ordinary" would have been precisely the expected value for all). That is, not just economic agents have homogeneous expectations (meaning that they have the same estimator functions with the same parameters), but that they all expect the same value for a given period. This is possible if and only if the forecast value reflects an equilibrium value. But when has the economy ever been at equilibrium?

Metaphors are powerful because they are simple to follow and to use for visualizing complex ideas and concepts, but this simplicity is what makes them dangerous as well. To quote Paul Valery (*Introduction to the Method of Leonardo da Vinci*—from Bartlett's *Familiar Quotations*): "The folly of mistaking a metaphor for a discovery, a metaphor for a proof, a torrent of verbiage for a spring of capital truths, and oneself for an oracle, is inborn in us." This is precisely what has occurred with regard to event studies.

"Abnormal returns," which is a misnomer at best and a downright fabrication at worst, has become a part of the finance jargon. Today, it does not matter a bit that the very same people who invented and propagated the metaphor have now denounced the market model, $R_i = a + bR_m$, from which "abnormal returns" are computed.[16] The metaphor keeps the concept alive, even though the "true" relationship that gave it birth seems to have been largely discredited.

In the preceding and this section, we have shown that practitioners have a very colorful language, and that academics have a very ideological one. One can enumerate more examples of these differences than we have done here, but the ultimate point is not how many examples one can come up with to make the case, but the significance of the difference. Does the difference between practitioners and academics run deeper than language? This question is addressed in the next section.

THE DUALITY OF THE LANGUAGE—ACADEMIC FINANCE AND PRACTITIONER FINANCE

There is academic finance and practitioner finance. There must be. After all, at one time or another, everyone in the field has declared or heard it declared with certainty and with feeling that some piece of written work is "academic finance" or "practitioner finance." When it comes to attaching the correct label, one knows it when one sees it—not unlike the notorious tongue-in-cheek definition of pornography.

How is it possible to recognize academic finance and practitioner finance? And why does the difference matter? There are three attributes of writing by which distinctions are made. The first is content; that is, its purpose or the issues, matters, or problems that it addresses. Academic finance concerns itself with the discovery and justification of theory; practitioner finance focuses on the application of theory. The second is method; that is, the approach, process, or technique by which the purpose is accomplished, the issue or matter is analyzed, or the problem is solved. Academic finance uses complex, sophisticated methods accessible only to those who have undergone advanced training in mathematics; practitioner finance uses comparatively simple, unsophisticated methods readily accessible to anyone with some experience in finance. The third is style, or the form of expression. Academic finance is symbolic and concise, with a fixed and very specific format; practitioner finance is verbal and comparatively drawn out, with a varying and unpredictable format.

There are no necessary associations among the three attributes. Theory need not be complex and sophisticated, nor must it be expressed in symbols. Application need not be simple and unsophisticated, nor must it be expressed in words. Clearly, the nature of the problem (the epistemology) ought to determine how it is solved (the method) and how that solution is communicated (the style). For many problems in finance, whose nature is fundamentally cultural, it may be wholly inappropriate that the problem be "solved" using an abstruse mathematical formulation and presented as a formal proof. Any work might appropriately combine academic and practitioner attributes.

"Academic finance" and "practitioner finance" are more than terms that can be applied independently to content, method, and style. They are two distinct cultures. The scholarly culture of academic finance is about the mind and thought. It is a "hard science" concerning factual judgments and testable facts. It is explanation and discovery. It must be expressed in a symbolic form accessible only to initiates. Regardless, however camouflaged, it is about control and exploitation: who is allowed to say what and when (as by imprimatur), who are the leaders and who are the followers—a process that had been termed "organized skepticism" by Robert C. Merton, but which evolved rather into the perpetuation of schools of thought.

The contrasting culture of practitioner finance is about the body and action. It a "soft art" often concerning value judgments and non-testable feelings. It must be expressed in words accessible to a mass audience. From the start, it is unconcealed control and exploitation.

As it is the editorial policy of journals to serve only one culture, writing must be clearly identified as belonging wholly to one or the other culture in order to be published.[17] Not only must the content, method, and style all be academic or all be practitioner, but they must also be unambiguously so. It is possible to recognize academic and practitioner finance so easily because, if it were not so easy to attach a label to a piece of writing, it would not have been published. It matters so much because it is necessary for both the work and its author to be part of a culture.

These answers lead to more provocative questions. Is this distinction between academic finance and practitioner finance meaningful? What is it of content, method, or style that is most important in making the distinction? What are the implications of having not merely separate literatures, but discrete cultures? Although a difference based on content may be meaningful or at least provocative, as a similar distinction in economics has been since John Neville Keynes' (1955) definition of normative and positive, this is not how the separation is made. Rather, the peculiarity is based on mathematics— not mathematics as method, but mathematics as style; not mathematics as science, but mathematics as art for art's sake.[18] This is indeed an insubstantial basis for a cultural divide that has proscribed numerous research opportunities that could surely contribute to a greater understanding of finance.

As a parallel, consider *Market Volatility* (Shiller 1990), a compendium of his highly regarded work on that subject. In the introduction of this work Robert Shiller contrasts economic models and popular models. According to Shiller's thoughtful reflection on the two cultures:

... popular models are the models of the economy held by the general public. These are not systems of equations, as are economists' models. As with popular music or popular periodicals, popular models are usually simple, unsophisticated, and spontaneous. Popular models consist of qualitative descriptions of causes, anecdotes as suggestions of what may happen, and presumed correlations, cycles, or other simple patterns. Associated with the transmission and implementation of popular models are patterns of investor behavior: communications patterns, reaction lags, habits, and social norms.... Popular models cause people to react incorrectly to economic data, and changing popular models cause price movements that bear no relation to fundamentals (1990, pp. 3-4).

The expressed and implied contrasts between economic models and popular models in the order in which they appear in this passage are:

Economic Models	Popular Models
Systems of Equations	Qualitative Descriptions
Complex	Simple
Sophisticated	Unsophisticated
Considered	Spontaneous
Comprehensive	Anecdotal
Statistical Patterns and Relations	Presumed Patterns and Relations
Complex Patterns	Simple Patterns
Instantaneous Comprehension	Lagged Reaction
Rational Responses Correct Reaction	Habits and Social Norms Incorrect Reaction
Rational Price Movements	Irrational Price Movements

Whitley (1986) considers the post-World War II history of the scholarly discipline of finance. He describes a transformation from business finance to financial economics that is effectively the replacement of one of the two cultures with another. His reflections on the transformation suggest a number of contrasts between the two cultures:

Financial Economics	Business Finance
Abstract and Formal Language	Ordinary Language
Restricted to Professionally Trained Researchers	No Specialized Training to Understand

Neoclassical Economics	Institutional Economics
More Scientific	Less Scientific
High Degree of	Low Degree of
Formalization/	Formalization/
Standardization	Standardization
Mathematical	Verbal
Valuation Processes	Operations of Particular
in Perfect Markets	Financial Institutions
Abstract	Descriptive
Theoretical	Practical
Idealized Problems	Real Problems

The two cultures are usually found in different institutional settings. The terms *academic finance* and *practitioner finance* themselves are naturally associated with universities and with profit-making enterprises, respectively.[19] What is of greater importance, however, is what the cultures are and not where they are, and what the cultures are is found in their writings. As discussed earlier in this chapter, there are apparent differences in content, method, and style, and most of the contrasts in the preceding subsection concern these three attributes. A number of contrasts, however, appear to concern a fourth attribute—how the two cultures view the world.

World View and Content

Although a number of contrasts between academic finance and practitioner finance clearly appear to concern differences between their perceptions of the world, it is questionable whether that world view really represents an attribute different from content or method. There are three ways to view the simplifications that distinguish the world view of academic finance from that of practitioner finance: (1) as negligibility assumptions (factors that have no effect on the truth of a theory), (2) as domain assumptions (factors that define the conditions for the truth of the theory), or (3) as heuristic assumptions (factors that are convenient for development of theory) (Musgrave 1981).

If the simplifications are the result of negligibility assumptions, then academic finance and practitioner finance have essentially the same world views, differing only in the minor matter of whether certain parts of the world are important enough to be considered. For example, both acknowledge the importance of investor expectations, but one assumes that differences in expectations among investors matter very little and can be ignored, whereas the other assumes that the differences can be significant.

If the simplifications are the result of domain assumptions, then academic finance and practitioner finance have totally different world views. In effect, they are concerned with different issues, matters, or problems; that is, different worlds. The content of their writings is substantially different. For example, one produces explanations that apply only when expectations are homogeneous; the other produces explanations that apply when expectations are heterogeneous as well.

If the simplifications are the result of heuristic assumptions, then they were made by academic finance for methodical (i.e., concerning method) reasons to transform complex problems into mathematically tractable ones. For example, the assumption of homogeneous expectations is merely a first step toward a more comprehensive theory incorporating heterogeneous expectations. Either the two cultures have essentially the same world view (simplifications are negligibility assumptions), or else the differences between their world views are matters of content (simplifications are domain assumptions) or method (simplifications are heuristic assumptions).

The preceding contended that, if the simplifications made by academic finance are domain assumptions, then there are substantial differences in content between academic and practitioner finance. Nowhere in the finance literature, however, does any author argue that academic finance is meant to apply only to a world in which such simplifications are literally true. Most authors would argue with Milton Friedman (1953) that the simplifications are negligibility assumptions meant to reduce a problem to its essentials, or with Karl Popper (1964) that the simplifications are heuristic assumptions meant to provide a simple starting point to be built on until a theory achieves sufficient realism—both sufficient explanatory and predictive power.

Is it really possible to make a meaningful distinction between description, explanation, theory, thought and laws and prescription, recommendation, practice, policy, action, and rules? The distinction between positive and normative, between what is and what ought to be, has never been considered as explicitly in finance as it has been in economics. As we have shown, even in the most famous works of finance concerning the Nobel prize-winning CAPM, there is considerable ambiguity about whether the authors consider their model to be positive or normative, and perceptions appear to have changed over time.

The very logic of inquiry in finance precludes a sharp distinction. Traditionally, practitioner finance is thought to "follow" academic finance, transforming descriptive, explanatory, theoretical laws into prescriptions of recommended rules for practice and policy. The theoretical laws, however, must have had empirical confirmation in order to have become laws; therefore, it must be that the recommended rules were already being followed. If normative follows positive, then in a practical sense, normative is valueless—one ought merely to continue to do what one is already doing. A positive theory can have normative value if it concerns whether one prescription "works" better than another; however, what it means for a prescription to "work" is itself a normative decision.

Since academic finance simplifications are not domain assumptions and since there is no unambiguous difference between positive and normative, academic finance and practitioner finance have essentially the same content. Hence, only method and style remain as bases for distinguishing one from the other.

Method

Academic finance is an objective science using sophisticated mathematics to discover theories of financial behavior and using statistics to test for the resulting complex patterns and relationships with ever-increasing volumes of data. Practitioner finance is a subjective art in which the unsophisticated assert simple patterns on the strength of limited casual observations and other anecdotal evidence. Are the two really so different as these contrasts make them appear?

Consider theory justification or empirical academic finance. Although sophisticated statistical tests performed on a large volume of data appear to be serious scientific attempts at validation, they are nothing of the sort. The structure and interpretation of such tests are severely biased in favor of finding whatever complex pattern or relationship one is looking for. The preceding chapter detailed this for event studies.

Even if tests were honestly structured, there is no way that a t-statistic showing significance at the five percent level would reflect on the *quality* of a theory. When one considers sample biases, several varieties of data mining, publication filters, and a host of other econometric intricacies and restrictive test assumptions that are usually violated, it is obvious that the numbers that result from all but the very simplest statistical procedures have no objective meaning that anyone is capable of asserting with any certainty. The conclusions of the Byzantine statistics of academic finance are unequivocally ad hoc. More importantly, a survey of the empirical literature on any issue in finance clearly shows that there is not now, nor has there ever been, such a thing as a definitive empirical test.

If there are no definitive empirical tests, what constitutes theory justification? The social history of the CAPM, outlined in Chapter VI, leaves no doubt that it is the perfectly subjective criterion of whether a theory makes sense. Although there have been few studies unequivocally supporting the CAPM, numerous studies rejecting the CAPM, and a strong argument that the CAPM was untestable and none of the studies meant anything (Roll 1977), the CAPM survives in all finance textbooks.

No matter how sophisticated the mathematics, all academic finance, both theoretical and empirical, ultimately means just what anyone wants it to mean. There is nothing factual, objective, or scientific about it. It is part and parcel of a value-laden, opinion-laden, subjective art, just as practitioner finance is alleged to be.[20] It is ad hoc in every sense of the word. This leaves only style to distinguish academic finance from practitioner finance.

Style

It is usually not even necessary to read a piece of finance writing in order to know whether it is academic finance or practitioner finance—the two not only look different at a glance, but are also printed on different paper.[21] When it comes to attaching the correct label, one knows it when one sees it. Academic finance has many long equations, fewer words, much white space on a page, and large numbers of footnotes and bibliographic references. Practitioner finance has fewer, shorter equations, more words, little white space on a page, and few if any footnotes and bibliographic references. Of course, on closer examination, there are other stylistic differences regarding word choice, illustrations, and the clarity and complexity of graphs and charts.

The most salient stylistic differences, however, have to do with the presence or absence of mathematics, but as we argued previously, the mathematics serves no scientific, methodical purpose. Metaphysical mathematics serves as the primary indicator in the writing of academic finance and as the centerpiece of the culture of academic finance.

CONCLUSIONS

Academic finance and practitioner finance coexist as two cultures. Each has its own journals, and what the cultures are is to be found in the writings that appear in these journals. The writings of both cultures cannot be distinguished by their content or by their method. They can be distinguished only by their style, and this style is largely a matter of the presence or absence of mathematics. It is the metaphysical, mystical power that mathematics has had since Plato and Pythagoras that has made it the *sine qua non* of academic finance.

Why should this matter? First, it is far too easy to mistake numerology for science when definitive tests are impossible. The two were virtually interchangeable until Newton and Galileo, and distinguishable thereafter only as a result of the successes of mathematics in the physical sciences. Many, if not most, of the applications of mathematics to the social sciences in general and to finance in particular have been a return to numerology without being recognized as such. Scientific method and numerological method can look very much the same, and only a thorough methodological analysis might tell them apart. Alas, methodology is not considered a fit topic for either academic or practitioner finance—the former not for its philosophical *method* and the latter not for its philosophical content. With its fixation on style, academic finance is left believing that it knows far more than it actually does.

Second, crucial issues that cannot be deformed into some sort of mathematical treatment are not addressed, for without a mathematical *method*, there can be no academic *style*.[22] The imperatives of style constrain the method. There are numerous qualitative methods in the social sciences that have the potential to make significant contributions to understanding financial behavior, but that are not permissible in academic finance for their lack of mathematics.[23] Furthermore, the constraints on the method impose constraints on the content as indicated by the dearth of methodological analyses in finance. Not only is one not allowed to study the usual finance problems in new and revealing ways, but also one is not allowed to venture into new territory, without one's work being academically proscribed.

Third, having two mutually exclusive cultures inhibits beneficial cross-fertilization. There is an informal academic prohibition against talking to practitioners, which is partly methodical—mathematics cannot be applied to a handful of conversations. Unfortunately, it is also partly cultural prejudice. According to academics, practitioners either are incapable of explaining the reasons for their financial behavior, or will lie about the reasons. There is also an academic aversion toward making academic finance comprehensible to practitioners unless induced to do so by large consulting fees. There is far less communication between academic finance and practitioner finance than there ought to be for the benefit of both.

Earlier chapters have implied the vacuity of a *methodologically* dubious finance that consists solely of deriving the logical implications of questionable assumptions, which are later tested with flawed statistical *methods*. In this chapter, we professed that academic finance is more form (style) than substance (content). The next chapter turns to how this worrisome state of affairs came about.

NOTES

1. Lately, the clock-speed of a CPU (central processor unit) is being replaced by MIPS (million instructions per second) as the commonly accepted measure of performance. The next generation of personal computers is pushing the 80 MIPS level. Although it is true that evaluating complex formulae involves, in many instances, hundreds of machine instructions, the speed of processing is still head-spinning.

2. The reference to "Wall Street," of course, is a synecdoche, meaning the investment community in general.

3. Military jargon in particular is full of acronyms, primarily for the sake of expedience. Circumlocution is deadly under battle conditions.

4. For example, many brokers come from retail sales. There are teachers, lawyers, historians, physicists, statisticians, actors and even physicians among financial analysts, research personnel and investment advisors, just to mention some of those we have met. It has been only during the 1980s that an influx of MBA's, many specifically trained in finance in academe, entered the profession. With the market crash of 1987 the hiring of MBA's seems to have slackened off.

5. The origin of the word use is in the folk saying of selling the skin of the bear before catching it, which served later as a metaphor for short sales. The bull is opposite of bear as bear-baiting is opposite to bull-baiting (in the sense that it was either this or that), a British "sport" until it was outlawed in 1835.

6. The word *security* comes from the combination of the Latin *se, sine* and *cura* (without worry). Accordingly, it is, in and of itself is deceptive. We know of no-financial asset that would be without disquiet to its owner.

7. In a way, *parachute*, meaning literally "a shield against falling" is a trope in itself.

8. AMEX, of course, is an acronym.

9. Strictly speaking, the term itself is a metaphor whose purpose is ideological. It causes one to presume a priori that the academics of finance is necessarily economics. Accordingly, all paradigms must be based on and consistent with the economic paradigm of *homo economicus*. Interestingly, the practitioners of finance are universally called financial analysts and not financial economists.

10. One textbook lists among the 12 principles of finance "the signaling principle," meaning that "actions convey information."

11. Faulty for Latin *sumpsimus*. A familiar story in which this error was made in the ritual of the Mass by an illiterate priest, who, when corrected, replied that he would not change his old *mumpsimus* for his critic's new *sumpsimus*. The term is used to portray a bigoted, adherent to be exposed, but customary error. Webster's *Third New International Dictionary*.

12. The authors thank Bill Lane for emphasizing the importance of this point.

13. Johnson's notation.

14. Of course, if one uses the CAPM to calculate expected returns, the assumption of equilibrium is explicit because of the model.

15. The homogeneous expectations assumption implies that there is an agreement in the market about the distribution of asset returns, about the parameters of the distribution and about estimator functions. The homogeneous expectations assumption in and of itself does not imply that each and every micro unit would have a singular outcome, given the fixed value of the independent variable.

16. See Fama and French (1992).

17. Although the stated purpose of *Financial Management*, the journal of the Financial Management Association (FMA), is "to serve both executives and academicians concerned with financial management of non-financial businesses, financial institutions, and public and private not-for-profit organizations," (*Financial Management*'s "Style Notes for Prospective Authors," any issue), the publication of a new journal, *Financial Practice and Education*, by the FMA in 1991 implicitly acknowledged that *Financial Management* was really committed to academic finance. The two cultures could not adequately co-exist within the same covers.

18. The mathematics in even the most esoteric journal of the field, *The Review of Financial Studies*, hardly goes beyond college calculus, difference equations and/or the algebra of Brownian motion.

19.   Government and not-for-profit organizations also have finance practitioners; however, real finance has traditionally been profit-making.

20.   This is not to say that it has no value in understanding financial behavior.

21.   Academic finance journals are exclusively printed on low-quality, matte paper (perhaps to symbolize frugality expected from academics), whereas practitioner-oriented journals are printed on high-quality, enamel paper.

22.   There is no shortage of very creative "deformations" in the academic finance literature.

23.   Often these qualitative methods involve time-consuming field research, which can be far more valuable than another event study with its pre-packaged method, but which takes too long to yield enough publications (if they could get published at all) to earn tenure at *soi-disant* "research" universities.

THE SOCIOLOGY OF FINANCIAL ECONOMICS

Chapter XI

How and Why This Happened

In recent years, one might have come across at least five papers, under different titles and in different journals, that discuss in essence the contribution of academic finance to financial practice. The gist of these papers is that 40 years of research have not greatly enhanced the arsenal of the financial decision maker. This conclusion holds true, even if one accepts without much criticism the accolades some distinguished academics bestow on subjects in which *they* made a seminal contribution.

Whether one looks at the field from the perspective of useful modeling, or from the vantage point of serious philosophical scrutiny, one must reach the conclusion that finance as a discipline has not created much and that finance as a methodology would have a difficult time demonstrating much independence.

On certain ceremonial occasions, worthy members of the academic finance profession are called upon to reflect in print on the profession's accomplishments. Faulhaber and Baumol (1988), Roll (1994), Merton (1994), Miller (1986) and Näslund (1986) are examples of such authors whose papers were published during the last decade. There are, however, just seven accomplishments listed in their five papers, and only four are cited in more than one paper. In roughly chronological order, these "accomplishments" are:

1. Capital budgeting, net present value, and duration (Faulhaber and Baumol)
2. Markowitz's mean-variance portfolio selection (Miller, Faulhaber and Baumol, Roll, Merton)
3. Modigliani and Miller's models of capital structure choice and dividend choice (Miller)
4. Sharpe's capital asset pricing model[1] (CAPM) (Näslund, Faulhaber and Baumol, Roll, Merton)
5. Fama's efficient markets hypothesis[2] (EMH)(Roll, Merton)
6. Black and Scholes' option pricing formula (Näslund, Faulhaber and Baumol, Roll, Merton)
7. Ross' arbitrage pricing theory (APT) (Näslund)

Present value, capital budgeting, and duration can hardly be attributed to a field that is called financial economics, which evolved as such since the first appearance of a journal circa 1972 bearing that term in its name, *Journal of Financial Economics*. The concept of present value, upon which both capital budgeting and duration build, has been with us more than 170 years.

The APT of Ross (1976, 1978) is really no more than the superimposition of the fiction of equilibrium on a system of linear equations, invoking the *deus ex machina* called arbitrage (see Chapter V). It is not testable and otherwise has no underlying statistical theory. We think that it is no coincidence that neither of these "accomplishments" is mentioned more than once—present value techniques by those who looked at the contributions of *economics* to the practitioner, and the APT by a comparative outsider who apparently was impressed by the volume of papers this theory elicited.

The question is: What makes a theory appear on lists such as this?

WHAT IS USEFUL AND TO WHOM

What do we expect from finance? What must a theory do in order for us to consider it noteworthy? Näslund (1988, p. 268) provides a convenient summary of his criteria for what makes for an important theoretical accomplishment:

1. The dynamics of the theory itself
2. The recognition it receives from other scientific disciplines
3. How practitioners relate to the theory and adapt their way of working because of what happens in the theory
4. The degree of financial innovation
5. The extent to which students are attracted to the field

This list of items, which is *de facto* an expansion of Friedman's definition of "fruitfulness," can be distilled into two by simply saying that something in finance is an accomplishment if practitioners use it (numbers 3 and 4) or if academics use it (numbers 1, 2, and 5).

If Practitioners Use It

Practitioners, also called financial analysts/corporate financial officers, come from backgrounds as varied as law, accounting, teaching, music, history, physics, and physiology. One of the authors has even met a physician who is a money manager. Knowing nothing about finance, the person nonetheless makes more money this way than as a general medical practitioner. What these finance practitioners consider useful is likely to be whatever helps them to make money. On the surface, this appears to be a very straightforward, very pragmatic (even very Friedmanian), criterion. If a theory can be used to boost returns, it is a good theory.

Unfortunately, the economy does not permit us to know whether a theory makes us more money, because we can never know how much we would have made had we not used the theory. Thus, we are forced to compare ourselves with others who are also out there trying to make money. Now, as hard as we might try, roughly half of us will always be below average, so a very desirable theory would be one that provides a justification for below-average returns. The concept of a risk-return tradeoff provides an ideal excuse for substandard performance in that low returns can be rationalized by low risk. Fortunately, risk cannot be measured as neatly as return, and the more measures of risk there are and the more controversies there are surrounding risk, the easier it is to use risk to "explain" low returns. And in the case of high returns, which need no "explanation," risk can conveniently be forgotten. Not only has the CAPM been a godsend to practitioners in this way, but also the more brouhaha it has stirred up, the better.

Along similar lines, no matter how meaningless a number might be, it is better than no number at all. Thus, when it is necessary to justify a rate of return in a public utilities commission hearing or to justify the valuation of a firm undergoing privatization in a formerly centrally planned economy, the CAPM provides not only a convenient, but also an essential, service to certify the return or the value.[3]

Personal computer, stereo component, and automobile manufacturers all advertise their technical features in order to differentiate their products from those of competitors. Finance practitioners are no different. We have already pointed out that there is no way of knowing whether a finance theory has any effect or not. But it doesn't matter that the latest finance theory is as useful as a synthesized voice announcing that a door is open, just so it sounds sexy enough to appeal to customers (hopefully sexier, however, than the synthesized voice). Shortly after Markowitz and Sharpe received the ultimate accolade for their work on MPT and the CAPM, one of the authors of this book observed that a local financial consultant was advertising the use of "techniques of Nobel prize-winners." It doesn't matter whether the consultant believed in the theories; in fact, he or she probably didn't. What mattered was whether the theories had a positive effect on customers. Of course, using the most *au courant* theories and buzzwords can also provide some extra insurance against possible below-par performance—if Nobel prize-winners can't beat the market, who can?

Thus, one of the most important qualities of a theory in the eyes of the finance practitioner is that it sound to someone, not necessarily the practitioner, as if it might work. Although unrealistic assumptions themselves do not sound good, they result in a logical consistency that sounds very good, and once a theory has been derived, the logical consistency stands out and the assumptions are buried in obscure academic papers. The CAPM is the paragon of a theory that makes sense, at least to those who have bought into the methodology. Ironically, however, theories can become self-fulfilling prophesies—if enough practitioners believe strongly enough (or are cynical enough) to use them, they just might work. There is a strong suspicion that the Black-Scholes/Merton Option Pricing Model is one of these, as trading screens scrupulously list actual option prices along with computations of what they "should" be according to the model.

Whether or not a practitioner buys into the Friedmanian methodology of finance, and many (if not most) don't, it certainly pays to buy its products. With such strong pre-existing demand, it would be foolish for rational finance academics not to provide a supply. This alone is sufficient to justify the positivist methodology that is so conducive to cranking out theory after theory with built-in obsolescence. But there is another game being played at universities for which positivism is even more suitable.

If Academics Use it

If extraterrestrial visitors were to evaluate finance, they are likely to comment on academicians' following a rigid regimen of form and language that is a combination of Gregorian chant and surrealism. This scenario is not so improbable, as these are often the comments of mathematicians describing economists. Must we conclude that extraterrestrials and mathematicians are so much more perceptive than researchers in finance and economics?

Consider Näslund's criteria for identifying a significant theoretical accomplishment from an academic perspective—the dynamics of the theory and its effects on one's reputation in the eyes of peers and students. Such criteria are strikingly similar to those one might apply to the efforts of an artist or the founder of a new religious sect. Szostak (1992) has written about economics as art rather than science, and about its transcendental allure.

Econ-art is capable of so much more than mere momentary refreshment. The true aficionado can be carried permanently away from the cares of this earth, to run carefree through a world far more well-behaved than our own. The beatific smiles of the foremost practitioners can be observed at conferences… It is the most peaceful of arts, the most contemplative, the most sublime (Szostak 1992, p. 70).

Who, though, that has ever taught international trade—drawn the Edgeworth box diagram, derived offer curves, illustrated the effects of tariffs with production possibility frontiers and indifference curves—who can have done that, that would not shed a tear if this elegant mass of theory had to be pushed to the background for the mere crime of only being a residual claimant on truth (p. 74).

Likewise, we have the Chicago/Rochester School of Finance—as if it were a school of art or literature. At conferences, the high priests of these schools pack hotel-ballroom luncheons (in spite of abysmal cuisine) and stalk the muted halls followed by their retinues of devoted disciples. Life has no gratifications quite like those of successfully explaining the CAPM to a classroom of undergraduates[4] or completing a *tour-de-force* derivation of the option pricing model before an auditorium of eager MBAs.

Unlike the world of art, however, there is no *Salon des Refusées* for those whose works are unacceptable to *l'Academie*. Whereas novelty and change eventually win at least a small audience of the most informed critics in literature, music, and painting (although the mass audiences cling to Twain's *Tom Sawyer*, Beethoven's Ninth Symphony, and Da Vinci's Mona Lisa), classical (or should we say neoclassical) finance expropriates almost all discourse.

Lest we dismiss finance academics as mere aesthetes or dilettantes (although some undoubtedly are), we must point out that there are very real reasons for the practice of unreal finance, thereby toeing the line drawn by the gurus of finance. In the following section, we conclude with the most likely explanation for Friedman's persistent influence on finance.

THE RATIONALE FOR THE POSITIVIST METHODOLOGY IN FINANCE

Jean Heck's (1995) *The McGraw-Hill Finance Literature Index* lists 60 publications in the domain of finance literature. Discounting journals of real estate, insurance, and a few others that are only tangential to the field, the number is still 54. The most senior of this set is the *Journal of Business*[5] the first volume of which appeared in 1928. Next, in the chronological order of their founding, are the *Journal of Finance* (1946) (JF), the *Financial Analysts Journal* (1960) (FAJ), the *Journal of Financial and Quantitative Analysis* (1966) (JFQA), and the *Journal of Money, Credit and Banking* (1969) (JMCB). This completes the list of journals in the field that were in existence before 1970. The bulk of the remaining 49 journals have a startup date after 1980.

Given the paucity of journal space during the early days of financial economics—even taking into account that some of the important papers of the time appeared in journals of economics (e.g., the *American Economic Review*, the *Quarterly Review of Economics*, the *Bell Journal of Economics*, the *Review of Economics and Statistics*, etc.)—the total number of articles published during the 1950s and most of the 1960s is quite limited. As a result, very few faculty employed at business school departments of finance during that time had an impressively long resume of peer-reviewed publications.[6]

Based on casual conversation with older faculty, we get the impression that it was quite possible to reach the rank of full professor (and of course to get tenure) without a single publication in a major academic journal (such as the JF or the JFQA).

The situation changed with the Soviets sending Sputnik into orbit and with the Carnegie report on higher education. Suddenly, at universities across the land, there was a drive for *scientification*: to position all their departments in line with the natural sciences and the methodologies used in these sciences. Because business schools never miss a chance to exploit an opportunity, they joined the ranks and, together with their brethren in departments of economics, fell into line. The natural physics envy of social scientists in general and economists, financial inclusive, in particular, added an extra, albeit not critical, impetus.

Suddenly, publication norms for faculty began to emerge, followed by new organizations for financial economists (the FMA, EFA, WFA, etc.), all starting their own publications. It is hard to fathom which process preceded which: the increased demand for scientific research, or the creation of newly established organizations for financial economists, all featuring annual meetings and paper presentations.

From the mid-1980s on, there were about 30 to 40 finance journals around, with a thin layer (of six to seven) forming an outlet for the aristocracy, By that time, even schools that were traditionally considered teaching schools, or "diploma-mills" in the parlance of academic pundits, required "research output," meaning a publication record, in order to be promoted or tenured. The differences between schools were along the lines of what constituted a "major hit" as opposed to a secondary or tertiary outlet, and how many of each were needed for tenure and for ascension in the professorial ranks. Here, one could observe wide divergence: from top schools, which required a minimum in the top seven journals, to schools where every publication (excluding trade journals but including textbooks) was considered a hit.[7]

Parallel, and independently, an upsurge in enrollment in MBA programs ensued, as a result of the meteoric expansion of financial markets and the lucrative starting salaries that financial institutions operating in these markets offered. Because of this surge of enrollment, the hiring of young and talented faculty became crucial. A large number of schools were eagerly searching for distinguished researchers to occupy newly endowed chairs or professorships (the ultimate dream of every academician), who could build around themselves a research program that would attract newly minted faculty and doctoral candidates to these schools. A market-for-researchers evolved where "value" was measured by how many JF's, JFQA's, JFE's (*Journal of Financial Economics*) and how many RR's (revise and resubmit) to one of these journals one had. During the last two decades, a trade in faculty evolved that is not quite dissimilar to, and just as burgeoning as, the trade in professional baseball players, albeit for much less money.

This system could be maintained (and still is maintained) only by the positivist methodology, its careful screening through the publication process (that does not tolerate criticism of the methodology), large electronic databases supplied by its major promoters, and high-speed computers. No "critical rationalism" of Popper, or in fact no critical thinking of any kind, could have sustained this market of arithmomorphy and the instrumentalist whirling of data-tapes—comparable to a thousand space-age Rumpelstiltskins, bent over, spinning gold from tiny rust-particle-coated magnetic media, on their magic electronic tape-drives.

Yet, Georgescu-Roegen (1979) many years ago already stated the obvious:

> [Besides] nothing can be derived from an analytical model that is not logically contained
> in its axiomatic basis. As has been argued by many famous mathematicians, any branch
> of mathematics is just a vast logical tautology (p. 321).

This is, and always must have been, known to all the academic practitioners of finance. The fact that we keep on doing what we have been doing since we condemned the early institutionalists of finance to a shameful intellectual demise shows that we are happy with a class system whose major concern is the preservation of an aristocracy rather than discovery.

If science is defined as the systematic search for the truth, then what is left of finance is its clever and elegant formalism pursued largely for the purposes of wealth and career enhancement. Consequently, it is not science. It is possibly art (something most, if not all, of its academic practitioners would vehemently deny), or perhaps more likely, meta-science. The choice we must face is either to openly recognize this or to search for a new methodology.

In their dedicated pursuit of professional recognition, finance academics seem to behave as if their sole influence on professionals is to feed them bits and pieces of knowledge that might in some way prove to be useful. Actually, the interplay among methodology, research and practice is much more complicated than that. This is the subject of the next chapter.

NOTES

1. With Sharpe having been awarded the 1990 Nobel Prize in economics, Lintner and Mossin, whose names have been traditionally associated with the CAPM, will be less and less quoted. Since Fama and French (1992) rechristened the model the SLB model (for Sharpe, Lintner and Black), and since the last two of the three are no longer among the living, we will hear less and less of the acronym CAPM.

2. Although Fama was not solely responsible for the EMH, he undertook some of the early empirical work and was responsible for a significant survey and theoretical exposition.

3.   German firms considering the purchase of Slovene companies required the firms' betas, even though circumstances were such that betas made no sense. The Slovenes were well aware of this but still were unable to convince the German purchasers, who may have known it too, but needed betas to justify the purchase price to someone else.

4.   It is doubtful, however, that anyone has yet scaled this Olympian peak.

5.   The *Journal of Business* is not exclusively dedicated to finance. Hence, the origin of the dedicated journals is the mid-1940s.

6.   Promotion and tenure data in most universities is sealed, and is confidential information. It is not possible to conduct research to determine what were the minimum requirements for promotion from assistant to associate, and from associate to full professor in what caliber schools. Information available on this subject is, necessarily, anecdotal.

7.   The orthodoxy was not just keen on counting only top journals, for publishing in what were considered second- and third-level journals counted against the candidate. Hence, faculty who had publications in inferior places were required to list those; omission was not permitted.

Chapter XII

The Profession and Practice

As we discussed in Chapter II, the behavior of most scientists implies their having made certain tacit Cartesian assumptions regarding scientific activity, namely: (1) there is a real external environment *out there* independent of science; (2) it is possible, at least in principle, to determine the truth of a scientific statement regarding the external environment; (3) scientists will never state all truths regarding the external environment; and (4) over time, scientists state more or better truths regarding the external environment. Of course, each of these statements has been a controversial issue in philosophy for quite some time, and there is as yet no consensus regarding the truth of the statements themselves. However, these statements are likely to characterize the beliefs of the majority of scientists, who are concerned more with their science itself and less with its philosophy.

And as we have asserted throughout this book, financial economists proceed as if their science is no exception. There is financial behavior *out there*, and financial economists empirically test theoretical statements regarding financial behavior to determine their truth, rigorously search for new theoretical statements regarding financial behavior, and periodically congratulate themselves on their successes. Because financial economists have not been as philosophically self-conscious as some other scientists, one can only infer the beliefs underlying their behavior. One belief seems to be that there are determinants of financial behavior in existence somewhere *out there*. Regarding accounting research, much of which resembles financial research, Chua (1986) writes:

> Mainstream accounting research is dominated by a belief in physical realism—the claim
> that there is a world of objective reality that exists independently of human beings and
> that has a determinate nature or essence that is knowable (p. 606).

However, the ontology of finance[1] is not what is implied by these assumptions-- (1) financial behavior is not independent of the science of financial economics; therefore, (2) the truth of scientific statements regarding the determinants of financial behavior is not a matter subject to determination,[2] (3) at all times, all current truths regarding the determinants of financial behavior have been stated, and (4) over time, financial economists state neither more nor better but, rather, different truths regarding the determinants of financial behavior. Actors know what determines their financial behavior, and these determinants change as the environment of the actors changes. Part of this environment is the science of financial economics itself. Financial economics is not a positive science of *what is* nor is it even a normative science of *what ought to be*. Rather, it is a rhetorical science of contention for *what will be*.

In the preceding chapter, we talked about some of the peculiarities of the finance profession that have shaped its research methodology. In this chapter, then, we will explain how that peculiar research methodology has a profound effect on the finance it purports to study. The explanation begins with a model of scientific activity. The model in its simplest form is descriptive of most science most of the time. Scientists formally select structures and tools from an intellectual environment and experiences from an external environment to create science. In subsequent sections, the model is refined to incorporate those complications that can affect all sciences some of the time and some sciences, notably financial economics, all of the time. These complications are the influence of science on the intellectual environment the informal use of structures and tools and experiences from the intellectual and external environments, and the influence of science on the external environment. The peculiar role of research in financial economics in light of these complications is discussed last.

A MODEL OF SCIENTIFIC ACTIVITY

Traditional scientific activity may be modeled as a Scientist creating Science out of structures and tools and experiences formally selected from the Intellectual and External Environments. The elements and the process incorporated in this simple model, true of most science most of the time, provide a framework for understanding the unusual nature of financial economics.

The Elements

An obvious definition of a Scientist is someone whose goals are among the conventional goals of Science.[3] These were listed in Chapter II—to understand, to explain, to find the truth of, to predict, to control, or to solve the problems of some part of the External Environment. Thus, broadly speaking, everyone is a scientist, for everyone must predict, control, or solve the problems of their own external environments in order to survive. So as not to construe scientific activity too liberally, it is desirable to define a Scientist more narrowly as someone who pursues the more elusive goals of finding truth, explaining, or understanding. A Scientist is interested in knowing *why*. Science, in turn, is the collective body of hypotheses, models, theories, principles, and laws by which Scientists achieve these goals.

Unfortunately, the terms *explaining, understanding, finding truth, hypothesis, model, theory, principle,* and *law* have not been wholly explicated nor wholly defined. Therefore, what a Scientist and Science truly are remains vague. Further, the aforementioned definition of a Scientist will create problems for methodological instrumentalists,[4] for whom theories are merely instruments for generation of predictions. Fortunately, the usefulness of the model of scientific activity for understanding the epistemology and ontology of finance is not determined by the precise characterization of a Scientist or Science. It is sufficient that there be financial economists that consider themselves to be Scientists and that there be a collective body of hypotheses (such as the EMH), models (such as the CAPM), theories (such as Arbitrage Pricing Theory), principles (such as the Principle of Diversification), and laws (such as The Law of Large Numbers) that may constitute a Science.

The Intellectual Environment, however, is a more critical element in the model. It is made up of the terms, concepts, patterns, representations, analogies, metaphors, rules of thought, and rules of investigation necessary for structuring the External Environment. The so-called *real* world does not necessarily present itself in a form that makes sense to its inhabitants. Sense has to be imposed on it. Broadly speaking, the Intellectual Environment is an individual's world view or *weltbild*. For a Scientist, the fundamental tools of inquiry—the scientific method, paradigm (Kuhn 1970), research program (Lakatos 1970), or research tradition (Laudan 1977)—are a part of the Intellectual Environment. Yet all of this is only the impersonal side of the Intellectual Environment. On the personal side lie the intuitions, emotions, and values reflected in an individual's culture, religion, or ideology.

Financial economics has an Intellectual Environment, parts of which it shares with other sciences and parts of which are peculiar to it. There are terms and concepts (debt, equity, capital structure, cost of capital), patterns (constrained optimization), representations (graphs, financial statements, mathematical notation), analogies and metaphors (signaling, markets for corporate control), rules of thought (economic intuition), and rules of investigation (methodology).[5]

The definitions of a Scientist, Science, and the Intellectual Environment all make reference to the External Environment. It is the reality *out there,* the facts, the truth. It is the observed, not the observations; the source of sensory input, not the input. It is often referred to as nature or the material world, though these terms may create difficulty for social scientists. Of course, the only perceptual contact anyone can have is with the Intellectual Environment, for the Intellectual Environment is the necessary means by which the External Environment is perceived. Accordingly, the ontology of an External Environment is problematic.

At one time, philosophical idealists denied its existence; however, philosophical naturalists, materialists, and realists (covering most modern scientists) believe that there is an External Environment. Without an External Environment, it would not be possible, even in principle, to determine the truth of a scientific statement. Without reality, truth would be moot. Truth would be a matter of convention among selected Scientists and not susceptible to independent determination by any one Scientist. Without an External Environment, it would not be possible to state more or better (broader or more general) truths. Unless there is some standard of reference, truths can be neither more nor better but merely different.

There is indeed some sort of External Environment of finance. After all, there is something called financial behavior, although it could hardly be characterized as a part of the natural, material, or physical world. Yet it is in a real sense *out there*. Financial institutions lend, corporations retain earnings, depositors deposit, investors invest, borrowers borrow, and widows and orphans receive dividends from public utilities. How is it that financial economists wield their intellectual structures and tools to create the science of finance; that is, the explanation, the understanding, or the truth of these activities—the determinants of financial behavior?

The Process

In the model, scientific activity begins as The Scientist formally selects certain structures from the (impersonal) Intellectual Environment, which in turn determine which observations or experiences will be formally selected from the External Environment. In some mysterious way, these combine to create the Science which enables The Scientist to understand, explain, or find the truth of the External Environment. This process is depicted in Figure XII.1.

There are obvious limitations to this model. The junction of the inputs from the Intellectual Environment and the External Environment seems to constitute some sort of context of justification for a hypothesis, model, or theory, yet a context of discovery does not appear present in the model. The context of justification is the confrontation of a statement in the form of a hypothesis, model, or theory with evidence from the real world to determine the truth of that statement. The context of discovery is the original creation of the statement in some way within the mind of the Scientist. Nonetheless, the model captures the essentials of what most scientists do most of the time.

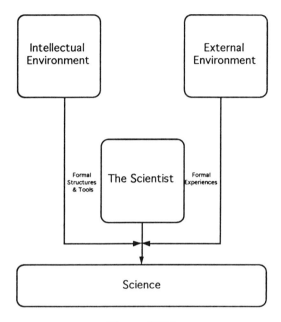

Figure XII.1.

Modigliani and Miller: An Example

How well does this model describe one of the classical endeavors of financial economics, Modigliani and Miller's (1958) "The Cost of Capital, Corporation Finance, and the Theory of Investment?" In the paper, the authors refer to the "search to establish the principles which govern rational investment and financial policy in a world of uncertainty" (Modigliani and Miller 1958, p. 263). This is evidence of their belief in an external environment in which there are such "governing principles"; that is, in which determinants of financial behavior do exist. Their empirical tests of their propositions is evidence of their belief in the possibility of determining the truth of a scientific statement. Their paper itself is evidence of their belief that not all truths regarding the cost of capital had been stated at the time it was written. Their criticism that the "certainty model has little descriptive value and provides no real guidance to the finance specialist or managerial economist ... " (Modigliani and Miller 1958, p. 262) is evidence of their belief in better truths over time. From their own statements, it is clear that Modigliani and Miller do indeed share with most other scientists the aforementioned implicit assumptions regarding scientific activity.

Their selections from the External Environment are straightforward— data regarding security yields and financial structures for electric utilities and oil companies for 1947 and 1948 and for 1953, respectively.[6] It is not possible to specify all that Modigliani and Miller selected from the Intellectual Environment, nor is it possible to classify it in any meaningful way. The structures and tools they used certainly include the concepts of cost of capital, debt, equity, profit, market value, maximization, certainty, uncertainty, equilibrium, arbitrage, and the relevant mathematics. In fact, it is impossible to precisely discriminate between their selections from the Intellectual Environment and their own original discoveries.

> A number of writers have stated close equivalents of our Proposition I although by appealing to intuition rather than by attempting a proof and only to insist immediately that the results were not applicable to the actual capital markets. Proposition II, however, so far as we have been able to discover is new (Modigliani and Miller 1958, p. 270).

Thus, it is difficult to specify exactly what Modigliani and Miller contributed to Science. The quotation suggests that their apparent contributions, Propositions I and II regarding the cost of capital, were not unequivocally new. In retrospect, their enduring contribution has been their methodology rather than their theory. (In effect, they contributed to the Intellectual Environment and not to the Science.) This includes their approach to the problem of the cost of capital:

> These and other drastic simplifications have been necessary in order to come to grips with the problem at all. Having served their purpose they can now be relaxed in the direction of greater realism and relevance, a task in which we hope others interested in this area will wish to share (Modigliani and Miller 1958, p. 295).[7]

It also includes the use of a proof based on arbitrage.

A retrospective in the *Journal of Economic Perspectives* confirms these impacts of the paper. Bhattacharya (1988) lists five key methodological contributions of the series of papers on the cost of capital, of which Modigliani and Miller's (1958) was the first. These were:

> (a) introduction of the risk-class (set of payoff patterns mutually replicable through trading) notion; (b) consideration of investor arbitrage (homemade leverage) in pricing securities; (c) initiation of integrated after-tax analyses of dividend and debt supply policies of firms; (d) consideration of empirical evidence and introduction of 'respectable' econometric methods in corporate finance; and (e) planting seeds for the development of economic modeling of unexplained phenomena, such as the 'informational content' of dividends for stock prices (pp. 135-136).

Stiglitz (1988) emphasizes the importance of their approach.

> Again ironically, some of the most productive responses to the Modigliani-Miller results have come from those who did not feel able to accept the conclusion that financial policy

is irrelevant. The Modigliani-Miller results forced these skeptics to identify which of the assumptions underlying the Modigliani-Miller theorem should be modified or rejected (p. 122).

Miller (1988) himself refers to the arbitrage proof: "The validity of our then-novel arbitrage proof of that proposition is also no longer disputed, and essentially similar arbitrage proofs are now common throughout finance" (p. 99).

Consistent with the simplest form of the model of scientific activity, Modigliani and Miller selected a variety of tools and structures from the Intellectual Environment and empirical observations from the External Environment in order to make a more truthful statement explaining the cost of capital and valuation. There are, however, important complications that must be added to the simplified model in order to make it a more accurate representation of how scientific activity actually occurs. The augmented model offers greater insight into Modigliani and Miller and into other work in financial economics.

INFLUENCE ON
THE INTELLECTUAL ENVIRONMENT

The Process

The first complication is the influence of Science on the Intellectual Environment. Hypotheses, models, theories, principles, and laws expand the stock of languages, concepts, patterns, representations, analogies, metaphors, rules of thought, and rules of investigation available to a Scientist. Changes occur in the world view or *weltbild*. Paradigms are overthrown by revolution and/or research programs degenerate. The influence of Science on the Intellectual Environment is what permits Science to advance. Without it, the Intellectual Environment would be rapidly depleted of its potential. With it, new observations and experiences are selected for extraction from the External Environment and old observations and experiences are used in new ways. This process is incorporated into the basic model in Figure XII.2.

Modigliani and Miller

Because their enduring contribution to science has been methodological, Modigliani and Miller necessarily have had an influence on the Intellectual Environment of subsequent work. Although it is by no means clear what a scientific revolution is, Modigliani and Miller (1958) would certainly be strong candidates for having effected one in financial economics. According

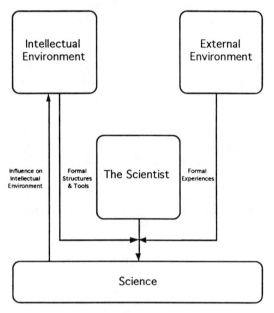

Figure XII.2.

to Ross (1988), "If the view of the progress of science that interprets it as one of changing paradigms has merit, then surely the work of Miller and Modigliani provides a laboratory example of a violently shifted paradigm" (p. 127).

For better or worse, the process of simplification, the mathematization, and the arbitrage structure of their proof have all had a profound impact on the way in which financial economics has proceeded since. In turn, they are intellectually indebted to their predecessors for their graphs, their diagrams, their notation, and whatever was referenced in their footnotes.

Nothing about the model of scientific activity in its Figure XII.2 form is surprising. It reflects scientific progress, not only through the creation of new hypotheses, models, theories, principles, and laws that explicitly constitute Science, but also through the creation of new structures and tools to facilitate the creation of Science. There are, however, additional complications of the model that introduce effects that are infrequently considered in science.

INFORMAL EXTRACTIONS FROM THE ENVIRONMENTS

The Process

All scientists bring something personal to their science. All have had their own informal experiences of the world and all have formed certain structure to comprehend these experiences. This must necessarily influence their science. Fay (1975) points out that it would be unreasonable to expect men and women to adopt one world view in their capacity as scientists engaged in study and another world view in their capacity as individuals engaged in the activities they have studied. Popper (1964) acknowledges the surprising relevance of this intuition for the natural sciences as well as the social sciences.

> It is undoubtedly true that we have a more direct knowledge of the 'inside of the human atom' than we have of physical atoms; but this knowledge is intuitive. In other words, we certainly use our knowledge of ourselves in order to frame hypotheses about some other people, or about all people.... The physicist, it is true, is not helped by such direct observation when he frames his hypotheses about atoms; nevertheless, he quite often uses some kind of sympathetic imagination or intuition which may easily make him feel that he is intimately acquainted with even the 'inside of the atoms'—with even their whims and prejudices (Popper 1964, p. 138).

This input is reflected in Figure XII.3.

The critical question; however, regards the importance of this informal input. According to Popper (1964),

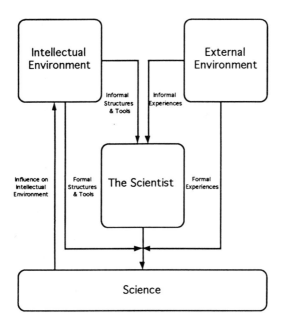

Figure XII.3.

> It is irrelevant from the point of view of science whether we have obtained our theories
> by jumping to unwarranted conclusions or merely by stumbling over them (that is,
> by 'intuition'), or else by some inductive procedure. The question 'How did you first
> *find* your theory?' relates as it were, to an entirely private matter (Popper 1964, p. 135).

What Popper must be taking for granted, however, is that there is no
significantly strong bias in favor of some "intuitive" theories and that "non-
intuitive" theories will always occur to someone. This is not true; for
example, Bowler (1989) makes a compelling case for the critical importance
of supposedly "non-scientific" considerations in the intellectual history of
the theory of evolution.

> Because he is a human being, living within a particular culture and society, it is difficult
> to believe that the ideas and values he has been taught will not play some role in
> stimulating his imagination in a certain direction. Existing theories are often perceived
> to have philosophical or ideological implications, so it does not seem unreasonable to
> suppose that (consciously or unconsciously) an awareness of these implications will
> shape the actual creation of each theory (p. 18).

The Case of Financial Economics

These informal selections of structures and tools from the Intellectual
Environment and experiences and observations from the External
Environment undoubtedly do play a role in the context of discovery for all
scientists, but especially interesting problems arise for financial economists.
Whereas vulcanologists are likely to encounter volcanoes only in their (the
vulcanologists') professional capacity, and particle physicists do not
consciously have face-to-face encounters with neutrinos outside the
laboratory, all financial economists have had particular experiences of their
own with finance. A consequence of this familiarity is that it is difficult
to create science that contradicts what they would expect their own behavior
to be.[8] The question, "What would I do?," provides the unacknowledged
context of discovery; and the question, "Would I do that?," the
unacknowledged context of justification for all financial economics. It
comes as no surprise that the most cherished hypotheses, models, and
theories make sense, as we discussed in detail in Chapter VI with the CAPM.
If they did not, they would never have been created.

This is not necessarily a bad approach. After all, financial economics is
ultimately concerned with individual financial behavior, and "laypersons"
will have much of the same common sense as financial economists. If a
financial economist can see himself or herself behaving in a certain way,
then that is confirmation that at least someone behaves that way, and others
probably behave that way as well. If he or she would not behave in a certain
way, that is evidence that some others probably will not. In this way,

common sense performs a useful function. However, in this sense, finance is more of an interpretive than a positive social science. There is no external rationality determining financial behavior. Rather, the apparent rationality underlying the financial behavior is simply some sort of expression or description in terms shared by both the financial economist and the layperson (Fay 1975).

Modigliani and Miller

Modigliani and Miller (1958) provide an especially interesting example of the relevance of common sense in science precisely because their conclusion appears to violate common sense. This problem is acknowledged in the original article: "The propositions we have developed with respect to the valuation of firms and shares appear to be substantially at variance with current doctrines in the field of finance" (Modigliani and Miller 1958, p. 455).

Later, Modigliani (1988) recalled that preceding the paper,

> In preparing my lecture dealing with the cost of capital, I was able to provide (for a world of no taxes) a sort of proof of Proposition I, based on arbitrage. I reported the result to my class the next day, adding that I didn't really believe my result and there probably was something wrong (Modigliani 1988, p. 149).

There are several references to an earlier paper by Durand's (1952) in which results similar to Modigliani and Miller's (1958) had been rejected because of the same problem: "A number of writers have stated close equivalents of our Proposition I although by appealing to intuition rather than by attempting a proof and only to insist immediately that the results were not applicable to the actual capital markets" (Modigliani and Miller 1958, p. 450).

And Modigliani later adds: "But mostly I listened to a paper by David Durand (1952) in which the possibility that financial structure would not affect the market valuation or the cost of capital was suggested, only to be rejected as not relevant to the actual capital markets" (Modigliani 1988, p. 149). And Miller continues: "But he [Durand] rejected this possibility in favor of his other extreme, which he believed closer to the ordinary, real world way of valuing corporate shares" (Miller 1988, p. 101).

If Durand had rejected his theory because of its conflict with common sense, why didn't Modigliani and Miller? They didn't because they devised an alternative common-sense intuition or rationale. Their initial article contained an extended analogy with a dairy farmer who is unable to raise the value of his whole milk by skimming off the cream and selling it separately from the skimmed milk. This is said to be analogous to a corporation whose cash flows are worth only so much regardless of how they are distributed among the firm's securities.

200 / Toward Finance with Meaning

Once a common-sense intuition or rationale could be created, then the theory was worth pursuing. Modigliani (1988) is explicit about this:

> But not then when colleagues (academic and practitioner) took it as self-evident that there was a unique, value-maximizing debt ratio and regarded our propositions as plainly preposterous. There was therefore a need for rigorous and varied arguments to show the formal proof of the result and provide the 'new' intuition as to why it made sense (Modigliani 1988, p. 150).[9]

However, Modigliani (1988) goes on to say:

> It [the article] was really addressed to finance specialists and it was written tongue-in-cheek, not really to demonstrate that leverage could not possibly affect market values in the actual world but to shock those who accepted the then-current naive view that some debt in the capital structure had to reduce the cost of capital" (Modigliani 1988, p. 150).

This is difficult to believe. The empirical section in the original article in which the propositions are formally tested, although seriously flawed as far as econometrics goes, is, nevertheless, hardly consistent with a tongue-in-cheek attempt to be shocking. One would not make a test of something if one did not expect that it might be true, especially not a revolutionary new theory. Modigliani also remembers that it was Miller's recollection of an earlier paper that appeared to provide empirical support for their proposition that caused them to undertake the formal development (Modigliani 1988).

Both Durand and Modigliani and Miller support the contention of this paper regarding the critical influence of common sense on financial economics. Very simply, theories must agree with common sense. Without agreement, it is the theory that is rejected. The interesting issue arises when there is more than one common sense. Modigliani and Miller retained their theory on the strength of an analogy that supplied a common-sense rationale for the theory's implications, yet this common sense (which of course was not yet *common*) conflicted with the prevailing common sense. This introduces the final complication to the model of scientific activity in which science has an impact on the object of that science.

THE INFLUENCE ON
THE EXTERNAL ENVIRONMENT

The Process in Financial Economics

A marked peculiarity of financial economics is that its object of study is the behavior of a few thousand people—all of whom are aware of the

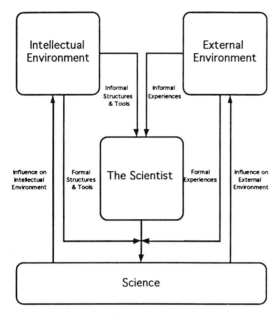

Figure XII.4.

science of financial economics. Although everyone engages in financial activity of one sort or another, only the decisions of a relative few have a significant impact. And most of these few have been educated in the science of financial economics and stay informed to some extent through professional literature of the changes in financial economics.[10] Science feeds back on the external environment so that there is effectively no *there* out there independent of the science.[11] Figure XII.4 incorporates this influence, completing the model of scientific activity.[12]

If financial economists were to come up with a plausible reason for behaving in a certain way, then people *might* begin behaving in that way. These behaviors then become imbedded in the common sense and reinforce that behavior in future science. The Black-Scholes/Merton option pricing model, for example, may well explain option pricing behavior only because the model itself is the source of pricing behavior. The model was published shortly after the opening of the first specialized options exchange, and, within months, traders were consulting Black-Scholes' tables of calculations as to what options "should be" worth.[13] Until expiration, options are worth only what someone is willing to pay for them. Once there is general agreement that the Black-Scholes model provides that value, then the model explains option pricing behavior, albeit in a very peculiar way. The model did not say what pricing behavior was nor did it say what pricing behavior should be. Rather, it convinced traders, and they made it what pricing behavior would be.

Financial economics is a rhetorical science in that plausible stories compete for the attention of the finance public. Whichever makes the most sense is what people will do. This then constitutes the explanation of behavior until another more plausible story comes along. Nothing ensures that the process leads to the fulfillment of any norms. If everyone could be convinced that it made sense to use astrological forecasts to form stock prices, then it would make sense to use astrological forecasts to form stock prices. Stocks are worth what the astrological forecasts, via the believers, say that they are worth. Anyone, who believed that the value of stocks depended on some sort of fundamental economic value would find that it simply was not true. This is the peculiar rationality of Keynes' notorious "beauty contest" in which the task is not to pick the person you think is the winner, but to pick the contestant whom the other judges will pick as the winner.

It is important to emphasize that financial economics does not *determine* financial behavior—the Black-Scholes option pricing model is an extreme example of the effect. In many, if not most, cases, financial economics is treated with extreme skepticism by practitioners. Often, as described in Chapter X, financial economics is written in a formal language that practitioners cannot comprehend. But, to be empirically tested, the formal language must be translated into an observation language that *would* be familiar to practitioners; there are numerous journals that interpret financial economics for practitioners (see Chapter VII); and textbooks used in the education of practitioners are largely catalogues of simplified research findings.

The important point is that the results of financial economics shape financial behavior either positively or negatively to a greater or lesser extent by influencing the beliefs of practitioners. Some of the practitioners are scientists, who form their subsequent theories out of their own behavior and the behavior they observe among others—behavior that was shaped by earlier theories. The biological constraints referred to as "human nature" do form an external reality of sorts; however, it is unlikely that even the most ardent sociobiologist would argue for a genetic basis for capital structure or option pricing.

Modigliani and Miller

With their contentions regarding the irrelevance of capital structure for the cost of capital and its attendant common-sense rationale, Modigliani and Miller entered the contest for the hearts and minds of corporate treasurers. If everyone were to believe that the cost of capital was independent of capital structure, then the cost of capital would become independent of capital structure. There are no deeper rules or laws or no incontrovertible "human nature" governing the process. The relationship between the cost of capital and capital structure is and, in fact, must be, precisely what the consensus common sense says that it is. Much as some may want to believe that finance is physics,[14] it is not.

What has occurred has been that Modigliani and Miller's rhetoric has simply not been as convincing as what, in 1958, was and now still is the conventional wisdom regarding the cost of capital and capital structure. The article is honored for its methodology, not its theory. Unfortunately, this methodology perpetuates the myth that there is a real world of the determinants of financial behavior *out there* that it is possible to explain or understand. Explanation and understanding are indeed possible, albeit in a much different way.

IMPLICATIONS FOR FINANCE

Beyond Positivism

The first implication is the necessary abandonment of the pretense of positivism in finance. There is simply nothing of importance *out there* to be positive about. The belief that there is has led to some peculiar research. In one article on the subject of capital structure, DeAngelo and Masulis (1980) told a plausible story that firms with larger non-debt tax shields (depreciation, for example) should have less debt in their capital structures, for more debt might cause the firms to lose the tax benefits of their deductible expenses. The favorable reception of this paper was a clear indication that DeAngelo and Masulis' rationale or intuition made sense.

A problem arises when empirical researchers set out to determine whether this plausible story is indeed true. There are only two ways in which this effect could ever be observed. The first is that financial managers already know the story and are indeed reducing their debt in line with increases in their non-debt tax shields. If this were true, then DeAngelo and Masulis may have performed some clever mathematics, casting the principle in a language with which practitioners might be unfamiliar, but essentially did not tell anyone anything that was not already known. There is certainly enough contact between financial economists and the finance community that someone from the former would have heard about such a principle from someone in the latter at some time.

The second way in which this effect could be observed is that firms that do link their debt to their non-debt tax shields are successes and firms that do not are failures, without, of course, anyone's realizing why the success or failure occurred. It is doubtful that any economy is so highly competitive that a minor matter such as this could have led to natural selection pronounced enough for its effect to be detected.

Now, the appropriate way to evaluate DeAngelo and Masulis' theory is as a plausible story. Some firms may believe it and begin to apply it; others may not. At some point, someone may concoct a plausible story that recommends the opposite, and the ideas will be in contention. It would be stretching a point to call DeAngelo and Masulis' story a normative theory; after all, there is no guarantee that the benefit will be worth the effort. Not every theory that can be used ought to be used. It simply sounds as if it makes sense, and it might be worth trying out. Thus, one function of financial economics is to tell plausible stories and attempt to convince the finance community that the recommended behavior be adopted. As discussed in the previous chapter, the true test of a theory is not whether it explains or predicts, but whether it is used. This is the marketplace of ideas.

Though the fact is rarely acknowledged, many of the greatest discoveries in economics have not come as the outcome of the manipulation of mathematics, but from someone's devising a plausible reason for behaving in a certain way. The theory of comparative advantage sounds wholly counter-intuitive at first, but, with a little thought, can easily see why it might work. Now, it is an important argument in the debate over free trade—but only *one* argument among many others. The same is true of Keynesian economics, which originated with an idea that it might make sense to behave in a certain way, though the story had never been told in quite that way before (Stewart 1979). The profound historical impact of "Keynesianism" on economic policy came from its power as a plausible recommendation of what might work, not as a description of how things had worked.

The Methodology of Finance

The second implication is that methodology in financial economics requires radical revision. Actors know the reasons for their financial behavior. They may have to be prodded to recognize them, and they may lie about them, but they do know them. They act in accordance with their beliefs, and these beliefs are the explanations for their actions. Because no theory in finance can exist without a rationale or common-sense interpretation, it is appropriate to go directly to the rationale rather than attempt to concoct a specious theory. The capital structure of a firm is what it is for the reasons given honestly by the corporate treasurer. If no one ever says that they use changes in capital structure as signals, then signaling theory is not an explanation of capital structure even though it may look as if there is signaling. The fundamental methodologies of finance are appropriately the qualitative techniques discussed in Chapter XIV that directly investigate behavior, provided they are not contaminated by the researcher's preconceived theory, (Glaser and Strauss 1967; Burrell and Morgan 1979).

Once data regarding the beliefs that motivate financial behavior have been obtained, the data may be unified not on the basis of some underlying rational behavior, but on the basis of the ebb and flow of ideas—of argument and counter-argument. Financial activity is not a consequence of rational behavior, but the current outcome of an intellectual history. There has been a substantial expenditure of resources to derive hypotheses, models, and theories of finance from Von Neumann and Morgenstern's (1947) fundamental axioms of rational behavior.[15] Agency theory, signaling theory, differential information theory, and a number of others have been devised to achieve this end. On the surface, it does indeed appear as if the demonstration that all finance is the outcome of- rational behavior constitutes understanding or explanation (by Kitcher's 1989 definition), if not the truth. Yet one cannot help but wonder with agency theory, signaling theory, and differential information theory, whether rationality is capable of an infinite expansion to encompass all behavior. If all behavior is rational, and if the current concept of rationality fails to capture a certain behavior, then rationality can and will be stretched to fit it in. The speed of this process is limited only by the ability of financial economists to create the necessary mathematics. McCloskey (1985) argued for the relevance of a rhetoric in economic methodology. In financial economics, the economics itself is a matter of rhetoric as academics and practitioners convince each other not what they are doing, but what it might make sense to do.

Counterintuitive Macrobehavior

Although it is true that a true theory of individual behavior is unlikely to contradict what an individual, including a financial economist, would report as his or her behavior under the circumstances, it is quite possible that the observable large-scale *outcome* of individual behavior may be counterintuitive. Aggregation of individual behavior is not necessarily a simple matter of summation. Unfortunately, there appears to have been little work in this area. Hayek (1967) referred to these sorts of problems as problems of complexity and argued that the traditional mathematical methodology was incapable of dealing with them.

> The statistical method is therefore of use only where we either deliberately ignore, or are ignorant of, the relations between the individual elements with different attributes, i.e., where we ignore or are ignorant of any structure into which they are organized. Statistics in such situations enables us to regain simplicity and to make the task manageable by substituting a single attribute for the unascertainable individual attributes in a collective. It is, however, for this reason irrelevant to the solution of problems in which it is the relations between individual elements with different attributes which matters (p. 30).

Schelling (1978) has offered numerous examples in which the summary outcome of individual rational behavior, which may make common sense, does not necessarily appear as rational behavior on an aggregate level. A serious impediment to progress in this area is the unwritten requirement that economic intuition (in effect, common sense) underlie every theory. Since all theory begins with intuitive rational behavior, it takes an extraordinary financial economist to make the leap of imagination to what a differential outcome will be in the aggregate for which the intuition may be quite obscure.

In financial economics, there is no strictly external environment of any significance. There is no *there* out there. Without an external environment, it is not possible, even in principle, to determine the truth of a scientific statement. Truth is a matter of convention among financial economists and practitioners and not susceptible to independent determination by anyone. Without an external environment, it is not possible to state more or better truths. Unless there is some standard of reference, there are neither more nor better but merely different truths. Whatever might pass for truth is really a reflection of the current relative dominance of beliefs in the struggle among them.

This situation calls for changes in the way research in financial economics is done. A theory that sounds good (i.e., makes sense) is worth consideration. If it is truly original, then empirical confirmation is not simply unnecessary, but impossible. If the object is to explain behavior, then the appropriate methodology is to determine what that behavior was and is and how it came to be that way. Finance is done for the honest reasons that those doing it give for their doing it, and it is necessary to abandon the prejudice against survey research and experimentation in order to acquire this information. If there is a more recondite role for financial economics, it is to discover those circumstances under which the interactions among individuals lead to unintended results. Doing so requires a great leap of imagination and a much reduced role for statistical methods. These are the issues to which we turn in the concluding chapters of this book.

NOTES

1. Here, the term *ontology of finance* means the nature of being or existence of determinants of financial behavior.

2. To clarify the terminology being used here, a "statement regarding the determinants of financial behavior" is the same as a "theoretical statement regarding financial behavior," which is the phrase used in the preceding paragraph. These are explanations or *why* statements. They are different from "statements regarding financial behavior," which are descriptions or *what* statements.

3. Capitalization is used to indicate reference to the elements of the model.

4. Recall that this is a label applied by Boland (1979) to those subscribing to Friedman's (1953) methodology which he himself called "positive."

5. In the vernacular sense of *approach* or *technique*.

6. Actually, selections from prior studies that had made the selections from the External Environment.

7. Although new to finance, this approach was not uncommon elsewhere. It resembles what Popper (1964) refers to as "the method of logical or rational reconstruction, or 'zero method'" (Popper 1964, p. 141). He in turn likens it to the "compositive" method of Menger and von Hayek. Popper also notes its use in economics by Marschak and Florence prior to its use by Modigliani and Miller. It was certainly implicit in Descartes as we noted in Chapter II.

8. Similar to the difficulties in comprehending the implications of relativity and quantum mechanics, that structure the world quite differently than the apparent structure of the world at the scale at which all live.

9. One wonders whether it was the formal proof or the intuition which was expected to be convincing.

10. The meaning of "relative few" is that the number of corporate financial executives or institutional investment managers whose decisions determine market variables is small relative to the numbers whose earnings determine national income or whose votes determine election results, for example. The important consideration, however, is their awareness of the studies of their own behavior.

11. This is not the same phenomenon as the impact of the act of measurement on the object of the measurement (an erroneous interpretation of the Heisenberg uncertainty principle). It also differs from the Copenhagen interpretation of quantum reality in which the act of measurement forces the object of the measurement to assume a certain state. Financial economics does not merely impact an external environment or reveal an external environment; it shapes the perceptions that substitute for an external environment.

12. Financial economics is not the only science for which this effect occurs. It is true of any science, all or at least most of the objects of which are aware of the science. International political economy is another example of a science for which this effect may be important.

13. The chronology is discussed in the *Economist* article, "Of Butterflies and Condors." Prior to Black and Scholes, traders were using tables of Sprenkle's "unknown parameters," for which Black and Scholes supplied values. Financial folklore has it that Black and Scholes traded on the basis of their formula for some time before publication of their work. Options have been in existence for centuries; however, one still wonders if there is a sufficiently large uncontaminated sample of option prices available against which to test the theory.

14. The increased attention being devoted to formal models of market equilibrium with taxes does suggest, however, that the MM perfect-world models have finally become assimilated. Like their counterparts in physics, they have served to define the boundary limits within which acceptable solutions are constrained to lie (Miller 1986, p. 408).

15. The traditional view of rational behavior is that it *is*, or at least *ought to be*, "human nature."

Section 6

FINANCE WITH MEANING

Chapter XIII

Meaning

Early in this book, we introduced Descartes' method of enquiry, of which the current methodology of finance is a direct descendant. In subsequent chapters we showed how that methodology has been refined and enshrined as scientism, how that methodology has inherent limitations and contradictions, and how that methodology has been sustained in spite of its shortcomings.

The usual response to such criticism is to demand an alternative. In one way, this demand is valid. Scientists must do something, and if it should not be done according to Descartes' method, what should it be done according to? But as the post-empiricist historians and philosophers of science have shown, scientists have never, and indeed *can* never, follow Descartes' method, even in its refined and developed form "positivism." Throughout history, scientists have practiced an alternative without really understanding it, claiming to have done one thing while actually having done another.[1] Descartes' method has been more of a rational reconstruction than a procedural guide.

We might speculate on the implications of the unconscious reversal of the logic that to discover laws, we must follow a certain method; that is, if we follow certain methodological rules, then we must discover laws. Finance papers invariably have a section on "methodology." As we have insisted, however, what appears in such sections is really "method." Of course it is impossible for a paper not to have a method, which is nothing more than how what was done was done. By calling "method" "methodology" and by prescribing certain methods and proscribing others, we attempt to guarantee that we find the kinds of knowledge (laws) that we believe to be there.

In another way, this demand for an alternative is inappropriate. The very idea of a scientific method is itself part of the Cartesian philosophy. If the universe is governed by laws, then there must be methodological rules by which the laws can be known. In effect, there must be a law for discovering laws. But if there are parts of the universe that are not governed by laws, then how we are to know these parts?

Human society has always been a thorn in the side of science. Is there or is there not a unity of science according to which the methods of the physical sciences and the social sciences are the same? If human affairs are governed by nomological (lawlike) associations between causes and effects as the physical universe appears to be, then there may very well be a unity of science. If not, there may or may not be.

The issue of the unity of science is thus closely related to that of free will versus determinism. This is a venerable philosophical debate which the authors are by no means qualified to summarize let alone contribute to, and which would be yet another inappropriate direction for this book. We can only admit our belief that there are methodologies and methods, in addition to those of the physical sciences which can contribute to understanding in the social sciences, including finance. This belief is based on our observation that finance has failed to provide any real results (comparable to those of the physical sciences) after decades of diligent and sophisticated effort.[2] Therefore, something must be missing, and there are a number of intellectual and philosophical traditions to suggest what that something might be—meaning.

MEANING

The title, *Toward Finance with Meaning*, implies that "meaning" is something that finance doesn't currently have but ought to have. But what is "meaning" and why is it so important? To answer this question, let us consider three intellectual traditions that have attempted to introduce "meaning" into the social sciences: structuralism, hermeneutics, and critical theory.

Structuralism

The structuralist approach to social science has a foot in the modernist tradition in its propositions that there are universal, general *structures* underlying all human behavior and that these structures can be discovered through systematic analysis (Gardner 1973; Kurzweil 1980). This certainly resembles the Cartesian ontology and epistemology that there are laws governing the universe (here, human behavior) and that these laws are in principle knowable through the scientific method.

Structuralism does, however, make a significant departure from Cartesian modernity. Human behavior cannot be understood as a series of events linked together as causes and effects as in the physical sciences, but as events that have functional meaning within the society in which they occur. Things are not important for the properties they possess, but for their relations with and differences from other things. As Whitehead put it,

The misconception which has haunted philosophic literature throughout the centuries is the notion of "independent existence." There is no such mode of existence; every entity is to be understood in terms of the way it is interwoven with the rest of the universe (quoted in Culler 1986, p. 14).

The best way to study the functions and relations is through language (Culler 1986), and Saussure's structuralist theory of linguistics has unexpected relevance to finance. Language is a system of signs; a "sign" being a combination of a "signified" (the idea or meaning) and a "signifier" (the acoustic form or image). There is not a set of universal concepts or signifieds "out there" awaiting a language to supply its own names or signifiers. Rather, a language structures the world to a certain extent through its choice of a set of signifieds and the rules by which one signified is distinguished from another. If this were not true, language translation would be very simple (a signifier in one language would be perfectly equivalent to a signifier in another), and the evolution of a language would be a clear process of changes in signifiers and the gains and losses of signifieds. According to this theory, a language is a system of signifieds and signifiers defined not by any property they possess independently, but by their relationship to other signifieds and signifiers.

Finance constructs theories using signifiers such as "interest," "dividends," "debt," "equity," "risk," "return," "private investors," "institutional investors," "corporations," and "markets" which have meaning (are attached to signifieds) within the highly stylized system of theoretical finance. But if the purpose of finance is to predict something, to control something, to solve the problems of something, to understand something, to explain something, or to find the truth of something having to do with a real economy, then all these signifiers must also represent real signifieds within that economy. Since the signifieds in a real economy have meaning only within the system of that economy's institutions, the signifieds will differ from country to country and from historical period to historical period.

To put it another way, finance theory is made up of words (signifiers) that are defined (attached to signifieds) within the theory. But when we try to use theory to say something about a real economy, we implicitly assume that the same words (signifiers) used in both the theory and in the economy have the same meanings (signifieds) in the economy as they do in the theory. Finance makes the bold assumption that the words in our theory not only mean the same things in the theory as they do in the economy from which the theory was developed, but also mean the same things in all other economies as well.[3] The signifiers are inappropriately assumed to have universal value. This was the underlying message of Chapter VII.

The "meaning" of Fujitsu dividends is different from the "meaning" of Apple dividends; and Carnegie Steel dividends, from USX dividends, because all the attendant institutions are to some degree different for each firm. Without first understanding the meaning or function of dividends within individual economies rather than assuming some sort of identity across economies solely because they use the same word, we can never hope to penetrate the underlying structures that govern dividends across systems. There is no reason not to propose, in advance, an underlying structure; however, it is arrogant to assume that one system (i.e., the financial markets and institutions of the late twentieth century United States) should provide the model for this structure.[4]

Hermeneutics

Returning to the purposes of science, we find that five of the six—to predict something, to control something, to solve the problems of something, to explain something, and to find the truth of something— appear, at least at first glance, to be fully consistent with a Cartesian philosophy, which presupposes objectivity, that there are things out there, that those things have properties, and that the things and properties are independent of whoever or whatever is observing them. To understand something is something more,[5] for understanding implies that there is a connection between the observer and the thing observed[6]—that the thing has a "meaning" that the observer understands or comprehends.[7]

Hermeneutics is a tradition that acknowledges the importance of the observer and understanding, not just in the social sciences but in the natural sciences as well. No observer can avoid his or her own history and own prejudices; therefore, there is no such thing as objectivity.[8] In fact, that objectivity is a desirable value is itself a consequence of history and prejudice, albeit one that we are so steeped in that we do not recognize it as such.[9] This echoes the statement made earlier in this book that belief in the scientific method is unscientific, for the scientific method cannot justify itself.

In positivism, the role of understanding (or *Verstehen*), in the sense of understanding someone's intentions, was as a source of hypotheses, but it played no role in the scientific process itself. The original *Verstehende*, or hermeneutic theorists, contended that, in the social sciences, it was not possible to explain why something occurred without understanding its meaning within the specific context in which it occurred; therefore, understanding was a necessary part of the scientific process. Gadamer's contention is that understanding is not limited to the conditions surrounding an occurrence, but is concerned with seeing the truth of something. Truth itself is something to be understood, rather than known. Knowledge is made, not found (Warnke 1987).

This is not to say that truth or reason is purely relative or idiosyncratic, but that what is true or rational comes out of a shared tradition. This idea closely resembles the post-empiricists' concept of a research paradigm, program, or tradition and also resembles philosophical pragmatism.

> There is no thinking which does not present itself on a background of tradition, and tradition has an intellectual quality that differentiates it from blind custom. Traditions are ways of interpretation and of observation, of valuation, of everything explicitly thought of. They are the circumambient atmosphere which thought must breathe; no one ever had an idea except as he inhaled some of this atmosphere (John Dewey, quoted in Tiles 1988, p. 22).

Referring to the purpose of science which is to find the truth of something, Dewey's comment on truth reflects its hermeneutic nature.

> The best definition of *truth* from the logical standpoint which is known to me is that of Peirce: "The opinion which is fated to be ultimately agreed to by all who investigate is what we mean by truth and the object represented by this opinion is the real" (John Dewey, quoted in Tiles 1988, p. 106).

Charles Sanders Peirce, the pragmatist philosopher referred to in this quotation, himself challenged the Cartesian scientific method, arguing that the acquisition of knowledge (of the truth) is a much less structured process. It arises out of an assortment of information, results, conjectures, opinions, and arguments assembled by a "community of inquirers" (Bernstein, 1983).

In signaling theory, finance has adopted a concept that depends very much on understanding and meaning, yet has managed to divorce itself from understanding and meaning. To reiterate, the origin of the word *signaling* is in a seminal paper by Spence (1973), who developed a model for a very specific, well-defined, and constrained situation in which signals are exchanged between an interviewer (the signalee) and a job-seeker (the signaler).

Clearly, a signal depends very much on a signalee's understanding a meaning implicit in an action of a signaler. To do so, the signalee must be able in some hermeneutic sense to put himself or herself in the position of the signaler. To the best of the knowledge of the authors, there is not a single study that attempts to verify this—that signaling was management's original intention and that it was clear both to management and, to the best of their understanding, to the signalees that the signalees decoded the signal properly. Although the very nature of signaling would seem to make it very context-dependent, finance treats signaling as if any signalee is able to perfectly interpret any signal by any signaler.

Critical Theory

Considering again the purposes of science, we have concluded that hermeneutics focuses on understanding. Shifting the focus to control introduces an entirely new set of issues. However benign its application, the idea of control is inseparable from the idea of power. It is naive to believe that the knowledge obtained by finance or by any science will not be used in some way or another to exercise power within the community of scientists and in society in general.[10] In turn, the prospect of power must influence how the science is conducted. Habermas identifies three processes of inquiry—empirical-analytic [Cartesian], which yields technical knowledge of laws in the natural and social sciences; historical-hermeneutic, which yields understanding of meaning in the social sciences and humanities; and critically oriented sciences, which concern ideology and yield what he refers to as emancipatory potential (McCarthy 1978).

That a not insignificant number of the most famous finance professors have left their universities for Wall Street, either to join existing financial firms or to form their own and that many others do substantial consulting work on the side indicate that finance has its payoffs. It would be naive to believe that research is conducted without an eye toward these opportunities. Critical theory considers how science and society interact.

Earlier in this book, there was an incomplete quotation from Husserl, which we now present in its entirety.

> [Modern science operates] like a machine, reliable in accomplishing obviously very useful things, a machine everyone can learn to operate correctly without in the least understanding the inner possibility and necessity of this sort of accomplishment (Husserl, quoted in Held 1980, p. 167).

The important idea here is that there are values implicit in the scientific method and that these values both reflect the values of society and reinforce the values of society, thereby acting as a conservative force to preserve the status quo.

Consider that the scientific method is especially well designed to serve what we have called the practical or economic purposes of science, and less obviously geared toward the epistemological ones. The centrality of the practical is not coincidental. Consider also the assumptions of objectivity implicit in Cartesianism. The values of the Enlightenment and Modernity are usefulness, efficiency, and rationality, and these values are best served by a formalist mathematical approach to science (Held 1980).

The formal system at the heart of finance theory works to reinforce existing behavior. If the principles on which the system has been developed were taken from existing behavior, they take on the appearance of incontrovertability. "Positive" principles become "normative" ones. Then, not only do the principles explain behavior, but also behavior inconsistent with the principles is labeled "irrational."

Sociobiology uses similar reasoning. As finance attempts to derive all financial behavior from what are essentially fundamental biological principles (such as *maximization*), sociobiology is an attempt to concoct evolutionary histories for all human behavior. If adaptation leads inevitably to optimization, then *what is* is *what must be*. It would be suboptimal to be anything else. This is reflected in Lumsden and Wilson (1981):

> Only with difficulty can individual development be deflected from narrow channels along which the great majority of human beings travel. In most conceivable environments, and in the absence of a forceful attempt to produce other responses, these behaviors will persist as the norms of culture in most or all societies (pp. 357-358).

In effect, what *is* is transformed into what *has to be*. Then, of course, there is a thin line between what *has to be* and what *ought to be* (Kaye 1986). Once certain behavior is certified as normative by theoreticians, then that certification reinforces the continuation or multiplication of the behavior. Financial behavior that may (or even may not) have been appropriate in the culture in which the theory originated is extended to another culture where the theory is adopted. Since the biological behavior is the same there, why should finance be different if financial behavior is simply an extension of biological behavior?

Kitcher (1985) attacks this reasoning with devastating results. He contends that creating an evolutionary history of a phenotype is a complex matter in which accident may play an important role along with natural selection. And how natural selection works depends on what it has to work with. This is likewise true regarding the derivation of accounting and financial behavior from biological principles. For example, the capital markets and financial institutions currently observed are more likely the result of complex social and historical processes than any rational natural selection. As Sahlins (1976) puts it:

> For between the basic drives that may be attributed to human nature and the social structures of human culture there enters a critical indeterminacy. The same human motives appear in different cultural forms, and different motives appear in the same forms. A fixed correspondence being lacking between the character of society and the human character, there can be no biological determinism (p. 11).

For a number of reasons, *what is* is not *what has to be*. Marx even argued that there are no economic laws, for the economy is a consequence of the vicissitudes of its historical development. Any presumptive economic laws simply serve to solidify the status quo (Keat and Urry 1982).

Modernity and Post-Modernity

Considering these very brief comments on structuralism, hermeneutics, and critical theory, we see that finance lacks real meaning in at least three different senses: it presupposes the meaning of words independent of languages, it presupposes the meaning of interactions independent of actors, and it presupposes the meaning of knowledge independent of the uses to which that knowledge will be put. In essence, finance has been inappropriately extracted from culture, without which it has no meaning. Let us briefly consider what might be called a "post-modern" culture in which "meaning" is important[11] as an alternative to the scientistic modern culture in which the ontology and epistemology of finance have been rooted.

The term *post-modern* has been used in many different contexts, and not always consistently. It has, in fact, become a sort of academic flavor-of-the-month in a number of disciplines. This popular treatment, however, should not detract from its intellectual importance and its possible contribution to finance.

Perhaps the greatest value in the notion of post-modernity is its contrast with certain features of modernity. Modernity is rooted in facts and objects; post-modernity in the models or images constructed out of those facts and the uses of the objects (Wakefield 1990). As described earlier in this book, modernity begins with things (objects) and the properties of the things, and the purpose of science is to discover the facts about them; that is, the laws which govern how properties change and how things relate. In post-modernity, what is important is how things and so-called facts are used within a culture, which, of course, changes as culture changes. In modernity, there is an inherent meaning to objects; in post-modernity, the meaning lies in their appearance.

Modernity believes that truth is an objective attribute; that is, it is in principle possible to determine whether a statement is true by comparing it with some outside reality. This is a transcendental realism, that the existence of things transcends how an observer sees them or knows them. In post-modernity, as in pragmatism, what is true is what is persuasive given the current belief system. Modernity has a whole, rigid, all-encompassing system (Descartes' fantasy); post-modernity has fragmented, flexible relationships (Bennington 1988). Modern explanations rely on cause-and-effect relationships; post-modern, on the interplay between interpretations of meaning (Norris 1987). Gane (1991) describes the modern concern with cause and effect very dramatically:

> The hysteria of causality [is] the delirium of trying to explain everything and to reference everything. The mass expands and becomes a fantastic encumbrance, a growing mass of interpretations which has little relation to any objective (p. 177).[12]

Foucault has coined the term *episteme* to accommodate the changing environment of post-modernity.

> [An episteme is] an epistemological space specific to a particular period, [a general form of thinking and theorizing that establishes] what ideas can appear, what sciences can be constituted, what experiences can be reflected in philosophies, what rationalities can be formed, only, perhaps, to dissolve and vanish soon afterwards (Foucault, quoted in Miller 1993, p. 150).

Modernity is only one among many styles of reasoning. In fact, one of post-modernity's strongest arguments is one presented earlier in a different form, that science cannot contain its own justification; that is, the modern can only justify itself within the realm of the post-modern.

What we hope to have shown in this chapter is that there are a number of well-known philosophies or methodologies for the social sciences that incorporate "meaning," an attribute that has been missing from the Cartesian methodology of finance and that the authors claim is the reason for the failure of finance. Finance has become so detached from its cultural meaning that it has little useful to say about society. What this chapter has not shown, however, is what scientists ought to do as an alternative to what they are doing now. In the following chapter, we will discuss a number of alternative methods consistent with these alternative methodologies.

NOTES

1.   An exploration of the implicit alternatives, however, would take this book off in an inappropriate direction. Those who are interested in more details should see Kuhn (1970), Lakatos (1978), and Laudan (1977) for further discussions.

2.   We understand that this section might offend those in finance who would agree with Lionel Robbins' observation concerning economics: "The efforts of economists during the last hundred and fifty years have resulted in the establishment of a body of generalisations whose substantial accuracy and importance are open to question only by the ignorant or the perverse" (Robbins 1952, p. 1).

3.   For example, liquidity preference is a technical concept of economics: it is not generally used by business men in the conduct of their affairs, but by the economist who wishes to explain the nature and consequences of certain kinds of business behaviour. But it is logically tied to concepts in business activity, for its use by the economist presupposes his understanding of what it is to conduct a business, which in turn involves an understanding of such business concepts as money, profit, cost, risk, and so forth. It is only the relation between his account and these concepts which makes it an account of economic activity as opposed, say, to a piece of theology (Winch 1958, p. 89).

4.   But ideas cannot be torn out of their context in that way; the relation between idea and context is an internal one. The idea gets its sense from the role it plays in the system. It is nonsensical to take several systems of ideas, find an element in each which can be expressed in the same verbal form, and then claim to have discovered an idea which is common to all the systems (Winch 1958, p. 107).

5.   Human science too is concerned with establishing similarities, regularities, and conformities to law which would make it possible to predict individual phenomena and processes… But the specific problem that the human sciences present to thought is that one has not rightly grasped their nature if one measures them by the yardstick of a progressive knowledge of regularity… The individual case does not serve only to confirm a law from which practical predictions can be made. Its ideal is rather to understand the phenomenon itself in its unique and historical concreteness. However much experiential universals are involved, the aim is not to confirm and extend these universalized experiences in order to attain knowledge of a law… but to understand how this man, this people, or this state is what it has become or, more generally, how it happened that it is so (Gadamer 1993, p. 4).

6.   An 'explanation' requires the application of theoretical propositions to facts that are established independently through systematic observation. In contrast, 'understanding' is an act in which experience and theoretical apprehension are fused…. In understanding I transpose my own self into something external in such a way that a past or foreign experience again becomes present in my own (Habermas 1971, p. 144).

7.   We begin with this proposition: 'to understand means to come to an understanding with each other.' Understanding is, primarily agreement. Thus, people usually understand each other immediately, or they make themselves understood with a view toward reaching agreement. Coming to an understanding, then, is always coming to an understanding about something. Understanding each other is always understanding each other with respect to something. From language we learn that the subject matter is not merely an arbitrary object of discussion, independent of the process of mutual understanding itself. And if two people understand each other independently of any topic, then this means that they understand each other not only in this or that respect, but in all the essential things that unite human beings (Gadamer 1993, p. 180).

It is true that the German language uses the word for 'understanding' also in the sense of a practical ability…. But this seems essentially different from the understanding that takes place in science and that is concerned with knowledge. If we examine the two senses more closely, we can see that they have something in common; both senses contain the element of recognition, of being well versed in something (Gadamer 1993, p. 260).

"We are 'thrown' into the world as beings who understand and interpret—so if we are to understand what it is to be human beings, we must seek to understand understanding itself, in its rich, full, and complex dimensions. Furthermore, understanding is not one type of activity, to be contrasted with other human activities…. Understanding is universal and may properly be said to underlie and pervade all activities (Bernstein 1983, p. 112).

8.   "There is no knowledge without preconceptions and prejudices" (Bernstein 1983, p. 128).

Does being situated within tradition really mean being subject to prejudices and limited in one's freedom? Is not, rather, all human existence, even the freest, limited and qualified in various ways? If this is true, the idea of an absolute reason is not a possibility for historical humanity. Reason exists for us only in concrete historical terms—i.e., it is not its own master but remains constantly dependent on the given circumstances in which it operates (Gadamer 1993, p. 276).

9.   The recognition that all understanding inevitably involves some prejudice gives the hermeneutical problem its real thrust…. The fundamental prejudice of the Enlightenment is the prejudice against prejudice itself, which denies tradition its power. This history of ideas shows that not until the Enlightenment does the concept of prejudice acquire the negative connotation familiar today. Actually, 'prejudice' means a judgement that is rendered before all the elements that determine a situation have been fully examined…. The only thing that gives a judgement dignity is its having a basis, a methodological justification (and not the fact that it may actually be correct). For the Enlightenment the absence of such a basis does not mean that there might be other kinds of certainty, but rather that the judgement has no

foundation in the things themselves—that is, that it is 'unfounded.' This conclusion follows only in the spirit of rationalism. It is the reason for discrediting prejudices and the reason scientific knowledge claims to exclude them completely. In adopting this principle, modern science is following the rule of Cartesian doubt, accepting nothing as certain that can in any way be doubted, and adopting the idea of method that follows from this rule (Gadamer 1993, p. 270).

10.   "So to understand the activities of an individual scientific investigator we must take account of two sets of relations: first, his relation to the phenomena which he investigates; second, his relation to his fellow scientists" (Winch 1958, p. 84).

11.   Only in the last 25 years, however, have academic philosophers in Britain and the United States generally shared his [Wittgenstein's] underlying perception that 'meaning' cannot be analyzed as a timeless relationship between propositions and states of affairs alone, but must be understood always in relation to one or another larger behavioral context (Toulmin 1990, p. 187).

12.   This quotation bears a striking resemblance to the comments of the modernists on the medieval schoolmen, which were quoted in Chapter II.

Chapter XIV

Alternative Methods

THE QUANTITATIVE RESEARCH TRADITION

Consistent with the Cartesian philosophy on which it is based, quantitative research regarding securities prices dominates finance.[1] The "accomplishments" of finance enumerated earlier—notably the EMH, the CAPM, the APT, and the Black-Scholes/Merton option pricing formula—are archetypal products of theoretical quantitative research, and tests of these and other hypotheses, models, theories, and formulas constitute empirical quantitative research. For the last three decades, such research papers have so dominated the finance literature, one might argue, that they serve not as *examples* of finance research, but as *definitions* of such research.

Quantitative research has most certainly led to the creation of new financial instruments and markets for use by investors, contributed to a deeper understanding of market behavior, and informed the development of market regulatory policies, so it cannot be said that there has been no social effect, and some of it may even have been beneficial.

Do not forget, however, the advantages that accrue to finance academics as a result of their efforts, as was discussed in Chapter XI. Prominent financial scholars enjoy the professional respect of their colleagues, are compensated with salaries much higher than those of other faculty, and are able to take advantage of lucrative consulting opportunities. The most famous scholars have actually founded ideological dynasties at their universities (The Chicago School, The Rochester School, etc.) and even received Nobel prizes. Through their joint control of the editorial boards of the major finance journals and the political and social processes that underlie doctoral education, these researchers can ensure the perpetuation of their methods as the sole form of legitimate inquiry and guarantee their own future success. In view of these advantages, it would be foolish for a scholar of finance to pursue anything but traditional (also called "modern finance") quantitative research!

223

Herein lies a paradox. Is it not ironic that those scholars who have enlightened us regarding the correlation between risk and the rate of return are the same scholars who are able to achieve the highest professional returns by choosing the path of least intellectual risk?[2] Unfortunately, this irony is overshadowed by a more pernicious note. Unless there is a downside to quantitative research, quantitative researchers are compelled to blindly defend their intellectual monopoly, repudiating any arguments challenging the supremacy of such research and ostracizing scholars advancing such arguments. Their actions, of course, are justified in the spirit of the rational economic man inhabiting all of their theories.

Let us summarize the principles that govern the quantitative research tradition in finance as they were introduced in Chapter II and augmented and expanded on throughout the book.

1. An underlying cause and effect mechanism animates all financial activity. Connections exist between initial conditions and final outcomes.
2. These connections are determinable, and if conditions were to be completely specified, which it is in principle possible to do, then outcomes could be predicted with certainty.
3. The free will of the human beings by whom and for whom all financial activity is undertaken can be ignored. All relevant human behavior is governed by the cause and effect mechanism.
4. All financial activity can be quantified, and the logic of statistical analysis and inference applies to all measurements.
5. All human beings have equal access to the institutions and systems within which financial activity is undertaken.

Now consider this research tradition within a broader social science perspective, using a scheme developed by Burrell and Morgan (1979)—a scheme that has already proven useful for analyzing research in accounting (Tomkins and Groves 1983a, 1983b; Willmott 1983). The scheme has had its critics, but it does provide us with an excellent way to summarize a number of debates regarding the nature of social science research and to identify two crucial issues that must be addressed prior to any study: the nature of social science research and the nature of society. One's position regarding these issues locates one's research on a corresponding two-dimensional grid. The nature of social science research is an objective-to-subjective axis, and the nature of society is a consensus-and-compromise to contention-and-domination axis.

To identify social science research as objective or subjective, Burrell and Morgan consider four factors:

1. Ontology (What is knowable?)
2. Epistemology (What is knowledge?)
3. Human Nature (How do humans interact?)
4. Methodology (How is knowledge acquired?)

The first four principles of traditional quantitative research listed above clearly label it as objective. There is a cause-and-effect mechanism underlying all natural and human activity (ontology); it is known through the set of law-like connections between initial conditions and final outcomes (epistemology); humans interact with each other and with their environment in accordance with this mechanism (human nature); information regarding all natural and human activity can be acquired through observations and measurements unaffected by individual perceptual differences (methodology). All told, the deterministic world of finance research is not unlike that of statistical mechanics.

At the subjective end of the continuum, things are quite different. Although financial activity itself is still quite real, there is no unchanging deeper reality animating it (ontology). Therefore, there is no list of invariant laws; rather, one knows finance as a subtle interplay of changing perceptions and patterns (epistemology). Financial activity is undertaken by idiosyncratic humans, aware of their own and others' actions and aware of the self-analysis of financial research, as was pointed out in Chapter XII. Their interactions with their environment and with each other are voluntary, and can be described and interpreted, but not predicted (human nature). The acquisition of knowledge requires the close observation of financial activity. Since the judgment and biases of the observer are an inseparable component of the process, all knowledge is researcher-specific. Many events cannot be quantified, and even if they could, the interactions of the measured variables would be intractable in mathematical terms (methodology).

We are not so foolish as to accuse finance researchers of believing that financial activity is the outcome of inelastic collisions (interactions) between fundamental particles (human beings). We would, however, go so far as to accuse them of behaving as if such objectivity were their belief. They look at debt, for example, as if it were a proton. Just as all protons that exist or have ever existed anywhere in the universe are identical and there are laws governing the behavior of these protons, so is it also for debt. There is no other explanation for the equal treatment in capital structure theories of the debt of Citibank and the Industrial Bank of Japan, of Dell Computer Corporation and International Business Machines, or of Carnegie Steel Corporation in 1886 and United States Steel in 1986. In finance research, debt is debt, and there must be invariant laws that govern it.[3]

Objectivity, of course, has its attractions. In the natural sciences, where objectivity is a more (but not completely) defensible position, accomplishments have been astonishing. There is a natural tendency to want to duplicate the methods of the natural sciences in order to duplicate their successes, but this cannot be done without making the assumption of objectivity implicit in the methods. The implications of this tacit assumption are never addressed. Objectivity also has the appearance of certainty that is missing from subjectivity. It is comforting to believe that a measurement is correct or incorrect or that a theory is verified or falsified regardless of who it is making the measurement or testing the theory. With objectivity, we can pretend to ignore the disturbing ambiguity about things that are neither right nor wrong, good nor bad.

The second issue used to position social science research concerns how human beings have contrived to define the character of society. At one extreme, we assume that people have voluntarily agreed to the institutions and customs that govern social interaction. Research is concerned with how this system works and why it has developed as it has. At the other extreme, the viewpoint focuses on how society changes and how power structures exist to repress certain groups in favor of others. Research seeks to discover the hidden patterns of power and emancipate the repressed groups. Burrell and Morgan call these two views regulation and radical change, with the former implying consensus and compromise and the latter contention and domination.

The fifth principle listed above places finance research at the regulation end of the continuum. Whether one is a widow, an orphan, or a Wall Street banker, one has equal access to the financial system, and a dollar is a dollar, whether it belongs to Warren Buffet, Warren Beatty, or Warren Peace. Although power struggles certainly occur, they do so within the rational confines of the so-called "market for corporate control." This telling metaphor is indicative of voluntary exchange, not of the involuntary seizure that is often characteristic of such power struggles.

Together, the opposing views regarding the nature of social science research and the nature of society define four different research programs, as shown in Figure 1. Traditional finance research is firmly embedded deep in the lower right functionalist corner. Its underlying belief structure holds that knowledge is quantifiable and stable. Society has certain immutable rules that researchers can discover. Having discovered these rules, researchers can then specify how future behaviors will unfold, because they are predictable from the rules. Furthermore, the rules are set by voluntary consensus, and radical change is both undesirable and unlikely. This view of finance is almost indistinguishable from that of natural science. The logical methodology is totally quantitative, since the researchers believe (implicitly or explicitly) that their measurements capture an objective reality that exists independent of the observers.

Radical Change, Conflict, Domination

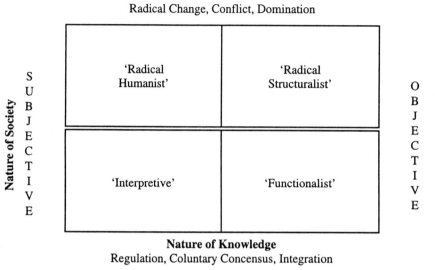

Nature of Society

'Radical Humanist'	'Radical Structuralist'
'Interpretive'	'Functionalist'

SUBJECTIVE

OBJECTIVE

Nature of Knowledge
Regulation, Coluntary Concensus, Integration

Figure XIV.1.

There is no "right" place to be within this scheme. Where you are, as a researcher, should be a function of your personal beliefs and the subjects that interest you, not a reflection of what is fashionable. What might radical structuralist, interpretive, or radical humanist finance be if such alternatives were to become a professional possibility? We can speculate; however, it is only speculation. Since little or no finance research is done in quadrants other than the functionalist, there is no way to say for certain what it might really be.

Consider, for example, research regarding capital structure. The traditional finance research program (functionalist) proceeds on the belief that firms have an intrinsic value equal to the discounted value of their future cash flows. The market value of the firm may differ from the intrinsic value only for short periods of disequilibrium. The goal of research regarding capital structure is to determine how the mix of financial claims issued by a firm affects (if at all) its intrinsic value.

The radical structuralist program would take a Marxist approach. One attribute of this approach is the belief that products have a use value dependent on their labor content and an exchange value in the marketplace. Under a capitalist system, firms attempt to exploit the laboring class for the benefit of the owners of the firm and the institutions under their control.

228 / Toward Finance with Meaning

Here, the goal of research regarding capital structure would be to discover the rules that govern how this value appropriated from labor is distributed among the capitalists and what effect that distribution has on relative power.

Although this appears to be a "radical" perspective by conventional finance standards, the underlying idea is unexpectedly familiar. It is not too different from the concept of agency theory, in which managers are thought to attempt to appropriate wealth from owners, who are attempting to prevent them from doing so. Agency theory, however, is an attempt to cast this not as a power struggle with strong overtones of domination and contention, but as an inevitable friction of the system that demands an appropriate "rational" response to eliminate it. It is also not too different from the theory of shareholders' attempting to appropriate wealth from bondholders through their choices of capital investments for the firm. Here again, the power struggle is solved "rationally" through the structure of debt contracts. Although everyone in this world, by their very nature, desperately wants to, no one ever breaks the rules, which are the model of impartiality.

In an interpretive research program, any objective value that a firm or its claims might have is subordinate to their sign values. This sign value locates a firm or claim within its culture and determines how other members or elements of that culture relate, respond, or react to it (Kellner 1989). Sign value is not an indication of reality, it creates reality. Reality and sign values are constantly changing. Interpretive research regarding capital structure would seek to determine what effects a firm sought to have on investors when it chose which claims to issue and what those effects turned out to be. It might also consider the historical paths by which certain claims came to have certain meanings. Debt in an interpretive research program is not just debt, but a claim whose sign value will always be quite different depending on who issued the debt, when, and under what circumstances.

Interestingly enough, the concept of a signal, which has become quite common in finance research, bears a strong resemblance to sign value. A functionalist research program uses the metaphor of a signal to mean that the firm's managers use capital structure, for example, to transmit information to investors regarding intrinsic value (or market value in equilibrium). In an interpretive program, however, the signification works in the other direction with market value communicating something about sign value. Using the metaphor of a signal implies a "rational" process of communication in which a deliberate message is encoded by the sender and correctly decoded by the receiver or by anyone else. "Debt" means something; everyone knows what it means; and the intention of the firm issuing debt was the communication of this meaning. Unfortunately, we know of no published finance research that ever asked a firm what it was signaling when it issued debt or asked an investor what debt meant to him or her.

A radical humanist program more or less combines features of the interpretive and radical structuralist programs[4] Here once again, the emphasis is on sign value, but signs signify the dominance of one group over another. The capital structure of the firm is a reflection of a power struggle within the firm issuing the claims, within the investment bank managing the issuance of the claims, and/or within the community or investors. Signs are manipulated by contending groups to enhance their power.

To reiterate, there is no "best" social science research program. All four can contribute to knowledge and understanding of capital structure, or any other matter in finance, although for them to do so, one must believe that knowledge and understanding is a much more complicated goal than simple predictability, as Friedman (1953) asserted. It must include *meaning*. Although traditional finance research appears to recognize that there is a wide variety of financial activity going on out there, it attempts to squeeze everything into a rational, objective, quantitative functionalist program through such questionable devices as agency theory and signaling theory.

Isn't it possible that finance issues have been so exhaustively studied in a single way that such studies have reached the point of diminishing returns? In regard to this question, Campbell, Daft, and Hulin (1982) point out that the popularity of a particular research program does not necessarily have a positive relation to its relative contribution to knowledge. On the contrary, it is often creative, innovative, and sometimes controversial pursuits that contribute most to the knowledge we acquire. Do we really learn much of value from yet another event study or another calculation of implied volatility using a hitherto unmined dataset or a recently discovered statistical procedure? Chapter XI offered some suggestions as to why finance research has the limited scope it has. Now we turn to what financial researchers might actually *do* to put some *meaning* into financial research.

NEW DIRECTIONS IN FINANCE

Unfortunately, many writers emphatically argue that traditional quantitative methods are incompatible with different, more qualitative, methods.[5] However, a growing number of researchers have begun to advocate a blend of these seemingly dichotomous methical approaches.[6] Qualitative and/or normative finance research (e.g., approaches traditionally associated with sociological and anthropological research) will enable scholars to examine aggregate market behavior in conjunction with ethical, cultural, ecological, political, and social issues.[7] In breaking the mold of tradition, emerging trends in the finance literature may, at long last, be again characterized by robustness, creativity, insight, multidimensionality, and a renewed applicability in addressing and analyzing the complex problems of a diverse world economy.

Some important topics require qualitative methods if we are to investigate them in any meaningful way. Finance researchers must examine the questions that are important in the world—they cannot pass by them simply because they don't fit into a quantitative framework. We suggest three such important issues, but there are certainly others.

One is the nature of finance itself; what it is, how we understand and define it, and where it fits into society. Other social sciences and humanities disciplines have well-established and continuing debates about their own nature and deep assumptions, but this discussion is lacking in the finance literature. We do not think that a legitimate academic field can achieve maturity without such a debate. We hope that this book will be an early contribution to a growing body of qualitative research into the nature of finance research.

A second emerging area is the effect of cultural and social differences on financial practice. International business and international finance are academic fields that expand as global trade grows. We observe that there are significant differences in financial practices and institutions among countries, and that these differences persist. We cannot reasonably maintain that there is one universal quantitative theory to explain these practices. The obvious place to look for part of the explanation is in the historical and cultural effects, and such research must be partly or wholly qualitative. The essential differences between Japanese and North American business culture and practice or even between North American business culture and practice at different times in history, are not neatly summarized and explained in a system of differential equations or a table of statistics.[8]

If the problems science sets out to solve and how it sets out to solve them are consequences of the social environment in which the science is undertaken and the historical trajectory that led to it, then science cannot be understood without reference to this socio-historical context (Kellner 1989).

Ethics in finance and business is another emerging field that is occupying more of finance teachers' time, but there is almost no research. Sessions at conferences focus on how to teach ethics, and publications are exclusively case studies for use in teaching.[9] We cannot imagine studying ethics without focusing on the qualitative effects of financial decision making, since it is the quality of what happens that poses ethical dilemmas. Ang (1993) presents a far-ranging discussion of financial ethics, based on a written exchange of letters with nine academics and practitioners with experience in this field. One of the striking features of the discussion is the extent to which qualitative rather than quantitative concepts underlie any attempt to understand and apply ethical standards. Stephen Loeb, one of the participants, notes the unsuitability of the reward structure for accountants who might be interested in accounting ethics, and Ang's concluding remark is:

Specifically, it is questionable that faculty members would be recognized for doing teaching and research in financial ethics and whether mainstream finance journals would publish theoretical, empirical, or case studies in this area. Without the proper incentive, like ethical choices, it would be a tough and brave decision for the finance faculty to make (Ang 1993, p. 56).

For those willing to make the tough and brave decision to broaden their horizon by entering into qualitative research, such a departure from tradition would undoubtedly require a great deal of academic retooling. However, as a starting point for those willing to boldly go where few in finance have gone before, there are resources from other disciplines to point the way.

ALTERNATIVE METHODS

First, to assist in formulating strategies for theory development, *The Discovery of Grounded Theory* (Glaser and Strauss 1967) and *Critical Issues in Social Theory* (Rhoads,1991) both provide valuable, historical insight pertaining to the origin and evolution of competing theories. Second, to assist in the integration and unification of competing paradigms, *The Design of Inquiring Systems* (Churchman 1971) and *Sociological Paradigms and Organizational Analysis* (Burrell and Morgan 1979) both provide critical insight regarding the framing of research paradigms in a general systems context. Finally, to assist in planning and operationalizing new directions in financial research, Morgan (1983) provides a useful framework that requires the researcher to evaluate his or her view of the social world, define his or her epistemological stance, and eventually, select an appropriate methodological approach consistent with his or her social views and epistemological grounding. The papers that make up the bulk of Morgan (1983) provide a wide variety of views on methodologies located in each of the four major quadrants in Figure XIV.1.

Following, we provide some very brief examples of different qualitative methods that seem appropriate for use in finance. In a more general sense, the entire field of philosophy that we have tried to introduce in this book provides a qualitative methodology and method for investigating the ontological and epistemological issues that are a critical part of the development of any social science. Now, we offer some examples of more specific methods.

Grounded Field Theory

Glaser and Strauss (1967) describe grounded field theory as a method to develop theory by probing deeply into what a number of actors—investors, companies, mutual funds, and so on—do when they are making the decisions that interest us. The investigation typically involves long interviews and subsequent interpretation of them.[10] From the interpretation, one or more theories or hypotheses arise, and are refined as more interviews and interpretations are completed. These may be competing or complementary theories. The researcher can then try to test these theories with other quantitative or qualitative methods, whichever seem appropriate.

The contrasting purely quantitative method is to develop a theory by building on first principles. Once the researcher builds some structure, usually with mathematical modeling in modern finance, he or she tests it to find if it has any resemblance to reality. (Of course, it must have some resemblance to reality, or at least the researcher's perception of reality, for that is where the first principles and the idea for the theory must have come from in the first place.) We think grounded field theory is both suitable and particularly important for finance, in which there seems to have developed an increasing gap between researchers' perceptions of reality and reality itself. Some researchers, however, seem to be using grounded field theory implicitly.

A recent example of grounded field research in accounting is Gibbins, Richardson, and Waterhouse (1990). They interviewed key accounting personnel to find out how they decide on their accounting policies. From their analysis of the interview data,[11] they hypothesize that policies are set either opportunistically to take advantage of some perceived financial advantage or ritualistically in accordance with established customs. The received wisdom on the question is positive accounting theory, which concerns itself only with the opportunistic theory because it agrees with the standard assumptions about economic behavior that we use when building theories from first principles. They may then test their hypotheses using more conventional quantitative techniques.

Gibbins et al. (1990) follow Glaser and Strauss (1967) explicitly. One often-cited work in finance, Lintner (1956), does grounded field research without this guidance. Lintner forms his theory of how corporate executives make dividend payout decisions by interviewing a number of the executives. His theory of sticky dividend payouts holds up well today, in spite of the hordes of subsequent papers building ever more complex signaling, agency, and taxation models to provide excuses for re-running CRSP tapes.

O'Barr and Conley (1992) interviewed institutional money managers extensively to find out how they make their decisions. Both authors are trained in cultural anthropology. They report that the supposedly quantitative, rational investment world is defined by its culture, and its decisions reflect that culture, rather than the rigorous economics that most outsiders (and finance theories) expect. Cray and Haines (1992) use deep interviewing techniques to find that pension fund managers don't use prescriptive textbook models because there is too much data to manage and they are subject to a "cleavage of interests." The cleavage is the competing political influence of all the different actors—investors, trustees, regulators, the managers themselves, competitors, brokers, and information sources.

The aforementioned paper by Ang (1993) is a very preliminary sort of grounded field research. Aside from that paper, we do not see finance researchers doing this kind of work. The authors of the two studies on the fund managers just cited work in other disciplines. Zipser (1994), discussing O'Barr and Conley, says that the academic field is ignoring their work, the money managers revile it, and few people seem interested in buying the book.

This sort of theory-building is essential if finance is to remain a relevant discipline, however. Cray and Haines conclude:

> As with many types of decision support tools, a focus on the technical aspects of the decision has led to inappropriate formalization and the neglect of human interaction. As a result, pension fund managers find such techniques both threatening and irrelevant. It is small wonder they are little used. The descriptions in this paper of the actual decision process used by pension fund managers can go some way toward alleviating this problem if they come to the attention of those who develop their models and if the form of the message does not immediately lead to the rejection of the content (Cray and Haines 1992, p, 58).

Ethnographic Analysis

Rosen (1990) critically analyzes numerous media statements of journalists and public finance figures during the market crashes of 1987 and 1989.[12] He argues that the stock markets are part of the essence of how Americans define themselves. When the markets went into free-fall, completely contradicting the EMH and any other positivist explanation based on past market data and research, the plunge threatened the very existence of the belief structure built by the American economy. Americans were confronted with chaos, and the cherished (and Nobel-Prize-winning) models of finance had nothing to say about it. Rosen further emphasizes the ethnographic nature of his research by noting that he was and is a licensed stockbroker, and thus was a participant-observer, rather than a researcher removed from the events he investigated.

If you think for a minute about the technical studies that have flooded the journals since 1987, about the effects of program trading on market efficiency, and other attempts to read the entrails of the price patterns around the time of the crashes, you can see the difference between quantitative and qualitative methods and the sorts of knowledge that each may bring to us.

A qualitative method like ethnography does not necessarily lead to testable quantitative hypotheses. For example, returning to dividend policy, we can consider Frankfurter and Lane (1992), who argue that dividends are part of the maintenance of social order in the same way that potlatches used to function for the aboriginal tribes of British Columbia. We cannot test such a theory quantitatively, we can only reflect whether it seems to agree with our view of society. That does not make it wrong or inappropriate as a way to advance our knowledge and understanding of dividend policy.

Historical Techniques

Historical research can be qualitative, quantitative, or a combination of the two. Studies using market price databases are both historical and archival, because they investigate data recorded in archival form.[13] Traditional finance studies have developed the quantitative side of the investigation without paying much attention to the qualities of the phenomena under consideration. The archival data does not exist in a vacuum—human beings interacting in complex societies create it. The character of the society and the people creating the data are essential to its meaningfulness, and qualitative historical techniques are useful in this regard. Business, economic, and accounting history are all well-established fields, with academics and journals devoted to them. We find these inquiries valuable to our understanding those subjects, which seems a valid reason for supposing that finance could benefit also.

For example, the accepted reason for the lack of banking failures in Canada during the depression of the 1930s is that Canada has a strong branch system, dominated by a few large banks. The greater financial strength and diversification of this system prevented failures at a time when thousands of small U.S. banks went under. Kryzanowski and Roberts (1993a) combines quantitative analysis of archival records of Canadian banks with textual research into what the politicians and bankers said about the problem at the time. They conclude that the Canadian banks were all insolvent for long periods of time, and only regulatory forbearance allowed them to survive. Kryzanowski and Roberts (1993b) continues the same theme with a case study of an insurance company.

Historical analysis also allows a more critical perspective of events. Whitley (1986) finds that the reason for the increasing emphasis on rigorous theory instead of description in the transformation of business finance into financial economics is the self-interest of the players, as we have discussed in Chapter XI, rather than any inherent intellectual superiority of accuracy of the latter view.

Case Study Research

Yin (1989) describes a detailed method for case study research. The investigator takes one or a few sites that embody whatever it is that he or she wishes to know more about, frames research questions and hypotheses, and collects very extensive and intensive data (documents, interviews, personal observations, etc.).[14] The questions are more effective if they are based on prior theory about the topic, but exploratory cases are also valuable. Case study research may include one or several sites, but always too few for statistical testing and generalization as in traditional finance research. The characteristic value lies in the multifaceted examination of some situation or problem or organization.

Statistical studies focus on a very few simple variables that are often weak proxies for the deeper questions we want to ask. Case studies are especially useful for asking why complex choices are made, for example.

Baker (1992) and Baker and Wruck (1989) are examples of finance case study research. The question of how changes in control of a company affect value have been investigated in many statistical studies. These two cases probe more deeply into why the values are affected, although still basing their inquiry on the ideas from the quantitative studies, both theoretical and empirical. As a result, we get a more thorough understanding of value creation and destruction.

Action Research

Our final example is a suggestion, rather than a specific example, since we are unaware of any finance research following this path. You might think of it as the logical extension of grounded field research. Suppose we want to know how capital structure is determined in practice. Suppose we have lots of time to spend around a big company, and the executives allow us to attend board and executive meetings. We sit in on the discussions of financing decisions and either tape them or make a lot of notes. After a while the people in the meetings get used to us and ask us to start participating. We introduce to them what we have learned about capital structure theory as academics, and what we know about practices at other companies. Gradually we become participants in the decisions, and we collectively develop a framework for how the company will make financing decisions in the future that is somewhat different (and better, we think) from the current policy. Then we withdraw from the engagement to write up a paper on this specific experience and how it adds to our knowledge of capital structure decisions. This research is quite different from sending a questionnaire to a number of executives and tabulating the answers. It goes much deeper, but there is no conventional quantitative evidence—there is a "sample" of only one. It is not a case study, either, because that is a pre-identified situation in which the case-writer does not participate.

Work of this sort is called action research (see, e.g., Susman 1983). Although the researcher need not worry about complex econometric problems, the issues of ethics and what constitutes valid observations are equally perplexing. In action research, the academic becomes explicitly a participant-observer, hoping that the deeper personal involvement in the research question will compensate for the loss of objectivity to create greater understanding.

In this chapter and the preceding chapter, we have seen that there are indeed alternative methodologies and methods, certainly no less scholarly and most likely more so, by which we can know more about finance. There is no need for the orthodox adherence to the discredited positivist/instrumentalist methodology and the severely abused mathematical and statistical models and procedures that are now tantamount to finance.

NOTES

1. A survey such as Fama's (1991) leaves no doubt regarding the central role of such research.

2. Excepting, of course, the hearty pioneers who did this research before it became fashionable.

3. The reader should note that Fama and French (1992) exclude financial institutions from the stock universe they study, because their leverage has a different meaning than the rest of the universe.

4. Some have expressed concern that there is no clear difference between the radical structuralist and radical humanist positions.

5. For futher insight into this debate, see Borman, LeCompt, and Goetz (1986), Krenz and Sax (1986), and Hammersley (1992).

6. See Bernard (1988), Kirk and Miller (1986), and Miles and Huberman (1984).

7. For a comparative historical analysis of numerous positive and normative research methodologies and ideologies, see Rhoads (1991).

8. Alfred Marshall criticized economists at the turn of the century for ignoring culture.

> The chief fault, then, in English economists at the beginning of the century was not that they ignored history and statistics; but that Ricardo and his followers neglected a large group of facts, and a method of studying facts which we now see to be of primary importance. They regarded man as, so to speak, a constant quantity, and gave themselves little trouble to study his variations. The people whom they knew were chiefly city men; and they took it for granted tacitly that other Englishmen were very much like those they knew in the city. They were aware that the inhabitants of other countries had peculiarities of their own; but they regarded such differences, when they thought of them at all, as superficial and sure to be removed as soon as other nations had got to know that better way which Englishmen were ready to teach them. The same bent of mind, that led our lawyers to impose English civil law on the Hindus, led our economists to work out theories on the tacit supposition that the world was made up of city men (Pigou 1956, p. 154).

Nothing has changed in a hundred years.

9. The best known of these in Arthur Andersen & Co. (1992).

10.   This textual analysis is a whole method in itself, though it can be used as a tool in other work.

11.   The textual analysis was a major research effort in itself, with two researchers independently following a specified method to extract meaning from the transcripts of the interviews.

12.   Similar textual analysis of newspaper descriptions of the crash of 1987 was conducted by Warner and Molotch (1993).

13.   The constrasting method is experimentation, in which the researcher creates the data himself or herself.

14.   Case studies as a teaching tool are somewhat different. A teaching case study, despite the standard disclaimer, seeks to illustrate for the student the lessons that the case writer/teacher already knows.

Chapter XV

Concluding Remarks

This book has been critical of financial economics or academic finance. In Section 2 we argued that the methodological foundations of the field are at best, shaky and, at worst, inconducive to the purpose of finding the truth (if there is one). Thus, even by rather dubious standards, finance cannot make contributions to knowledge. In Sections 3, we set out to show that the most cherished paradigms and theories are essentially meaningless, non-verifiable, or both. The subject of Section 4 was to show the duality of language and the duplicity inherent in its use. Section 5 delved into the sociological reasons and causes of how and why we reached the point we are, and Section 6 attempted to show how it is possible to infuse meaning into what finance is supposed to accomplish vis-a-vis what it actually achieves.

When the dismal state of the field is mentioned in private conversations with practicing academics in the corridors of annual conferences, the tag line of such conversations is usually, "What else is there?" Without an alternative, criticism is just so much pointless carping.

The logic that it takes a new paradigm to topple the old one is often attributed to Kuhn (1970), and is thus accepted as incontrovertible:[1]

> Once a first paradigm through which to view nature has been found, there is no such thing as research in the absence of any paradigm. To reject one paradigm without simultaneously substituting another is to reject science itself (p. 79).

There is no active alternative to what finance is now. It is sustained by a Catch-22. Criticism is forbidden without an alternative, but alternatives are impossible without criticism. Anything that looks different is considered insufficiently rigorous finance, or not considered finance at all. But developing an alternative is tantamount to putting one's career at peril. Even if an altruist in the pursuit of knowledge were to labor diligently on something new, he or she would be condemned to anonymity and unpublished to death.

What must be questioned, however, is whether finance has ever had what Kuhn (1970) would call a paradigm.

> Paradigms gain their status because they are more successful than their competitors in solving a few problems that the group of practitioners has come to recognize as acute (p. 23).

As we have tried to show, the finance of the last four decades has had no successes, especially with acute problems such as asset valuation, capital structure, and dividend policy; therefore, finance's so-called paradigm has nothing to do with any scientific achievement, but with a supposedly "scientific" method. Finance's paradigmatic method is justified by its rhetorical elegance, not by its results. Its ever-increasing quantitative sophistication resembles the jousting of a knight in armor who proved the purity of his heart by knocking off with a lance or mace another knight from a miserable horse, forced to carry on its back 350 pounds of warrior, weaponry and armor.

Even if we agree that one paradigm must be replaced by another, then for finance, this only means new methods. Since the old paradigm had no results, we cannot realistically expect a new one to immediately weigh in with any either.

But finance will never adopt new methods until it changes its methodology (the logic or philosophy of financial inquiry) and its sociology (what counts and what doesn't, who is its aristocracy, and what reward structure is to go hand in glove with both). In conclusion, we suggest these changes, methodological or otherwise, which must be seriously contemplated in order to move the field from its dead-weight point toward progress in knowledge and discovery.

1. What constitutes information. That practitioners either are ignorant or lie about what they are doing and that we can only tease the truth out of massive quantities of aggregate data is patently false, as is the implication that there is, in fact, a single underlying "truth" that corresponds with the "facts."

2. What constitutes evidence. The history of nearly every major theory in finance should make it painfully clear that there is no such thing as a definitive statistical test nor even a definitive set of tests. The results of empirical work will never unequivocally verify nor falsify anything. One person works with this data set and one with that; one person slices the data horizontally and one vertically; one person ARCHes and one GARCHes. We develop increasingly sophisticated tests to address the theoretical problems of simpler tests (and to show off our intellectual abilities), but we have less and less understanding

of what any of the numerical results truly *mean*. Even when we arrive at the same numbers, we interpret them differently. What is and what is not a "fact" is difficult to determine.

3. **What constitutes knowledge.** There is no immutable set of laws governing the social world as there appears to be governing the natural world. If there is, the laws are likely to be rather obvious and uninteresting. What we know of our societies, we know in the form of the stories we tell ourselves in which we assemble the "facts" as we perceive them into a whole that makes sense to us. For any set of facts, there are countless stories; as new facts emerge, stories change. Finance practitioners act on the basis of their stories, and even finance academics cast their beliefs in the form of stories. If we want to know finance, we must know these stories.

4. **What constitutes professional accomplishment.** That success in academic finance is based on the publication of articles is an imitation of the physical sciences in which there is a real possibility of progress and some sense of urgency to the dissemination of experimental results. In a competitive sense, there is some meaningful stake in precedence, and in a cooperative one, there is legitimate cross-fertilization among researchers. Finance has had only the illusion of progress; there is nothing urgent about its results.[2] Two things about the social structure of the academic finance profession must change. First, serious intellectual inquiry in finance requires a broader and deeper education outside the mathematics and economics that now constitute doctoral curricula, so that the Doctor of Philosophy degree means what it says. Second, serious intellectual inquiry is a painfully time-consuming process. One must do more than pull a set of statistics out of a set of data. The research process ought to yield a comprehensive, well-thought-out book rather than a series of fragmented, thoughtless, hit-and-run articles. A reputational system that acknowledges the difficulties of real intellectual accomplishment works successfully in European universities and in humanities departments in the United States. It could and should work for finance, as well.

5. **The need for standards.** A set of standards, describing what constitutes growth in scientific knowledge, must be developed in harmony with agreed-upon tenets of philosophy of science to supplement the reviewing process, currently ensconced in the leading journals of the field. The standards must include, but not be restricted to, such articles as realism of assumptions, the possible benefits of the proposed paradigm to its end-users, whether the possibility of expanding existing knowledge is real and whether the model is intellectually superior to that it purports to replace.

6. Who bears the burden of proof. Everyone bears the burden of proof
    for his or her own assertions. The burden should not fall solely on
    only those who doubt the status quo. The entrenched aristocracy
    should not be allowed to have its assumptions unquestioned and its
    assertions of progress unchallenged, simply because it got there first.

If we have created the impression in this work that we are self-loathing
finance academics, then we have pathetically missed our mark. Nor do we
suffer from sour grapes syndrome. We are more than happy to accept the
fact that finance is an emerging discipline and that it has accomplished
something—if in nothing else, then at least in earnestness and volume.
Provided that current research is conducted according to some agreeable and
rigorous **standards**, it certainly may yield surplus valuable information. But
there are other valid methods we must begin to use as well.

The finance pioneers whose names are attached to generally recognized
accomplishments are especially deserving of respect. That their efforts have
been unsuccessful is much less important than the imagination with which
they conceived them and the ardor with which they pursued them. When
they were doing their work, *it* constituted an alternative perspective. A
finance group that is willing to support and encourage a new methodology
now (instead of settling to be a poor imitation of the Chicago-Rochester
school) might become in the future a "school" of its own.

NOTES

1. "Financial economists" who are familiar with the rhetoric of Kuhn's "paradigms" seem
to draw upon him selectively and ignore the larger part of his message. If they believe in the
existence of paradigms, why do they reject the relevance of the history of finance?
2. Except perhaps in the rare instances when it discovers malfeasance in markets and
institutions.

References

Akerlof, George A. 1970. "The Market for Lemons: Quality Uncertainty and the Market Mechanism." *Quarterly Journal of Economics* 84: 488-500.

Ambarish, Ramasastry, Kose John, and Joseph Williams. 1987. "Efficient Signaling with Dividends and Investments." *Journal of Finance* 42: 321-343.

Ang, James, ed. 1993. "FM Forum on Financial Ethics." *Financial Management* 22:32-59.

Arnott, Robert D. 1983. "What Hath MPT Wrought: Which Risks Reap Rewards?" *Journal of Portfolio Management* 10: 5-11.

Arrow, Kenneth J. 1951. "Alternative Approaches to the Theory of Choice in Risk-Taking Situations." *Econometrica* 19: 404-437.

————. 1982. "Risk Perception in Psychology and Economics." *Economic Inquiry* 20: 1-9.

Arthur Andersen & Co., S.C. 1992. *Business Ethics Program: Finance Materials.*

Ashley, John W. 1962. "Stock Prices and Changes in Earnings and Dividends: Some Empirical Results." *Journal of Political Economy* 70:82-85.

Auerbach, Alan J. 1979. "Wealth Maximization and the Cost of Capital." *Quarterly Journal of Economics* 93: 433-446.

Baker, George. 1992. "Beatrice: A Case Study in the Creation and Destruction of Value." *Journal of Finance* 47:1081-1120.

Baker, George, and Karen Wruck. 1989. "Organization Changes and Value Creation in leveraged Buyouts: The Case of O.M. Scott & Sons Co." *Journal of Financial Economics* 25:163-190.

Ball, Ray and Philip Brown. 1968. "An Empirical Evaluation of Accounting Income Numbers." *Journal of Accounting Research* 6:159-178.

Baskin, Jonathan Barron. 1988. "The Development of Corporate Financial Markets in Britain and the United States, 1600-1914: Overcoming Asymmetric Information." *Business History Review* 62: 199-237.

Bell, Eric T. 1933. *Numerology.* Baltimore, MD: The Williams and Wilkins Company.

Bernard, H. R. 1988. *Research Methods in Cultural Anthropology.* Newbury Park, CA: Sage Publications.

Bennington, Geoffrey. 1988. *Lyotard: Writing the Event.* New York: Columbia University Press.

Benston, George. 1967. "Published Corporate Accounting Data and Stock Prices." *Journal of Accounting Research* (Supplement to Volume 5):1-63.

Berle, Adolf A. Jr., and Gardiner C. Means. 1932. *The Modern Corporation and Private Property.* Reprint 1968. New York: Harcourt, Brace & World.

Bernoulli, Daniel. 1954. "Exposition of a New Theory on the Measurement of Risk." *Econometrica* 22: 23-36.

Bernstein, Richard J. 1983. *Beyond Objectivism and Relativism.* Philadelphia: University of Pennsylvania Press.

243

Bernstein, Peter L. 1992. *Capital Ideas.* New York: The Free Press.

————. 1996. "The New Religion of Risk Management." *Harvard Business Review* March-April: 47-51.

Bhattacharya, Sudipto. 1979. "Imperfect Information, Dividend Policy and the Bird in the Hand Fallacy." *Bell Journal of Economics* 10:259-270.

————. 1980. "Nondissipative Dividend Signaling Structures and Dividend Policy." *Quarterly Journal of Economics* 95: 1-24.

Black, Fischer. 1993. "Estimating Expected Return." *Financial Analysts Journal* 49: 36-38.

————. 1995. *Exploring General Equilibrium.* Cambridge: MIT Press.

Black, Fischer, and Myron Scholes. 1973. "The Pricing of Options and Corporate Liabilities." *Journal of Political Economy* 81: 637-654.

Blaug, Mark. 1994. "Why I Am Not a Constructivist: Confessions of an Unrepentant Popperian." In *New Directions in Economic Methodology*, edited by R. E. Backhouse. London: Routledge.

Blume, Marshal E., and Robert F. Stambaugh. 1983. "Biases in Computed Returns: An Application to the Size Effect." *Journal of Financial Economics* 12: 387-404.

Boehmer, Ekhart, James Musumeci, and Anette Poulsen. 1991. "Event Study Methodology Under Conditions of Event-Induced Variances." *Journal of Financial Economics* 30: 253-272.

Boland, Lawrence A. 1979. "A Critique of Friedman's Critics." *Journal of Economic Literature* 17:503-522.

Boness, A. James. 1964. "A Pedagogic Note on the Cost of Capital." *Journal of Finance* 19: 79-106.

Borgmann, Albert. 1992. *Crossing the Postmodern Divide.* Chicago: University of Chicago Press.

Borman, K. M., M. LeCompt, and J. Goetz. 1986. "Ethnographic and Qualitative Research Design and Why it doesn't Work." *American Behavioral Scientist* 30(1):42-67.

Bowler, Peter J. 1989. *Evolution: The History of an Idea*, Revised edition. Berkeley, CA: University of California Press.

Brigham, Eugene F. and Louis C. Gapenski. 1987. *Intermediate Financial Management*, Second Edition. Chicago: Dryden Press.

Brown, Stephen J. and Jerold B. Warner. 1980. "Measuring Security Price Performance." *Journal of Financial Economics* 8: 205-258.

————. 1986. "Using Daily Stock Returns: The Case of Event Studies." *Journal of Financial Economics* 14: 3-31.

Burrell, Gibson, and Gareth Morgan. 1979. *Sociological Paradigms and Organizational Analysis.* London: Heinemann Press.

Caldwell, Bruce J. 1991. "Clarifying Popper." *Journal of Economic Literature* 29: 1-33.

Campbell, John P., Richard L. Daft, and Charles L. Hulin. 1982. *What to Study: Generating and Developing Research Questions.* Beverly Hills, CA: Sage Publications.

Carnap, Rudolf. 1962. *Logical Foundations of Probability*, Second Edition. Chicago: University of Chicago Press.

Charlesworth, James C. Ed. 1963. *Mathematics and the Social Sciences.* Philadelphia: The American Academy of Political and Social Science.

Cheng, Pao L. and Robert R. Grauer. 1980. "An Alternative Test of the Capital Asset Pricing Model." *American Economic Review* 70: 660-671.

Chua, Wai Fong. 1986. "Radical Developments in Accounting Thought." *The Accounting Review* 61:601-632.

Churchman, Charles W. 1971. *The Design of Inquiring Systems.* New York: Basic Books, Inc. Publishers.

Clark, J.B. 1893. "Insurance and Business Profit." *Quarterly Journal of Economics* 7: 40-54.

Cohen, Kalman J. and Jerry A. Pogue. 1967. "An Empirical Evaluation of Alternative Portfolio Selection Models." *Journal of Business* 40: 166-193.

Cohen, Jerome B., Edward D. Zinbarg and Arthur Zeikel. 1997. *Investment Analysis and Portfolio Management*, Fifth Edition. Homewood IL: Irwin.

Cooley, Philip L., Rodney Roenfeldt and Naval K. Modani. 1977. "Interdependence of Market Risk Measures." *Journal of Business* 50: 356-363.

Copeland, Thomas E. and J. Fred Weston. 1988. *Financial Theory and Corporate Policy*, Third Edition. Reading, MA: Addison-Wesley Publishing Company.

Cottingham, John. 1986. *Descartes*. Oxford: Basil Blackwell.

Cray, David, and George Haines. 1992. "Do as I Say, Not as You Do: Prescriptive and Descriptive Models of Decision Making in Pension Fund Management." *Alternative Perspectives on Finance Conference* Proceedings: 21-65.

Craver, Earlene. 1980. "The Emigration of the Austrian Economists." *History of Political Economy* 18: 1-32.

Crockett, John H. Jr. 1980. "Irving Fisher on the Financial Economics of Uncertainty." *History of Political Economy* 12: 65-82.

Cross, Rod. 1982. "The Duhem-Quine Thesis, Lakatos, and the Appraisal of Theories in Macroeconomics." *The Economic Journal* 92: 320-340.

Culler, Jonathan. 1986. *Ferdinand de Saussure*, Revised Edition. Ithaca, NY: Cornell University Press.

Cyert, Robert M. and James G. March. 1963. *The Behavioral Theory of the Firm*. Englewood Cliffs, NJ: Prentice-Hall.

Daston, Lorraine J. 1987. "The Domestication of Risk: Mathematical Probability and Insurance 1650-1830." In *The Probabalistic Revolution—Volume I: Ideas in History*, edited by L. Kruger, L. J. Daston and M. Heidelberger. Cambridge, MA: MIT Press.

DeAngelo, Harry, and Ronald W. Masulis. 1980. "Optimal Capital Structure Under Corporate and Personal Taxation." *Journal of Financial Economics* 8:3-29.

De Bondt, Werner F.M. and Richard Thaler. 1985. "Does the Stock Market Over react?" *Journal of Finance* 40: 793-805.

De Duve, Christian. 1991. *Blueprint for a Cell: The Nature and Origin of Life*. Burlington, NC: Neil Patterson Publishers.

David, Florence N. 1962. *Games, Gods, and Gambling*. New York: Hafner Publishing Company.

De Finetti, Bruno. 1972. *Probability, Induction, and Statistics*. London: John Wiley & Sons.

Demsetz, Harold. 1968. "The Cost of Transacting." *Quarterly Journal of Economics* 82: 33-53.

Denton, Frank T. 1985. "Data Mining as an Industry." *Review of Economics and Statistics* 67: 124-127.

De Wulf, Maurice 1956. *An Introduction to Scholastic Philosophy*. New York: Dover Publications, Inc.

Domar, Evsey D. and Richard A. Musgrave. 1944. "Proportional Income Taxation and Risk-Taking." *Quarterly Journal of Economics* 58: 388-422.

Edgeworth, F.Y. 1888. "The Mathematical Theory of Banking." *Journal of the Royal Statistical Society* 51: 113-127.

Elton, Edwin, Martin J. Gruber and Manfred W. Padberg. 1976. "Simple Criteria for Optimal Portfolio Selection." *Journal of Finance* 31: 1341-1357.

———. 1978. "Simple Criteria for Optimal Portfolio Selection: Tracing Out the Efficient Frontier." *Journal of Finance* 33: 296-302.

Fay, Brian. 1975. *Social Theory and Political Practice*. New York: Holmes & Meier Publishers.

Fama, Eugene F. 1991. "Efficient Capital Markets: II." *The Journal of Finance* 46: 1575-1617.

———. 1976. *Foundations of Finance*. New York: Basic Books.

Fama, Eugene F. and Kenneth R. French. 1992. "The Cross-Section of Expected Stock Returns." *Journal of Finance* 47: 427-465.

Fama, Eugene F. and James MacBeth. 1973. "Risk, Return, and Equilibrium: Empirical Tests." *Journal of Political Economy* 81: 607-636.

Faulhaber, Gerald R., and William J. Baumol. 1988. "Economists as Innovators: Practical Products of Theoretical Research." *Journal of Economic Literature* 26:577-600.

Faulk, Gregory, George M. Frankfurter and Herbert E. Phillips. 1996. "The Ex Post Performance of Four Portfolio Selection Models." Working Paper, Louisiana State University.

Feige, Edgar L. 1975. "The Consequence of Journal Editorial Policies and a Suggestion for Revision." *Journal of Political Economy* 83: 1291-1295.

Feldstein, Martin and Jerry Green. 1983. "Why Do Companies Pay Dividends?" *American Economic Review* 73: 17-30.

Fellner, William. 1943. "Monetary Policies and Hoarding in Periods of Stagnation." *The Journal of Political Economy* 51: 191-205.

Findlay, M. Chapman and E.E. Williams. 1980. "A Positivist Evaluation of the New Finance." *Financial Management* 9: 7-17.

Fine, Terrence L. 1973. *Theories of Probability*. New York: Academic Press.

Fisher, Irving. 1906. *The Nature of Capital and Interest*. New York: The Macmillan Company.

———. 1930. *The Theory of Interest*. New York: The Macmillan Company.

Foster, George. 1978. "Asset Pricing Models: Further Tests." *Journal of Financial and Quantitative Analysis* 13: 39-54.

———. 1986. *Financial Statement Analysis*, Second Edition. Englewood Cliffs, NJ: Prentice-Hall.

Foucault, Michel. 1994. *The Order of Things*. New York: Vintage Books.

Fouse, William L., William W. Jahnke and Barr Rosenberg. 1974. "Is Beta Phlogiston?" *Financial Analysts Journal* 30: 70-80.

Frankfurter, George M. and Thomas Frecka. 1979. "Efficient Portfolios and Superfluous Diversification." *The Journal of Financial and Quantitative Analysis* 14: 925-938.

Frankfurter, George M. and Christopher G. Lamoureux. 1989. "Estimation and Selection Bias in Mean-Variance Portfolio Selection." *The Journal of Financial Research* 12: 173-181.

Frankfurter, George M., and Herbert E. Phillips. 1982. "MPT Plus Security Analysis for Better Performance." *Journal of Portfolio Management* 8: 29-36.

Frankfurter, George M., and Herbert E. Phillips. (Forthcoming). "Normative Implications of Equilibrium Models: Homogeneous Expectations and Other Artificialities." *Journal of Economic Behavior and Organization*.

Frankfurter, George M., William Lane and Efraim Darom. 1994. "Expressed Cost Consciousness in the 'Letter to Stockholders'." *Review of Quantitative Finance and Accounting* 4: 253-264.

Friedman, Milton. 1953. "The Methodology of Positive Economics." Pp. 3- 43 in *Essays in Positive Economics*. Chicago: University of Chicago Press.

Friend, Irwin, Randolph Westerfield, and Michael Granito. 1978. "New Evidence on the Capital Asset Pricing Model." *The Journal of Finance* 33: 903-920.

Gadamer, Hans-Georg. 1993. *Truth and Method*, 2nd. Revised Edition. New York: Continuum.

Gane, Mike. 1991. *Baudrillard: Critical and Fatal Theory*. London: Routledge.

Gardner, Howard. 1973. *The Quest for Mind*. New York: Alfred A. Knopf.

Georgescu-Roegen, Nicholas. 1971. *The Entropy Law and the Economic Process*. Cambridge: Harvard University Press.

———. 1979. "Methods in Economic Science." *Journal of Economic Issues* 13:317-328.

Gibbins, Michael, Alan Richardson, and John Waterhouse. 1990. "The Management of Corporate Financial Disclosures: Opportunity, Ritualism, Policies, and Processes." *Journal of Accounting Research* 28:121-143.

Gigerenzer, Gerd, Zeno Swijtink, Theodore Porter, Lorraine Daston, John Beatty and Lorenz Krüger. 1989. *The Empire of Chance.* Cambridge: Cambridge University Press.

Glaser, Barney, and Anselm L. Strauss. 1967. *The Discovery of Grounded Theory: Strategies for Qualitative Research.* Chicago: Aldine Publishing Company.

Good, I.J. 1962. "Subjective Probability as the Measure of a Non-Measureable Set." In *Logic, Methodology, and Philosophy of Science,* edited by E. Nagel, P. Suppes and A. Tarski. Stanford, CA: Stanford University Press.

Gordon, Myron J. 1963. "Optimal Investment and Financing Policy." *Journal of Finance* 18: 264-272.

————. 1994. *Finance, Investment and Macroeconomics: The Noeclassical and a Post Keynesian Solution.* Hants: Edward Elgar Publishing Company.

Gordon, Myron J. and Eli Shapiro. 1956. "Capital Equipment Analysis: The Required Rate of Profit." *Management Science* 3: 102-110.

Gould, Stephen Jay. 1993. "Cordelia's Dilemma." *Natural History* 2: 10-18.

Grether, David M. and Charles R. Plott. 1979. "Economic Theory of Choice and the Preference Reversal Phenomenon." *American Economic Review* 69: 623-638.

Grossman, Sanford J., and Oliver D. Hart. 1982. "Corporate Financial Structure and Managerial Incentives." In *The Economics of Information and Uncertainty,* edited by J. J. McCall. Chicago: University of Chicago Press.

Habermas, Jürgen. 1971. *Knowledge and Human Interests.* Boston, MA: Beacon Press.

————. 1987. *The Philosophical Discourse of Modernity.* Cambridge, MA: MIT Press.

Hacking, Ian. 1975. *The Emergence of Probability.* Cambridge: Cambridge University Press.

————. 1990. *The Taming of Chance.* Cambridge: Cambridge University Press.

Hald, Anders. 1990. *A History of Probability and Statistics.* New York: John Wiley & Sons.

Hammersley, Martyn. 1992. *What's Wrong with Ethnography?* New York: Routledge.

Hamada, Robert S. 1969. "Portfolio Analysis, Market Equilibrium and Corporation Finance." *Journal of Finance* 24: 13-31.

————. 1972. "The Effect of the Firm's Capital Structure on the Systematic Risk of Common Stocks." *Journal of Finance* 27:435-452.

Hamilton, William Peter. 1922. *The Stock Market Barometer.* New York: Harper & Brothers Publishers.

Hammer, Jerry A. and Herbert E. Phillips. 1992. "The Single Index Model: Cross-Sectional Residual Covariances and Superfluous Diversification." *The International Review of Financial Analysis* 2: 39-50.

Hands, D. Wade. 1985. "Karl Popper and Economic Methodology: A New Look." *Economic Philosophy* 1: 83-99.

Harris, Roy. 1980. *The Language Makers.* Ithaca, NY: Cornell University Press.

Hardy, Charles O. 1923. *Risk and Risk Bearing.* Chicago: University of Chicago Press.

Hart, Albert Gailord. 1940. "Uncertainty and Inducements to Invest." *Review of Economic Studies* 8: 49-53.

————. 1965. *Anticipations, Uncertainty, and Dynamic Planning.* New York: Augustus M. Kelley Publisher.

————. 1965. "Risk, Uncertainty, and the Unprofitability of Compounding Probabilities." In *Studies in Mathematical Economics and Econometrics,* edited by O. Lange, F. McIntyre and T. O. Yntema. Chicago: University of Chicago Press.

Harrington, Diana R. 1987. *Modern Portfolio Theory, The Capital Asset Pricing Model, & Arbitrage Pricing Theory: A User's Guide,* Second Edition. Englewood Cliffs, NJ: Prentice-Hall.

Haugen, Robert A. and Lemma W. Senbet. 1978. "The Insignificance of Bankruptcy Costs to the Theory of Optimal Capital Structure." *Journal of Finance* 33: 383-393.

Hayek, Friedrich A. 1967. "The Theory of Complex Phenomena." In *Studies in Philosophy, Politics, and Economics*. Chicago: The University of Chicago Press.

Haynes, John. 1895. "Risk as an Economic Factor." *Quarterly Journal of Economics* 9: 409-449.

Held, David. 1980. *Introduction to Critical Theory*. Berkeley, CA: University of California Press.

Heidegger, Martin. 1984. *The Metaphysical Foundations of Logic*. Translated by Michael Heim. Bloomington, IN: Indiana University Press.

Hicks, John R. 1931. "The Theory of Uncertainty and Profit." *Economica* 15: 170-189.

————. 1935. "A Suggestion for Simplifying the Theory of Money." *Economica*, 1-19.

Hogben, Lancelot. 1957. *Statistical Theory*. London: George Allen & Unwin Ltd.

"The Human Factor." 1996. *Euromoney* (January): 30-35.

Jahnke, William W. 1994. "Requiem for Efficient Market Theory." *Journal of Investing* 3: 5-9.

Jensen, Michael C. 1986. "Agency Costs of Free Cash Flow, Corporate Finance, and Takeovers." *American Economic Review* 76: 305-360.

Jensen, Michael C. and William H. Meckling. 1976. "Theory of the Firm: Managerial Behavior, Agency Costs and Ownership Structure." *Journal of Financial Economics* 3: 305-360.

Jensen, Michael C. and Clifford W. Smith, Jr. 1985. "Stockholders, Managers and Creditor Interests: Application of Agency Theory." In *Recent Advances in Corporate Finance*, edited by E.I. Altman and M. G. Subrahmanyan. Homewood, IL: R.D. Irwin.

John, Kose and Joseph Williams. 1985. "Dividends, Dilution and Taxes: A Signaling Equilibrium." *Journal of Finance* 40: 1053-1070.

Kahneman, Daniel and Amos Tversky. 1982. "Intuitive Prediction: Biases and Corrective Procedures." In *Judgement Under Uncertainty: Heuristics and Biases, edited by D. Kahneman, P. Slovic and A. Tversky*. London: Cambridge University Press.

Kamin, Jacob F. and Joshua Ronen. 1981. "Effects of Budgetary Control on Management Decisions: Some Empirical Evidence." *Decision Sciences* 12: 471-485.

Kaye, Howard L. 1986. *The Social Meaning of Modern Biology*. New Haven, CT: Yale University Press.

Keat, Russell, and John Urry. 1982 *Social Theory as Science*, 2nd Edition. London: Routledge & Kegan Paul.

Kellner, Douglas. 1989. *Jean Baudrillard*. Stanford, CA: Stanford University Press.

Keim, Donald B. 1983. "Size-Related Anomalies and Stock Return Seasinality: Further Empirical Evidence." *Journal of Financial Economics* 12: 13-32.

Keynes, John M. 1891. *The Scope and Method of Political Economy*. London: Macmillan & Co.

————. 1936. *The General Theory of Employment, Interest and Money*. London: Harcourt Brace Jovanovich.

————. 1921. *A Treatise on Probability*. London: Macmillan and Co., Limited.

————. 1955. *The Scope and Method of Political Economy*. New York: Kelley and Millman.

Kim, E. Han. 1978. "A Mean-Variance Theory of Optimal Capital Structure and Corporate Debt Capacity." *Journal of Finance* 33: 45-64.

King, M. 1977. *Public Policy and the Corporation*. London: Chapman and Hall.

Kitcher, Philip. 1985. *Vaulting Ambition: Sociobiology and the Quest for Human Nature*. Cambridge, MA: MIT Press.

————. 1989. "Explanatory Unification and the Causal Structure of The World." In *Scientific Explanation*, edited by P. Kitcher and W. C. Salmon. Minneapolis: University of Minnesota Press.

Kirk, Jerome, and Mark L. Miller. 1986. *Reliability and Validity in Qualitative Research*. Beverly Hills, CA: Sage Publications.

Klamer, Arjo and Thomas C. Leonard. 1994. "So What's an Economic Metaphor?" In *Natural Images in Economic Thought*, edited by P. Mirowski. Cambridge: Cambridge University Press.

Klein, Benjamin and Keith B. Leffler. 1981. "The Role of Market Forces in Assuring Contractual Performance." *Journal of Political Economy* 89: 615-641.

Kline, Morris. 1953. *Mathematics in Western Culture*. New York: Oxford University Press.

Knight, Frank H. 1921. *Risk, Uncertainty and Profit*. Boston: Houghton Mifflin Company.

Koopmans, Tjalling C. 1947. "Measurement Without Theory." *Review of Economics and Statistics*. Reprinted in *Readings in Business Cycles*, edited by A.G. Robert and L.R. Klein. Homewood, IL: Richard D. Irwin.

Krenz, C., and G. Sax. 1986. "What Quantitative Research Is and Why It Doesn't Work." *American Behavioral Scientist* 30:58-69.

Kryzanowski, Lawrence, and Gordon Roberts. 1993. "Canadian Banking Solvency, 1922-1940." *Journal of Money, Credit, and Banking* 25:361-376.

———. 1993. "Capital Forbearance: A Depression Era Case Study of Sun Life." Concordia University Working Paper.

Kuhn, Thomas S. 1970. *The Structure of Scientific Revolutions*, 2nd Edition. Chicago: University of Chicago Press.

———. 1977. *The Essential Tension*. Chicago: University of Chicago Press.

Kurzweil, Edith. 1980. *The Age of Structuralism*. New York: Columbia University Press.

Kyburg, Henry E. Jr. and H. E. Smokler. Eds. 1964. *Studies in Subjective Probability*. New York: John Wiley.

Lakatos, Imre. 1970. "Falsification and the Methodology of Scientific Research Programmes." In *Criticism and the Growth of Knowledge*, edited by I. Lakatos and A. Musgrave. Cambridge: Cambridge University Press.

———. 1978. *The Methodology of Scientific Research Programmes*. Philosophical Papers, Volume 1, edited by John Worrall and Gregory Currie. Cambridge: Cambridge University Press.

Lambert, Richard A. 1984. "Income Smoothing as Rational Equilibrium Behavior." *Accounting Review* 59: 604-618.

Lamoureux, Christopher G. 1990. "Dividends, Taxes, and Normative Portfolio Theory" *Journal of Economics and Business* 42: 121-131.

Lamoureux, G. Christopher, and William D. Lastrapes. 1993. "Toward the Understanding of Stochastic Implied Volatilities." *Review of Financial Studies* 6: 293-326.

Laudan, Larry. 1977. *Progress and Its Problems: Towards a Theory of Scientific Growth*. Berkeley: University of California Press.

Lavington, F. 1912. "Uncertainty in its Relation to the Net Rate of Interest." *Economic Journal* 22: 398-409.

———. 1925. "An Approach to the Theory of Business Risks." *Economic Journal* 35: 186-199.

Lakoff, George. 1991. "Metaphor and War: The System of Metaphors Used to Justify the War in the Gulf." *Journal of Urban and Cultural Studies* 2.

Levinthal, Daniel. 1988. "A Survey of Agency Models of Organizations." *Journal of Economic Behavior and Organization* 9: 153-185.

Lintner, John, 1956. "Distribution of Income of Corporations Among Dividends, Retained Earnings, and Taxes." *American Economic Review* 46:97-113.

———. 1965. "The Valuation of Risk Assets and the Selection of Risky Investments in Stock Portfolios and Capital Budgets." *The Review of Economics and Statistics* 47:13-37.

Lichtenstein, Sarah and Paul Slovic. 1971. "Reversals of Preferences Between Bids and Choices in Gambling Decisions." *Journal of Experimental Psychology* 89: 46-55.

Lovell, Michael C. 1983. "Data Mining." *The Review of Economics and Statistics* 65: 1-12.

Lumsden, Charles J., and Wilson, Edward O. 1981. *Genes, Mind, and Culture.* Cambridge, MA: Harvard University Press.

Lyotard, Jean-Francois. 1984. *The Postmodern Condition: A Report on Knowledge.* Minneapolis, MN: University of Minnesota Press.

Machlup, Fritz. 1969. "Positive and Normative Economics: An Analysis of the Ideas." In *Economic Means and Social Ends: Essays in Political Economics,* edited by R. L. Heilbroner. Englewood Cliffs, NJ: Prentice-Hall.

Magee, Robert P. 1980. "Equilibria in Budget Participation." *Journal of Accounting Research* 18: 551-573.

Maistrov, Leonid E. 1974. *Probability Theory: A Historical Sketch.* New York: Academic Press.

Makower, Helen, and Jakob Marschak. 1938. "Assets, Prices, and Monetary Theory." *Economica* 5: 261-288.

Markowitz, H. M. 1952. "Portfolio Selection." *Journal of Finance* 7: 77-91.

———. 1959. *Portfolio Selection: Efficient Diversification of Investments.* New Haven: Yale University Press.

Marschak, Jakob. 1938. "Money and the Theory of Assets." *Econometrica* 6: 311-325.

———. 1941. "Lack of Confidence." *Social Research* 8: 41-62.

McCloskey, Donald N. 1985. *The Rhetoric of Economics.* Madison: The University of Wisconsin Press.

McNeill, B., S. J. Pauker, H. C. Sox and Amos Tversky. 1981. "Patient Preferences for Alternative Therapies." Working paper.

Merton, Robert, C. 1973. "Theory of Rational Option Pricing." *Bell Journal of Economics and Management Science* 4: 141-183.

———. 1995. "Influence of Mathematical Models in Finance: Past, Present and Future." *Financial Practice and Education* 5:7-15.

Miles, Mattew B., and A. Michael Huberman. 1984. *Qualitative Data Analysis: A Sourcebook of New Methods.* Beverly Hills, CA: Sage Publications.

Miller, James. 1993. *The Passion of Michel Foucault.* New York: Simon & Schuster.

Miller, Merton M. 1986. "The Academic Field of Finance: Some Observations on its History and Prospects." *Tijdschrift voor Economie en Management* 31:395-408.

———. 1988. "The Modigliani-Miller Propositions After Thirty Years." *Journal of Economic Perspectives* 2:99-120.

Miller, Merton H., and Franco Modigliani. 1961. "Dividend Policy, Growth and the Valuation of Shares." *Journal of Business.* 34:411-433.

Miller, Merton H., and Kevin Rock. 1985. "Dividend Policy Under Asymmetric Information." *Journal of Finance.* 40:1031-1051.

Miller, Merton H., and Myron S. Scholes. 1978. "Dividends and Taxes." *Journal of Financial Economics.* 6:333-364.

Mirowski, Philip. 1989. *More Heat Than Light.* Cambridge; Cambridge University Press.

Modigliani, Franco. 1988. "MM - Past, Present, Future." *Journal of Economic Perspectives* 2:149-158.

Modigliani, Franco, and Merton H. Miller. 1958. "The Cost of Capital, Corporation Finance, and the Theory of Investment." *The American Economic Review* 48:261-297.

Morgan, G. 1983. "Research Strategies: Modes of Engagement." In *Beyond Method: Strategies for Social Research,* edited by G. Morgan. Beverly Hills, CA: Sage Publications.

Musgrave, Alan. 1981. "'Unreal Assumptions' in Economic Theory: The F-Twist Untwisted." *Kyklos* 34:377-387.

Murray, A. 1990. "Three U.S. Economists Win Nobel Prize." *The Wall Street Journal,* pp. B1, B8.

Myers, Stewart C. 1972. "On the Use of Beta in Regulatory Proceedings: A Comment." *Bell Journal of Economics and Management Science* 3: 622-627.

————— . 1978. "On the Use of Modern Portfolio Theory in Public Utility Rate Cases: Comment." *Financial Management* 7: 66-68.

————— . 1984. "The Capital Structure Puzzle." *Journal of Finance.* 39:575-592.

————— . 1990. "Still Searching for Optimal Capital Structure." Keynote address delivered at HEC International Conference.

Myers, Stewart C. and Nicholas S. Majluf. 1984. "Corporate Financing and Investment Decisions When Firms Have Information That Investors Do Not Have." *Journal of Financial Economics* 13: 187-121.

Nagel, Ernest. 1961. *The Structure of Science.* New York: Harcourt, Brace & World, Inc.

————— . 1939. *Principles of the Theory of Probability.* Volume 1(6). *International Encyclopedia of Unified Science.* Chicago: University of Chicago Press.

Norton, John Pease. 1902. *Statistical Studies in the New York Money Market.* New York: The Macmillan Company.

————— . 1904. "The Theory of Loan Credit in Relation to Corporation Economics." *Publications of the American Economic Association* 5: 34-61.

Nunnally, J. 1960. "The Place of Statistics in Psychology." *Educational and Psychological Measurement* 20:641-650.

O'Barr, William, and John Conley. 1992. *Fortune and Folly.* Homewood, IL: Richard D. Irwin.

Ofer, Aharon and Anjan Thakor. 1987. "A Theory of Stock Price Response to Alternative Corporate Cash Disbursement Methods: Stock Repurchase and Dividends." *Journal of Finance* 42: 365-394.

Oldershaw, Robert L. 1990. "Mathematics and Natural Philosophy." In *Mathematics and Science,* edited by R. E. Mickens. Singapore: World Scientific Publishing Co. Pte. Ltd.

Passell, Peter. 1990. "Ideas That Changed Wall Street and Fathered Mutual Funds." *The New York Times,* pp. D1, D6.

Phillips, Herbert E. 1993. "Portfolio Optimization Algorithms, Simplified Criteria, and Security Selection: A Contrast and Evaluation." *Review of Quantitative Finance and Accounting* 3: 91-97.

Pigou, Arthur C. 1962. *The Economics of Welfare.* (Reprint of 1920 edition.) London: Macmillan & Co. Ltd.

Popper, Karl R. 1963. *Conjectures and Refutations: The Growth of Scientific Knowledge.* New York: Harper & Row Publishers.

————— . 1964. *The Poverty of Historicism.* New York: Harper & Row Publishers.

————— . 1968. *Conjectures and Refutations.* New York: Harper Torchbooks.

————— . 1979. *Truth, Rationality, and the Growth of Scientific Knowledge.* Frankfurt am Maine: Klostermann.

Porter, Theodore M. 1986. *The Rise of Statistical Thinking 1820-1900.* Princeton, NJ: Princeton University Press.

Poundstone, William. 1988. *Labyrinths of Reason.* New York: Anchor Press.

Ramsey, Frank Plumpton. 1931. "Truth and Probability." In *The Foundations of Mathematics.* London: Routledge & Kegan Paul Ltd.

Reichenbach, Hans. 1949. *The Theory of Probability,* Second Edition. Berkeley: University of California Press.

————— . 1978. "The Current Status of the Capital Asset Pricing Model (CAPM)." *Journal of Finance* 33: 885-901.

Reiter, Sara Ann. 1994. "Storytellers, Stories, and 'Free Cash Flow'." *The International Review of Financial Analysis* 3: 209-224.

Reinganum, Mark R. 1981. "Misspecification of Capital Asset Pricing: Empirical Anomalies Based on Earnings' Yields and Market Values." *Journal of Financial Economics* 9: 19-46.

Rhoads, John K. 1991. *Critical Issues in Social Theory.* University Park, PA: Pennsylvania State University Press.

Riley, John G. 1979. "Informational Equilibrium." *Econometrica* 47: 331-359.

Robbins, Lionel. 1952. *An Essay on the Nature and Significance of Economic Science*, 2nd edition. London: Macmillan and Co., Limited.

Roll, Richard. 1977. "A Critique of the Asset Pricing Theory's Tests." *Journal of Financial Economics* 4: 129-176.

––––––– . 1978. "Ambiguity When Security Performance is Measured by the Securities Market Line." *Journal of Finance* 33: 1051-1069.

––––––– . 1988. "R^2." *The Journal of Finance* 43: 541-566.

Roll, Richard and Stephan A. Ross. 1994. "On the Cross-Sectional Relation Between Expected Returns and Betas." *Journal of Finance* 49: 101-122.

Rosen, M. 1990. "Staying on the String: The Yo and the Market in Eighty-Nine." *Critical Perspectives on Accounting* 4:337-365.

Ross, Edward A. 1896. "Uncertainty as a Factor in Production." *Annals of the American Academy of Political and Social Science* 8: 92-119.

Ross, Stephen A. 1977. "The Determination of Financial Structure: The Incentive-Signalling Approach." *Bell Journal of Economics* 8:23-29.

––––––– . 1978. "The Current Status of the Capital Asset Pricing Model (CAPM)." *Journal of Finance* 33: 885-901.

Russell, Thomas and Richard Thaler. 1985. "The Relevance of Quasi-rationality

Rucker, Rudy von Bitter. 1982. *Infinity and the Mind*. Boston: Birkhauser.

Ryan, Robert J. 1982. "Capital Market Theory-A Case Study in Methodological Conflict." *Journal of Business Finance and Accounting* 9: 443-458.

Sahlins, Marshall. 1976. *The Use and Abuse of Biology: An Anthropological Critique of Sociobiology*. Ann Arbor, MI: University of Michigan Press.

Salmon, Wesley C. 1989. "Four Decades of Scientific Explanation." In *Scientific Explanation*, edited by P. Kitcher and W. C. Salmon. Minneapolis: University of Minnesota Press.

Samuelson, Paul A. 1966. "Risk and Uncertainty: A Fallacy of Large Numbers." In *The Collected Papers of Paul Samuelson*, edited by J. E. Stiglitz. Cambridge, MA: MIT Press.

Savage, Leonard J. 1972. *The Foundations of Statistics*, Second Revised Edition. New York: Dover Publications, Inc.

Schelling, Thomas C. 1978. *Micromotives and Macrobehavior*. New York: W.W. Norton & Company.

Schiff, Michael and Arie Y. Lewin. 1970. "The Impact of People on Budgets." *Accounting Review* 45: 259-268.

Scholes, Myron S. 1972. "The Market for Securities: Substitution Versus Price Pressure and the Effects of Information on Share Prices." *Journal of Business* 45:179-211.

"School Briefs: Of Butterflies and Condors." 1991. *The Economist* 318:58-59.

Scott, James H., Jr. 1977. "Bankruptcy, Secured Debt, and Optimal Capital Structure." *Journal of Finance* 32: 1-19.

Selvin, Hanan E. 1957. "A Critique of Significance in Survey Research." *American Sociological Review.* 22: 519-527.

Shackle, George L.S. 1940a. "The Nature of the Inducement to Invest." *Review of Economic Studies* 8: 44-48.

––––––– . 1940b. "A Reply to Professor Hart." *Review of Economic Studies* 8: 54-57.

––––––– . 1952. *Expectation in Economics*. Cambridge: Canbridge University Press.

Shanken, Jay. 1982. "The Arbitrage Pricing Theory: Is it Testable?" *Journal of Finance* 37: 1129-1140.

Sharpe, William F. 1963. "A Simplified Model of Portfolio Analysis." *Management Science* 9: 277-293.

––––––– . 1964. "Capital Asset Prices: A Theory of Market Equilibrium Under Conditions of Risk." *Journal of Finance* 19: 425-442.

_____ . 1972. "Discussion." *Journal of Finance* 27: 456-458.

Sharpe, William F. and Gordon J. Alexander. 1990. *Investments*, Fourth Edition. Englewood Cliffs, NJ: Prentice Hall.

Shaw, Alan R. 1988. "Market Timing and Technical Analysis." In *The Financial Analysts Handbook*, Second Edition, edited by S. N. Levine. Homewood, IL: Dow Jones -Irwin.

Shiller, Robert J. 1981. "Do Stock Prices Move Too Much to Be Justified by Subsequent Changes in Dividends?" *American Economic Review* 71: 421-436.

Simon, Herbert A. 1979. "Rational Decision Making in Business Organizations." *American Economic Review* 69: 493-513.

Snooks, Greame D. 1993. *Economics Without Time*. Ann Arbor, MI: University of Michigan Press.

Solomon, Ezra. 1963. *The Theory of Financial Management*. New York: Columbia University Press.

Sorenson, Eric H. 1985. "In Defense of Technical Analysis: Discussion." *Journal of Finance*. 40: 773-775.

Spence, Michael. 1973. "Job Market Signaling." *Quarterly Journal of Economics* 87: 355-374.

Sterling, Theodore D. 1959. "Publication Decisions and Their Possible Effects on Inferences Drawn from Tests of Significance—or Vice Versa." *Journal of the American Statistical Association* 54: 30-34.

Stewart, Ian M.T. 1979. *Reasoning and Method in Economics*. London: McGraw-Hill Book Company (UK) Ltd.

Stigler, Stephen M. 1986. *The History of Statistics*. Cambridge, MA: The Belknap Press .

Stiglitz, Joseph E. 1988. "Why Financial Structure Matters." *Journal of Economic Perspectives* 2:121-126.

Steindl, J. 1941. "On Risk." *Oxford Economic Papers* 5: 43-53.

Stoll, Hans R. 1978a. "The Supply of Dealer Services in Security Markets." *Journal of Finance* 33: 1133-1151.

_____ . 1978b. "The Pricing of Security Dealer Services: An Empirical Study of NASDAQ Stocks." *Journal of Finance* 33: 1153-1172.

Susman, G. 1983. "Action Research: A Socio-Technical Systems Perspective." In *Beyond Method: Strategies for Social Research*, edited by G. Morgan. Beverly Hills, CA: Sage Publications.

Szostak, Rick. 1992. "The History of Art and the Art in Economics." *History of Economics Review*, 70-107.

Tarski A. 1943-1944. "The Semantic Conception of Truth." *Philosophy and Phenomenological Research* 4: 341-376.

Thakor, Anjan, V. 1989. "Strategic Issues in Financial Contracting: An Overview." *Financial Management* 18: 39-58.

Titman, Sheridan and Brett Trueman. 1986. "Information Quality and the Valuation of New Issues." *Journal of Accounting and Economics* 8: 159-172.

Tiles, J.E. 1988. *Dewey*. London: Routledge.

Tobin, James. 1958. "Liquidity Preference as Behaviour Towards Risk." *The Review of Economic Studies* 25: 65-86.

Tomkins, Cyril, and Roger Groves. 1983. "The Everyday Accountant and Researching His Reality." *Accounting, Organizations, and Society* 8:361-374.

_____ . 1983. "The Everyday Accountant and Researching His Reality: Further Thoughts." *Accounting, Organizations, and Society* 8:407-415.

Tullock, Gordon. 1959. "Publication Decisions and Tests of Significance—A Comment." *Journal of the American Statistical Association* 54: 593.

Toulmin, Stephen. 1990. *Cosmopolis: The Hidden Agenda of Modernity*. New York: The Free Press.

Tversky, Amos, and Daniel Kahneman. 1974. "Judgement Under Uncertainty: Heuristics and Biases." *Science* 185: 1124-1131.

———. 1981. "The Framing of Decision and the Psychology of Choice." *Science* 211: 453-458.

von Mises, Richard. 1957. *Probability, Statistics, and Truth*. London: George Allen & Unwin.

von Neumann, John and Oskar Morgenstern. 1947. *Theory of Games and Economic Behavior*. Princeton: Princeton University Press.

von Wright, Georg H. 1957. *The Logical Problem of Induction*. Helsinki, Acta Philosophica Fennica, fasc. 3, 1941, 2nd rev. ed. Oxford: Basil Blackwell.

Wakefield, Neville. 1990. *Postmodernism*. London: Pluto Press.

Walter, James. 1963. "Dividend Policy: Its Influence on the Value of the Enterprise." *Journal of Finance* 18: 280-291.

Wang, Chamont. 1993. *Sense and Nonsense of Statistical Inference*. New York: Marcel Dekker, Inc.

Warner, Kee, and Harvey Molotch. 1993. "Information in the Marketplace: Media Explanations of the '87 Crash." *Social Problems* 40:167-188.

Warnke, Georgia. 1987. *Gadamer: Hermeneutics, Tradition and-Reason*. Stanford, CA: Stanford University Press.

Weatherford, Roy. 1982. *Philosophical Foundations of Probability Theory*. London: Routledge & Kegan Paul.

Weintraub, E. Roy. 1985. *General Equilibrium Analysis: Studies in Appraisal*. Cambridge: Cambridge University Press.

West, Bruce J. 1990. "The Disproportionate Response." In *Mathematics and Science*, edited by R. E. Mickens. Singapore: World Scientific Publishing Co. Pte. Ltd.

Weston, J. Fred. 1966. *The Scope and Methodology of Finance*. Englewood Cliffs, NJ: Prentice-Hall, Inc.

Whitley, Richard. 1986. "The Transformation of Business Finance into Financial Economics: The Roles of Academic Expansion and Changes in the U.S. Capital Markets." *Accounting, Organizations, and Society* 11:171-192.

Wigner, Eugene P. 1960. "The Unreasonable Effectiveness of Mathematics in the Natural Sciences." *Communications in Pure and Applied Mathematicss* 13: 1-14.

Willett, Allan H. 1901. "The Economic Theory of Risk and Insurance." In *Studies in History, Economics, and Public Law*. New York: Columbia University Press.

Williams, Joseph. 1988. "Efficient Signaling with Dividends, Investment, and Stock Repurchases." *Journal of Finance* 43: 737-747.

Williamson, Oliver E. 1964. *The Economics of Discretionary Behavior: Managerial Objectives in a Theory of a Firm*. Englewood Cliffs, NJ: Prentice Hall.

Willmott, High C. 1983. "Paradigms for Accounting Research: Critical Reflections on Tomkins and Groves' Everyday Accountant and Researching His Reality." *Accounting, Organizations, and Society* 8:389-405.

Winch, Peter. 1958. *The Idea of a Social Science*. London: Routledge & Kegan Paul.

Yin, Robert K. 1989. *Case Study Research: Design and Methods*, Revised Edition. Beverly Hills, CA: Sage Publications.

Young, S. Mark. 1985. "Participative Budgeting: The Effect of Risk Aversion and Asymmetric Information on Budgetary Slack." *Journal of Accounting Research* 23: 829-842.

Zipser, Andy. 1994. "What Tribe Is This?" *Barrons* 74:26-27.

INDEX

Agency theory, xvi, 52-53, 58, 205, 228, 229
    and dividend policy, 58
APT (*see* Arbitrage pricing theory)
Arbitrage mechanism, 42, 61
Arbitrage pricing theory, 4, 59, 61, 62, 95, 182
    vs CAPM, 86
Arrow, Keith, 62, 64, 133-134
Ashley, John W., 165-166
Asset valuation problem, 18, 83, 116
Asymmetric information, 52-53

Bentham, Jeremy, 46, 141
Bernoulli, Daniel, 109, 110-113
Bernoulli, James, 109-110, 111
Bird-in-the-hand models, 46, 55
Black-Scholes/Merton Option Pricing Model, 65, 184, 201
Burrell and Morgan's research analysis scheme, 224-227

Capital structure problem, 18
    and mechanical metaphor, 13-14
CAPM (Capital Asset Pricing Model), xix, 4, 7, 37, 38, 42, 51, 58-59, 74, 75, 79, 173
    and beta, 93-94
    and failure at prediction, 99

Fama and French's SLB model, 39, 42, 47, 96
institutional milieu, 92-94, 95
Sharpe's market model, 30-31, 78, 84-86
vs APT, 86
(*see also* Lintner, John)
CAPM-N (normative), 76-77
CAPM-P (positive), 76-77, 88-90
CAPM-U (useful), 77, 78, 90-92
CARs, change of meaning, 166
Chicago/Rochester School of financial economics, 59-60, 79, 166, 185, 223, 242
Cordelia's Dilemma, 39, 146, 152
Cost of capital theories, 50-52
Critical rationalism, and Popperian philosophy, 36
Critical theory, in social science, 216
CRSP seminars, xix, 59, 166

Data conjuring, 40-41
Data mining, 39, 151-152
Data snooping, 40, 151
Data storking, 41
de Rouvroy, Claude Henri, 25
DeAngelo and Masulis paper 1980, 203-204
Derivatives, 65
    and academic models, 65-66

Descartes,
  Cartesian Anxiety, 15, 95
  and mechanical metaphor, 13-14
  rational reconstruction vs pro-
     cedural guide, 211
  and universal laws governing the
     social world, 14, 140
Dividend,
  policy problem, 18
  signaling value, 49, 56-58
  and social order, 233-234
Dividend signaling, 56-58
DuPont method, 45-47
Durand, David, 199-200

Eastern Finance Association, xv
Econometrics, 67, 128
Edgeworth, F.Y., 117, 123, 184
Efficient markets hypothesis
     (EMH), 59-61, 163-164, 187
Eisenberg, Anne, 162
Episteme, 219
Estimation problem, 116, 121, 127
Event studies,
  and abnormal return metaphor,
     165-169
  and hypothesis testing, 143-148
  problems with samples, 149-151,
     152
  and types of missing data, 151
Evolutionary organicism, 25
Expected return-variance maxim,
     79-80
Expected utility, 109, 111, 113

Falsificationalism, 36, 148, 152
Fama, Eugene F., 87, 95
  Fama-French article, xix, 39, 42,
     88, 96, 187
  (*see also* Efficient markets
     hypothesis)
Farrington, Benjamin, 12
Ferguson, Robert, 142-143

Feyerabend, Paul, 17
Finance,
  and Kuhn's paradigm, 17, 240
  and limitations of research, 5,
     230
  ontology and epistemology, 4, 9,
     189-190
  and philosophy, 4-5, 6, 18
  and probability, 108
  scope and methodology, xvi
  and tenet of positive economics,
     xxi
Financial economics, xvi, 92
  academic vs practitioner, 169-176
  academics vested interests, 186-
     187, 216, 233
  accomplishments, 181
  as art, 36, 43, 67-68, 174, 187
  and external rationality, 199, 205-
     206, 226, 3, xviii
  fundamentals of modeling, 46,
     189, 201
  and numerology, 175-176
  practitioners, 182-184, 202
  a rhetorical science, 190, 202
  robo-finance, 54
  (*see also* Metaphors used in
     financial economics)
Fisher, Lawrence, 166
Foucault, Michel, 219
Free rider model, 43
Free-cash-flow hypothesis, 53, 54
Friedman, Milton, xviii, 7, 67, 73,
     173, 185
  and Cowles Commission, 27, 29
  importance of data, 27-29
  The Methodology of Positive
     Economics, 6, 77
  positivism/instrumentalism, 26,
     27, 47, 85
  theoretical assumptions, 29-31, 39
  vs Popper's philosophy of
     science, 35-38

Gibbins, Michael, 232
Glaser, Barney, 231-233
Gould, Stephen Jay, 39, 146

Hamada, Robert S., 50, 51, 52
Hayek, Friedrich A., 205-206
Heck, Jean, 185
Hermeneutics, in social science,
    214-215
Hicks, John R., 124-126
High frequency data in finance, 8
Huygens, Christian, 109, 110, 111

Index funds, 59, 91
Instrumentalism, 26-27
    and economics, xviii, 7
    and Friedmanian positivism, 26
    *The International Review of
        Financial Analysis*, xv

Jahnke, William, 59
Jensen, Michael C., 52-53, 58
The Journal of Investing, xix

Keynes, John Neville, 73, 170
Knight, Frank H., 101, 121, 123-
    128, 130
Kuhn, Thomas, 16, 239

Lane, William, xv
Language of finance,
    and common/formal language
        translation errors, 101
    figures of speech, 158, 162-165
    and jargon, 159-162
    and Saussure's structuralist the-
        ory of linguistics, 213-214
    and use of vague scientific termi-
        nology, 191
    (*see also* Metaphors)
Law of large numbers, 109, 110,
    111, 123, 124

and problems in financial mod-
    els, 115-116, 121, 134
Lintner, John, 51, 85-86, 96, 187,
    232
Liquidity preference model, 83-84
Logical positivism (LP), 25
    and the verification principle, 26

*The McGraw-Hill Finance Litera-
    ture Index*, 185
Market,
    micro-structure, 66-67
    personification, 158
Markowitz, Harry, 74, 79, 81-83, 84,
    91, 117
    (*see also* MPT)
Meaning,
    in finance, 3, 218
    in the social sciences, 212-217
Meckling, William H., 52-53
Merton, Robert C.,
    option pricing, 65
    theory of finance, 5
Metaphors used in financial eco-
    nomics,
    abnormal vs residual, 166-167
    market for capital control, 163
    neutral mutations vs anomalies,
        163-164
Methodology in financial econom-
    ics, 3, 190, 204-205
    areas for change, 240-242
    and behavioral work, 65
    criteria for theoretical accomp-
        lishment, 182
    limits of useful work, 181
    Popperian monism, 36
    return to numerology, 175-176
    roots in the revolution of the
        Enlightenment, 11
    and scientific revolution of
        Modigliani and Miller,
        195-196

Micro Structure, xvi
Miller, Merton H., 162-163
  (*see also* Modigliani and Miller
    theories)
Modigliani and Miller theories, 42,
    46, 47, 68, 163, 193-195
  and common sense, 199-200
  cost-of-capital, 47-49, 194-195,
    202-203
  dividend policy theory, 49-50
  MPT, 84, 116, 117, 183
    Markowitz-Sharpe sources of
      bias, 168
Multi-index model, 62
Murderers Row, xix, 59

Normative models (capital ration-
    ing and portfolio theory),
    47, 79, 80-83

Objectivism, 15
Organizational theory, 54-55
Overreaction hypothesis, 62-63

Paradigm, 16-17, 239
Pecking-order hypothesis, xvi, 53,
    54
Performance evaluation, 81
Pierce, Charles Sanders, 215
Popper, Karl R., 27, 148, 152, 173,
    187
  and intuition, 197
  Popperian philosophy of science,
    35-36, 52
  Portfolio theory (modern) (*see*
    MPT
Positivism,
  and economics, xviii, 73, 74, 203
  origins, 25
  and simplifying assumptions,
    135
  vs normativism, 73-74
  (*see also* Logical positivism)

Post-empiricism, 16-18
  *The Structure of Scientific Revo-
    lutions*, 16
Post-modernity vs modernity, 218-
    219
Probability theories, 102-109
  behavioral probability (Px4), 103,
    105-106
  classical probability (Px0), 102,
    103
  and early economics theoreti-
    cians, 109-113, 117-135
  and languages, 106-109
  logical probability (Px2), 102,
    105
  mathematical expectation, 109,
    111
  relative frequency probability
    (Px1), 102, 103-104, 113
  subjective probability (Px3), 102,
    105
  (*see also* Bernoulli, Daniel; Ber-
    noulli, James; Huygens,
    Christian
Publication filter, 152)

Qualitative and/or normative
    financial research, 211-212,
    217, 229- 236
  action research, 235-236
  Burrell and Morgan's research
    analysis scheme, 224-227
  case study research, 234-235
  ethnographic analysis, 233-234
  grounded field theory, 231-233
  historical techniques, 234
  radical humanism, 229
  radical structuralism, 227-228
  (*see also* Research open issues)
Quantitative research, 5
  and creation of new financial
    instruments, 223
  data and methodology, 5, 14

data requirements of Friedmanian instrumentalism, 27-29, 37
data requirements of Popper's critical rationalism, 36
mathematics and the appearance of science, 139, 142-143, 153, 170, 175, 226
and problems with statistical significance, 148-151
requirements of Friedman and Popper, 36-38
and theory confirmation, 147, 174
underlying principles, 224
and unpredictability of stock market, 147

Rationality hypothesis, 64
Reference class problem, 104, 105, 115, 123, 124, 131-132
and early theoreticians, 121, 129
and scientific theory of choice, 133-134
Research open issues,
cultural and social difference in financial practice, 230
ethics, 230
nature of finance, 230
Return-variance efficient portfolios, 83-84
Ricardo, David, 141, 236
Richardson, Alan, 232
Risk measurement, 7
and early theoreticians, 109-113, 117-135, 183
and relative frequency probabilities, 113, 116
vs uncertainty, 101, 130-131
(*see also* Probability theories)
Roberts, Harry, 166
Roll, Richard, 88-89, 94, 95, 96
Ross, Stephen, 59, 86-87, 88-89, 96, 164

(*see also* Arbitrage pricing theory)

Scale effect, and logarithmic transformation, 39
Science,
and belief in governing principles, 191, 193
and different societies, 12
emphasis in U.S. academia after Sputnik, 186
experience vs experiments, 29
and financial economics academics, 170, 174
and mathematical models, 106, 139, 216
a philosophy, 9, 10-11, 16, 32, 99
and Popperian philosophy, 35-36
scientific methods, 4-5, 10, 14, 87, 190-195, 211
Scientism, 15, 18, 139, 211
The Scope and Methodology of Finance, xv, xvi, xxi, 3
Sharpe, William F., 30-31, 38, 47, 67, 74, 81-83
classical financial doctrine, 85
(*see also* CAPM; Markowitz-Sharpe portfolio model)
Signaling Theories xvi, 55-58, 164-165, 205, 215
and sign value, 228
Signifieds and signifiers in financial theory, 213-214
Situational logic, 35
Sorites paradox, 134
Spence, Michael, 164, 215
Statistical significance, 150-151
Sticky dividend payout theory, 232
Stoll model of bid-ask spread, 66
Strauss, Anselm L., 231-233
Structuralism, in social science, 212-214

Tobin, James, 51, 83, 84
Trade-off theory, 50-51
Treynor, Jack, 142-143

Valuation model, 4
Value,
  present, 182
  valuation model, 4
Verification vs confirmation, 26
Verstehen, 214

Vienna Group, 25, 73

Wang's paradox (*see* Sorites
    paradox)
Waterhouse, John, 232
Wealth maximization, xvi, 46, 62,
    163
Weatherford, Roy, 102
Weston, J. Fred, xv, xvi, xxi
Wittgenstein, Ludwig, 25, 26